CISTERCIAN FATHERS SERIES: NUMBER SEVENTEEN

Aelred of Rievaulx

THE MIRROR OF CHARITY

CISTERCIAN FATHERS SERIES: NUMBER SEVENTEEN

AELRED OF RIEVAULX

THE MIRROR OF CHARITY

Translated by
Elizabeth Connor, ocso

Introduction and Notes by
Charles Dumont, ocso

Cistercian Publications
Kalamazoo, Michigan
1990

C Translation copyrighted by Cistercian Publications Inc., 1990

This translation is based on the critical edition of C. H. Talbot, *Liber de specvlo caritatis*, Turnhout: Corpus Christianorum Continuatio Mediaevalis.

The work of Cistercian Publications is made possible in part by support from Western Michigan University to the Institute of Cistercian Studies.

Available through bookstores or directly from the publishers:
Cistercian Publications
Distribution
St Joseph's Abbey
Spencer, Massachusetts 01562

Available in Britain and Europe from:
Cassells plc
Artillery House Artillery Row
London SW1P 1RT

Library of Congress Cataloguing-in-Publication Data
Aelred, of Rievaulx, Saint, 1110-1167.
The mirror of charity.
(Cistercian Fathers series ; no. 17)
Translation of: Speculum caritatis.
Bibliography: p.
    1. Love (Theology)—Early works to 1800. I. Connor,
        Elizabeth. II. Title. III. Series.
BV4639.A3413   1983   241'.4   82-12821
            ISBN 0-87907-217-2
            ISBN 0-87907-717-4 (pbk.)

Printed in the United States of America

TABLE OF CONTENTS

LIST OF ABBREVIATIONS

CC	Corpus Christianorum series. Turnhout, Belgium. 1953–
CCCM	Corpus Christianorum series. Continuatio Mediævalis. Turnhout, Belgium, 1971–
CF	Cistercian Fathers series. Spencer, Massachusetts, Kalamazoo, Michigan, 1970–
Ep	*Epistola*
PG	J.-P. Migne, *Patrologiae cursus completus, series graeca*, 162 volumes. Paris, 1857–1866.
PL	J.-P. Migne, *Patrologiae cursus completus, series latina*, 221 volumes. Paris, 1844–1864.
Sat	*Satira*
SCh	Sources Chrétiennes series. Paris, 1941–.
Serm	Sermo(es)

Works by Aelred of Rievaulx

Adv	*Sermo de adventu Domini*
Anima	*De anima*
Ann	*Sermo in annuntiatione Beatae Mariae*
Ben	*Sermo in natali sancti Benedicti*
Gen Angl	*Genealogia regum Anglorum*
Iesu	*De Iesu puero duodenni*
Inst incl	*De institutione inclusarum*
Nat Dom	*Sermo in natali Domini*
Oner	*Sermones de oneribus*
OS	*Sermo in festo omnium sanctorum*
Orat past	*Oratio pastoralis*
Palm	*Sermo in ramis palmarum*

Pent Spec car *Sermo in die Pentecosten Speculum caritatis*

Works by Bernard of Clairvaux

Assumpt	*Sermo in assumptione B.V.M.*
Apo	*Apologia ad Guillelmum abbatem*
Conv	*Sermo de conversione ad clericos*
Csi	*De consideratione libri v*
Dil	*Liber de diligendo Deo*
Div	*Sermones de diversis*
Pre	*Liber de praecepto et dispensatione*
QH	*Sermo super psalmum Qui habitat*
SC	*Sermo(nes) super Cantica canticorum*

Other Patristic Works

Augustine of Hippo

Conf.	*Confessiones*
De Gen. ad lit.	*De Genesi ad litteram*
De Trin.	*De Trinitate*
Enarr in Ps	*Enarrationes in Psalmos*
Ep Ioh.	*In epistolam Iohannis*
In Ioh. tract.	*In Iohannem tractatus*

Gregory of Nyssa

Comm. in Cant.	*Commentarium in Cantica canticorum*

TRANSLATOR'S PREFACE

Undertaking the translation of a work like the *Mirror of Charity* of Aelred of Rievaulx is like setting out on a spiritual journey. This long work, composed while Aelred was still a rather young monk, before he had been entrusted with an abbot's responsibilities, does, in fact, present to us a spiritual itinerary.

Early in Book I this 'Bernard of the North' sets out the major lines of the doctrine of the human person as image of God. Four different states are described: the human person as created by God, happy, unmarred by sin; after sin, when the image has been disfigured but not destroyed; the progressive restoration of likeness by participation in grace coming from Christ's death and resurrection; and finally, the perfect happiness which will be reached only in the life to come.

The rest of the *Mirror of Charity* is largely a development on the third state, our present condition in this life—this *interim*—where charity and self-centeredness co-exist in the soul. As charity gradually grows by the action of grace and with the co-operation of our own moral effort, self-centeredness lessens. And this is the purpose of monastic observance: the increase of charity. Aelred readily refers to the tradition of the apostles and the Fathers, and his teaching, with its articulations *theoria-praxis, spiritalia-corporalia,* is solidly founded in this tradition.

The affable, mild-manner Aelred was a man, a monk, of many-sided character. The *Mirror of Charity* shows us, besides the monastic theologian, a philosopher who could rival the Scholastics, and a monk speaking to God in sublime prayers and meditations. His extraordinary capacity for relating to others and for friendship is well-known. In the last chapters of Book II, where he caricatures the monks in choir and those who have fallen prey to curiosity or a desire to dominate, his humor also appears.

In the struggle between charity and self-centeredness in the soul it is essential for the monk to understand the significance of Christ's New Commandment that his followers love one another. And so Book III begins with a development of the three loves: God, neighbor, and self.

Certain simply untranslatable words in medieval texts can present problems for a translator. Fortunately Aelred himself defines some of his key words; *affectus* and *officialis*, for example. Others he assumes his readers understand; something true in the twelfth but no longer in the twentieth century. The notes on *affectus* and *mens* are called to the readers' attention.

I wish to express my thanks to my former abbess, Mère Françoise Lemieux, who permitted me to embark upon this work, to Father Charles Dumont, who not only contributed the Introduction and the End Notes, but shared his knowledge of Aelred's doctrine with me, to Dr Rozanne Elder for her valuable advice, and to Sr Thérèse Sincery of Saint-Romuald for her help with the proofs.

Aelred was a man of peace. The *Mirror of Charity* is a work of peace. May we all share in that peace.

Elizabeth Connor, ocso

Saint-Romuald, Québec

INTRODUCTION

AELRED OF RIEVAULX: HIS LIFE AND WORKS

Charles Dumont, ocso

The Cistercian School of Charity according to Saint Aelred

*I*f cenobitic monastic life is to succeed in visible form, masters and disciples must seek together, in pursuit of a definite end, by determined, freely-chosen means. The goal is deifying union with God. The monk-believer knows that God alone can give him hope; the christian monk 'puts all his hope in that one alone who saves the whole person'.[1] On this direct route set out by the Gospel, the holiness of the Church points out his way; the guideposts are holy monks. From both grace and nature they have received the gift of being able to help their brothers in sincere and intelligent seeking, and in this way the Holy Spirit has accomplished through them his work of sanctification. To establish the link between means—both divine and human—and their common ultimate end is the task of those who by a continuing tradition pass on from generation to generation the form proper to the monastic state. Because of greater talent and more favorable human circumstances, certain monks have succeeded in doing this with greater brilliance and more lasting effect than others. Cîteaux certainly represents one of the 'eras of explosive vitality' about which Henri de Lubac has spoken.[2] And for those who are still followers of Cîteaux in their daily lives, as

---

1 Bernard *QH* 15.5
2 *Paradoxes* (Paris: Seuil, 1958) 38.

11

well as for monasticism in general, it remains one of those beacons which mark the route through the course of the ages.

The best of the cistercian historians, Louis Lekai, brought out very well the personality of Stephen Harding when he described him as 'the first person in the Order's history who can unmistakably be recognized as a creative genius'.[3] In 1109 he received the charge of one of the countless reform abbeys of that period.[4] Only four years later, in 1113, did Saint Bernard enter Cîteaux. In him, Stephen saw 'a God-sent genius'.[5]

In England, twenty years later, the same phenomenon recurred. Rievaulx was founded in 1132 by monks of Clairvaux. The superior was an Englishman, William, Bernard's own secretary. Two years later, in 1134, the monastery had the good fortune of having as a novice one of the most distinguished personalities of his time: Aelred. Giving up a promising career at the royal court of Scotland, he had become a Cistercian at the age of twenty-four.

The third great luminary of twelfth-century cistercian monasticism,[6] Aelred did not possess Saint Bernard's power of thought or William of Saint Thierry's mastery of theology, but he equalled them in pastoral insight, particularly in his ability to form monks. Having himself been educated by one of the best disciples of the first abbot of Clairvaux, Aelred, unlike William of Saint Thierry and Guerric of Igny, had never attended the schools and so received his formation in both theology and monastic life at the same time within the monastic tradition. Moreover, he alone of the first four great abbots had previously been novice master; not very long—scarcely two years— but long enough to remain something of a novice master throughout his life as abbot. If we study him attentively, even a little, we encounter one of the best possible

3. *The Cistercians. Ideals and Reality* (Kent, Ohio: Kent State University Press, 1977) 17.

4 *Ibid.*

5 *Ibid.*, 34.

6 *Ibid.*, 232.

sources for our knowledge of the cistercian spirit as it was manifested in exercises of the spiritual life as well as in exterior observances.

When Aelred entered Rievaulx, the Order was in a period of expansion, and the spiritual doctrine of the school of charity was already widespread in the claravallian filiation. The principles of this spirituality had been developed in a masterful synthesis by Saint Bernard, but it was Aelred, as an intelligent and enthusiastic disciple, who was to emphasize them and give them a new attractiveness by a pedagogical and even systematic application, particularly in the practice of meditation on the Gospel.

Because of a certain lack of historical perspective and a naive assimilation of monastic life to the evangelical life, reading the Gospel and meditating on it were not only actualized (*sicut praesens*), but life at Rievaulx was itself seen as a summary and fulfillment of tradition.

> To summarize many things in a few words, I hear nothing about perfection in the precepts of either the Gospel or of the apostles, I find nothing in the writings of the holy Fathers, I understand nothing in the sayings of the ancient monks which is not in harmony with this order and this profession.[7]

Aelred possessed a personal charm which drew disciples naturally to him. His own experience of human weakness in a worldly life made him a beautiful example of the humble compassion which he had found in Saint Bernard. A person can speak only of what he knows, and he can know only by experience. The fundamental human experience is one of liberty fettered by the passions, and of love led astray by self-centeredness and envy.

By seeking to reach fulfillment without God, by blind desire, by loving oneself wrongly, humankind lost itself in

---

7 *Spec car* II.**17**.43; CCCM I:821–26.

losing God.[8] 'Man' remains dissatisfied, and this unrest is a
sign both of his capacity for happiness and, at the same time,
his inability to attain it. This experience of exile in a region of
essential unlikeness is the starting point for the whole itinerary
of return to God. 'Man', having loved himself in the wrong
way (*perverse*: 'in spite of good sense'), turns once again
toward the natural and adequate object of his saved love.[9]
What is described as knowledge of our radical unhappiness in
Bernard's first degree of humility in Aelred takes the form of
an anxious uneasiness of conscience. In modern language,
this experience can be expressed by the formulation given it
by Sartre: 'The human reality is suffering... perpetually
haunted by a totality which it is without being able to be it....
[It] therefore is by nature an unhappy consciousness....'[10] But
whereas the atheist sees his consciousness as being 'with no
possibility of surpassing its unhappy state', and condemned to
useless suffering, Aelred follows a patristic tradition and in this
human situation recognizes forgetfulness of God, error of the
mind, and reversal of love.[11] The image of God in the human
person no longer 'responds' to the divine model, but it has not
been irremediably destroyed. Memory, intellect, and desire
can recover their original, innate orientation. On hearing
Scripture, the soul in its depths will remember God. There
knowledge rediscovers truth, and love its natural object,
which is infinite. Man, deformed, takes form once more. It is
here that monastic formation should be situated.

Immediately after describing the human condition and
hope, as we have just summarized it, Aelred speaks of the
growth of the soul as that of a little bird growing wings in the

---

8 *Spec car* I.4.12 (161)

9 *Oner* 29 (30);PL 195:487B. For the numbering of these sermons in
Migne, see Charles Dumont, 'Autour des Sermons *De Oneribus* d'Aelred de
Rievaulx', *Collectanea OCR* 19 (1957) 114–121, esp. 115, n.2.

10 Jean-Paul Sartre, *Being and Nothingness*. Translated by Hazel E.
Barnes. (New York: Washington Square Press, 1972) 141.

11 *Spec car* I.4.12 (180–182).

nest of discipline. Yet the first lesson to be learned in this school of charity will be Jesus crucified, a lesson which will last an entire lifetime. In a beautiful prayer to the Crucified, Aelred three times repeats the word *interim*: meanwhile—that is to say, during this life. It is from the Lord Jesus that he expects the full restoration of divine likeness. His memory, he says, wants to embrace Jesus in a meditation which will save it from forgetfulness; his intellect henceforth wants no knowledge but that of his crucified Lord, so it may not stray from firmness of faith; and he asks Christ's love to absorb all the desires of his heart.[12]

Charity, therefore, is learned from God contemplated in his humanity. The true meaning of the imitation of Jesus Christ lies in this moral conformity to Christ. The root of love, in all its forms, is to will what another wills. In friendship, as in obedience, fraternal charity, or sacrifice, the essence of love resides in this quality of the will which consents to the divine will and adheres to it.[13] Aelred points out this *ordo voluntarius*, which for him is the free gift of self, as being the special characteristic of religious life,[14] and he makes a strict distinction between it and the redundant non-essentials of sensible emotions. It is the passions which hinder the freedom of the spirit cleaving to the divine Spirit. Following the monastic tradition—and especially Cassian whom he expressly quotes[15]—Aelred gives particular attention to them, and teaches that, to do away with this obstacle, to reject all the superfluous things that have come to weigh upon man and bend him down toward earth, is to free the spontaneous dynamic of love and once more open to it the way of return to its source, which is also its fullness.

In an ordered way, then, monastic formation includes education in faith, moral reform, and discipline of body and soul.

---

12 *Spec car* I.**5**.16 (225–240), cf. I.**8**.23 (331–340).
13 *Spec car* II.**18**.53 (975–994)
14 *Spec car* III.**36**.96
15 *Spec car* III.**33**.79 (1516)

There is an unvarying continuity in the school of charity. From the outset, the inclination of the will draws after it the two other faculties of the soul: intellect and memory. It is this unwavering attachment (*affectus*) of heart and will which sustains the thrust of the soul throughout its return journey to God. Charity is at once both the goal and the principle which gives order and form to the virtues and which triumphs over the passions. It is charity which gives meaning to monastic observances. The discipline of a physically harsh life, the application of the thoughts and affections to the things of God, and the practice of fraternal charity in community pre-suppose observances, but only charity gives them their true meaning.

Reciprocally, these dispositions condition a type of life which removes everything that fetters the soul and weighs it down. Without love, these observances lose their meaning and, consequently, their thrust. They become an unbearable burden. To show this was Aelred's point in writing *The Mirror of Charity*.

Continuity is determined by the nature of the ultimate end. Mystical union itself has a moral character in the sense that it is still the will, or love, which is predominant in the experience. Consciousness simply grasps what it can. If love consists in willing what the loved one wills, it is the very fact of this conformity of wills, this *connaturality*, which makes possible union with God. To be like is to be ontologically united even before one is aware of it. This is why the experience of human friendship, as well as brotherly love in community, was of such great pedagogical importance to Aelred. Formation therefore consists of restoring the deformed creature to its original form, in order that it may be deified in being made conformable to its divine archetype. This form is Christ, the Wisdom of God.

Aelred presented this teaching at the beginning of his commentary on Isaiah, where we find clearly described his concept of monastic teaching:

Wisdom passes into holy souls to form friends and prophets.[16] Through them she has produced Holy Scripture for us as the source of all erudition.... Therefore, with regard to what the prophet wrote at the inspiration of the Spirit, I will say what the same Spirit has suggested to me for your edification. I recognize that in all respects I owe you something for your advancement, on account of my charge, of course, but especially on account of my affection for you.... Progress in the understanding of Scripture is not given to me for myself. I have no illusions about that. But rather it is transmitted to you through me. Quite obviously it should not be attributed to my merits, because I am a sinner, nor to [my] education in school, because, as you know, I have almost no formal education. You must not even see in it a result of my application to study, because I rarely have free time and am often taken up with other occupations. Everything comes from God, therefore. It is entrusted to me and transmitted to you.

Then follows his prayer:

You who inspired Isaiah to write, inspire me that I may understand what he wrote. You inspired him that I may believe, and it is written that 'unless we believe, we will not understand'.[17]

In its transmission, therefore, the monastic tradition is deeply rooted in the mystery of faith and the charity which has been 'poured into our hearts by the Holy Spirit'.[18] Personal, subjective liberty expresses itself only under the action of grace, which maintains it in the divine objectivity of faith, hope, and charity. In consent to this radical dependence, liberty is saved from intellectual singularity.

---

16 Wis 7:27
17 Quoting Is 7:9 (LXX) in *Oner* 1(2); PL 195:363–65.
18 Rm 5:5

Like all christian teaching in the Middle Ages, monastic education was based directly on Scripture interpreted according to the patristic four senses: historical, moral, allegorical and anagogical. If the moral (tropological) sense is more notably developed in Aelred than in Bernard, it remains true that Aelred, like his master, always grafts this on to the allegorical sense. Thus it is solely in the mystery of the union of Christ and the Church, of which the monastic community is an image, that union of the soul with the Word, Love and Wisdom, will be realized.

To form a monk is something completely different from putting him into a mold or making him into a slavish copy of a model, even a saintly model. The creation of a work of art is sparked and guided by the exigencies of the form. In the same way, the discipline of the rule frees the thrust of spiritual love from everything which hampers and weighs it down. Just as the first Cistercians refused superfluous land and revenues, the monk is to free himself from the shackles of the passions and, by renouncing them, to restore the divine image within himself to its original simplicity and beauty. It is a voluntary self-stripping which consists of taking up the Cross of Christ and of taking on his yoke of obedience. *Ordo noster crux Christi*, Aelred wrote elsewhere: Our way of life is the cross of Christ.[19] But Christ's cross and yoke unite. It is a weight which gives wings.[20]

The spiritual art is not learned by abstract, theoretical notions. It is properly-oriented *praxis* which leads to *theoria*, not the reverse. It is likewise by practice that monk-masters are formed. They may be compared to master-builders or overseers, who have first served an apprenticeship as rank and file construction workers.[21] The sober purity of line that we admire in the abbeys of Fontenay, Sénanque, or Rievaulx

---

19 *Palm 1*; PL 195:263D.
20 *Spec car* I.**27**.78 (1258).
21 Bernard, *SC* 23.6 (*discipulus, socius, magister*). (CF 7:30).

echoes the sobriety of life and the simplicity acquired by the monks who built them.

For twenty-five years Aelred never stopped teaching the stages of a Cistercian's formation in the school of charity. After the monk's conversion to Christ, he remains hidden in the secret of God's face, letting himself be formed anew to God's incarnate Image by ascetical and spiritual exercises under the direction of a master in the regular discipline. Then he, in turn, can become a master, a *forma gregis*, a form for the flock, and the example, *exemplar*, of what the Spirit calls each monk to become.[22] In this way he is a mediator of the monastic vocation. And so the monastic tradition reveals itself as a relay of reflections of Christ—*vices Christi*—which the Holy Spirit manifests to the eyes of the disciple. Aelred intimates this relay by witness in a beautiful text where he describes once again the degrees of formation:

> You who until now have heard said to you 'Come', say it now yourself in your turn.[23]

And for someone who was a new guide for his brothers, he added two practical recommendations: he was to ask advice with great discretion and prudence, because he lacked experience, especially in outward matters; and above all, he was unceasingly to remember the road by which he had travelled to arrive at this care of souls, so that, having warred against his passions, he might not now succumb to that plague of the human race, the passion to dominate (*libido dominandi*).[24] A monk expresses himself most truly in prayer, and it is in Aelred's *Pastoral Prayer* that we find most clearly stated his concept of, and experience as, spiritual father and monastic educator.[25]

---

22 *Oner* 29 (30); PL 195:487D.
23 *Oner* 28 (29); 484AB.
24 *Oner* 28 (29); 484B, cf. *Spec car* II.**26**.
25 *Orat Past* 1–10 *passim*.

Reading the history of Aelred's life now, in the light of the principle lines of his teaching we have outlined, will permit us to grasp how he profited from his own experience, and to see how he formed his disciples, among whom we may include ourselves.

The Life of Aelred: From the Royal Court of Scotland to the Desert of Rievaulx

Although we have a Life of Aelred written shortly after his death by Walter Daniel, a monk of Rievaulx and his abbot's secretary and infirmarian, it is in Aelred's own works, especially in the first book of the *Mirror of Charity* that we can best discover his personality. There, like Saint Augustine, he makes a confession, both to reveal God's grace in himself and to call his readers' attention to it in themselves. Sometimes, when our heart with its conflicts and sentiments recognizes itself in his, he seems very close to us. But often, when so many aspects of the world in which he lived eight hundred years ago escape us, he seems very far away. There are no two people, he said, for whom the same exterior norms are equally suitable.[26] What then should we say about the interior life, which is the true life of a monk? We need only say that a type of psychology naively simplified—or even a type highly perfected— necessarily remains on the threshold of the drama which takes place in the human conscience, with its refusal and consent that are unforeseeable and indistinguishable from the simultaneous action of grace and liberty. And yet, in its very liberty all interior life is largely conditioned by the exterior circumstances which surround a person from birth to death.

Aelred was born in 1110, at Hexham, in Northumberland, about as far north as Newcastle and not far from Durham, the centre of christian culture where he received his early education. Hexham had been a focal point of christian and monastic life during the seventh century and Aelred was to relate the

---

26 *Spec car* III.**31**.75 (1404).

history of the saints of the church of Hexham, where his father and grandfather had been pastors.[27]

At the age of about fourteen, he had the privilege of being accepted into the court of David I of Scotland.[28] There he found himself in the company of Simon and Waldef, the two sons of Queen Matilda by her first marriage to a nephew of William the Conqueror, and Henry, her third son whom she had by David. Henry died young, in 1152, one year before his father's death.[29]

Until 1124 and his accession to the throne of Scotland, David had lived at the court of England with his sister, Queen Maud, who was the wife of Henry I Beauclerc, son of the Conqueror. Aelred therefore fell heir to an anglo-norman culture. French was spoken at the court as much as was English [30] and he had leisure time to pursue a classical education. We know he assiduously read Cicero's treatise *On Friendship*, to Laelius.

When he was about twenty, Aelred discharged at court the not very well identified function of *dispensator*—steward, seneschal, or majordomo. He was responsible for the royal table. In their correspondence, he and Bernard would make allusions to this role: Bernard seeing in it a preparation for Aelred's role as an author; Aelred claiming with humility that before entering the monastery he had known nothing but life in the kitchen.

Aelred often hints at a licentious life during this period. In Book One of *The Mirror of Charity* he goes so far as to say that although everyone envied his apparent happiness, his conscience tormented him to the point of making him think of

---

27 'On the Saints of Hexham', in *The Priory of Hexham*, edited by J. Raine (Surtees Society XLIV, 1864) 173–203.

28 See his *Gen Ang*; PL 195:713–716, 737.

29 *Gen Ang*; PL 195:736–37.

30 As regards English being spoken at court, cf. II.**17**.51, where Aelred speaks of the popular stories about King Arthur. Queen Maud also spoke English. Aelred's everyday speech was a casual mixture of languages. 'As he was dying, he would say,"*Festinate* for Christ luve"'. Walter Daniel, *The Life of Ailred of Rievaulx*, LIV, translated with Introduction and Notes by F.M. Powicke (London: Thomas Nelson, 1950) 60.

'the worst remedy of despair'.[31] A bit earlier he had said that he would pass over in silence many things he could have said against a vice of the flesh (in a passage where he was mentioning scriptural texts), because he knew the great modesty of Bernard, for whom the work was destined.[32] In a work he wrote for his sister, he was to recall how distressed she had once been at the frivolity of his conduct.[33] In spite of this confession, for which Aelred borrowed from Augustine's references to his illicit liaison,[34] it is impossible to know to what exactly he was referring. When he speaks of the torments which trouble the soul in worldly friendship, he means envy, suspicion, anxieties, and death, which puts an end to them.[35] Walter Daniel, who in his zeal as hagiographer pretended that Aelred had lived as a monk at the court of Scotland, found himself criticized on this point by two canons.[36] His reply shows great embarrassment, but he never denies Aelred's culpable liaison. He retorts that the critics know nothing of the rhetorical art and claims that actually, because a monk is characterized by the virtues of humility and chastity, he had simply been using a stylistic expression. He was only focusing on Aelred's humility by synecdoche (*intellectio*), whereby a part is taken for the whole and the whole for a part.[37]

Walter Daniel thus forgot the eulogy he had made of his abbot's sincerity: that he 'refused to put grammar rules before truth, but everywhere put truth before them. He despised the vain pursuit of eloquence, and preferred the pure, undiluted truth of the matter about which he might be speaking.'[38]

---

31 *Spec car* 1.**28**.79 (1301–1308).

32 *Spec car* 1.**26**.76 (1202–1211).

33 *Inst incl* 32 (CF 2:92–97).

34 Cf. *Spec car* I.**28**.79, and Augustine, *Conf* II, 1–2.

35 *Spec car* I.**25**.71 (1120–1125).

36 *Vita* 76: Letter to Mauritius: 'Nam quid cause pretendunt? Idcirco videlicet quod Aelredus eodem tempore virginitatem suam aliquociens defloraverit talem hominem a me non debuisse monacho comparari.'

37 *Vita*; Powicke, p.761.

38 *Vita* XVIII; p.27.

In the *Life of Saint Waldef,* the king's son who died as
cistercian abbot of Melrose—a *Life* we will mention again with
reference to *The Mirror of Charity*—we also find an account of
Aelred's years at the royal court. The following incident tells
us something of his experience there. It was Waldef, not
Aelred, who in reality lived in the world like a monk. Waldef
was different from his companions, who wanted to corrupt
him and put him in contact 'with a young girl of the nobility
who had a seductive glance'. After the two had seen one
another several times, she offered him a golden ring inlaid
with a precious stone as a sign and pledge of her love. When
Waldef put this ring on his finger, one of the young men
declared to the others, Aelred no doubt among them, 'Look!
Waldef has become one of us. He's in love!' As soon as Waldef
heard that, he tore the ring from his finger and threw it into the
fire. His biographer expresses his admiration for Waldef's
heroic detachment from riches! 'Plenty of people can be found
who easily overcome pride, gluttony, or lust', he says, ' but
those who succeed in despising gold are rare.'[39] This comment lets us feel the distance separating us from the Middle
Ages, even in what concerns a moral judgement of an incident
we can quite easily imagine.

Few details of Aelred's life at the royal court are known to
us, and those which Walter Daniel relates must be sorted out
from the heap of rhetorical flowers beneath which he has
buried them. By temperament and preference Aelred was
closer to Waldef and Henry, the king's own son, than to the
knights who thought of little but hunting and fighting. Both
were of exemplary conduct, and it is in comparison with their
virtues that Aelred's statements about his waywardness should
be judged.

An incident related in the *Vita Ailredi* (we find his name
spelled this way in the *Vita*) proves that Aelred's situation
provoked envy among the courtiers. It especially provoked a
rude knight who made accusations about him to the king in

---

39 *Vita S. Waltheni Abbatis* 1.16–17; *Acta Sanctorum,* August 1:252–253.

language so indecent that it could not be written down, according to Walter Daniel. In this way he avoids revealing the substance of the accusations, even though we can suspect their nature. By this account we learn that Aelred held the purse strings of the royal treasury. As he would himself say in a simpler way when telling of his conversion, it was when everyone around him believed him happy and envied his success that he felt most profoundly unhappy.[40] In reply to the charge made against him that he had failed in his fidelity to the king, he answered that if he had sinned, he had done so in the eyes of the king of heaven.[41]

Waldef left his father's court to enter the Canons Regular. At the time Aelred was nearly twenty years old. He was to remain with the king for another four years, but there is no doubt that this event had an influence on his vocation. During this entire period, moreover, Aelred was in contact with the religious world, and one of his former masters, a monk of Durham named Laurence, dedicated to him a *Life* of Saint Brigit, a new edition in good Latin of a rather barbaric text.

Aelred's father, Eliaf, whom Laurence calls his friend, had asked him to undertake the work. The manuscript was sent to the *dispensator* of the royal house, and in his dedicatory letter Laurence alluded to the interest his former student continued to have in literature and study.[42] The saints' *Lives* he published in correct Latin—like the *Life of Saint Ninian* Aelred was to write—gave eloquent witness to the twelfth-century Renascence.

When did Aelred begin to think about entering monastic life? According to Walter Daniel he seems to have had this intention from the time of Waldef's departure, but he concealed it from those around him. So absorbed by this desire was his mind that he was wasting away because of it, but even more—and this remark is interesting—he was doing violence

---

40 *Spec car* I.**28**.79 (1301–1308)

41 *Vita* III; 5–7.

42 See Anselme Hoste, OSB, 'A Survey of the Unedited Works of Laurence of Durham', *Sacris Erudiri* 11 (1960) 248–265.

to himself so as not to seem the man he was or wished to become.[43]

This awareness and these, no doubt vague, desires do not detract from the spontaneity of his decision to become a monk. He made the decision in particular circumstances; we find the account of them in the *Vita*. Here again, historical truth has to be sifted from numerous edifying clichés.

In 1134, when Aelred was twenty-four, he was sent by King David to Thurstan, archbishop of York. Through a friend who dwelt close to the city, perhaps Waldef, who was at the time prior of the Canons Regular at Kirkham, north of York, he heard of a small community of 'white monks' who had recently arrived in Yorkshire and made a foundation at Rievaulx. Once their mission to York had been completed, Aelred and his companions went to the castle of Walter Espec, at Helmsley, just next to Rievaulx. The monks of Clairvaux had been directed there by King Henry two years earlier, in 1132, and Espec had given them land. Later we find Espec leading the English forces against the Scots at the battle of the Standard, whose history Aelred was to relate. He died in the cistercian habit at Rievaulx after founding several monasteries.

But let us return to 1134. The day after Aelred's arrival, Espec took his guests to visit the new monastery. The *Vita* gives us a detailed account of the ritual for receiving guests, just as it describes the surrounding countryside and the life of the monks.[44] The affected style of the biographer contrasts painfully with the simplicity and the rejection of superfluity which he eulogized with every intention of sincerity!

The following day, after passing a second night at the castle, Aelred left on horseback for Scotland. With his companions he passed along the crest that overlooks the valley of the River Rye. At the point where the road leading down to the monastery turned off, Aelred brought his mount to a halt and asked a member of his entourage if he would like to return to see the

---

43 *Vita* IV; 10.
44 *Vita* VIII; 10,16.

monks again, to know more about them. This incident, which
aroused the biographer's emotions, does not lack interest for
us—not for the reason Walter Daniel gives but because by the
account of it which Aelred himself was later to give, his
decision depended on the accord of two wills, the same
accord by which he would one day, and invariably, define
friendship and charity itself.

It was then, after a second interview with the monks, that
Aelred abruptly decided not to return to the king's court, but
to stay with the monks. Less persuasive or less given to
proselytism than Bernard, he succeeded in keeping only one
member of his company with him. All the others refused. After
passing the four days required by the Rule at the guesthouse
he was received into the novitiate, but not before first telling
the assembled community of his decision to become a monk.

During his year of novitiate, his biographer continues, he
excelled in the three things that make a monk: meditation,
pure prayer, and useful labor. From a jumble of considerations, where Daniel is no doubt describing his own meditations while telling us that Aelred did not linger over such
subjects, let us pick out several lines:

> The whole strength of his mind was poured out like a
> flood upon God and his Son; it was as though he had
> fastened to the Crucified Christ a very long thread whose
> end he had taken back as far as the seat of God the
> Father. By this thread I mean the strain (*intentio)* and the
> concentrated vigour of his mental being (*intellectus*).[45]

We find here an image of devotion to the humanity of Christ
and particularly to Christ on the cross, as Saint Bernard practised and taught it. But if it was Bernard who laid down the
principles of meditation on the Gospel with application of
the senses (*sicut praesens*), as it would later be developed,
notably by Saint Ignatius Loyola, it was Aelred who gave the

---

45 *Vita* X; 19.

most fully-elaborated examples in his treatise *On Jesus at the Age of Twelve*, and in the triple meditation which forms the last part of his *Rule of Life for a Recluse*. Both are practical exercises in the monastic method of *lectio-oratio-meditatio*. One he sent to his friend Yvo, a monk of Wardon who was his interlocutor in Book One of *Spiritual Friendship*; the other he sent to his sister, a recluse. Both had asked him for them. These two works doubtlessly date from the end of his life, and in a way he summarizes in them the entire practice of this pedagogy he employed during his years as abbot.

Like Bernard before him, Aelred was not to write until he had had ten years' experience in monastic life. Walter Daniel brings out several characteristics of the cistercian life as Aelred practised them before he introduced others to them by his teaching. The alternation of occupations to which he attributed the power of pacifying man and assuring an equilibrium in his life made him put aside prayer to employ himself with some kind of manual work, at which he did not spare his delicate hands. At every moment, obedience dictated to him what his duty was. He never did more or less than he was told, thus avoiding vanity as well as laziness. Daniel also mentions the alternation of contemplation and compassion. This latter term designates community life. For it he renounced his self-will and was at the service of his brothers. This is true martyrdom, but no one has greater love than he who gives his life for those he loves. The biographer recites his lesson well here, because these elements are indeed the very ones we find in the ascetical and spiritual teaching of his abbot.

Aelred was still a young monk when his abbot took him into his council. Soon he was sent on a mission to Rome to present to Pope Innocent II the abbot's point of view in the dispute over a successor to Archbishop Thurstan of York, who had recently (1140) died at Pontefract in the cluniac habit. We need not go into this situation, which was complicated by entrenched political interests and dragged on for many years. It had the happy side effect of causing Aelred to pass by Clairvaux in the spring of 1142. There he was entrusted with

some letters Saint Bernard had written to the pope. Bernard's
Letter 347 presents to the pope some *viri simplices*, among
whom we can recognize Aelred and the other monks dele-
gated by their superior. Bernard must certainly not have been
ignorant of Aelred's existence. He was the Father Immediate
of Rievaulx, and although he most probably never crossed the
English Channel, the abbot of Rievaulx, his own former secretary who had once continued writing while rain fell all around
them but left them dry, surely had not failed to write to him
about this very promising monk.

In Aelred, Bernard met a disciple twenty years younger than
himself who, nevertheless, by his literary formation corre-
sponded to his own monastic ideal and especially to the role
of defender and theologian of the cistercian reform, which he
had himself played with such ardor and intelligence. Almost
twenty years had passed since Bernard had written his *Apology*. The Order had grown, and the phenomenon of seduction
that the white monks had exercised on other religious elsewhere was now being reproduced in England. From the
moment the claravallian monks arrived at Rievaulx (1134), the
'conversion' of the monks of Saint Mary's, York, began. Soon
there was an increasing stream of individual and collective
transfer to Cîteaux, including all the houses of the Congregation of Savigny in 1147.

But this invasion of black monks and Canons Regular soon
provoked difficulties. Aelred witnessed them and was obliged
to take account of them. The monks and canons who had
been formed in a less rigorous discipline than that of Cîteaux
and then 'reformed' by Cistercians who had been sent to them
or who received them into community, objected that the
cistercian observance was physically too hard. According to
them, excessive austerity was an obstacle to the free flowering
of a life of charity and contemplation.

Bernard, who was not insensitive to this criticism, encouraged Aelred to write a treatise which would reply to these
objections. *The Mirror of Charity* is that treatise. Aelred had
already composed notes on the subject, and even a reply in

the form of letters to a monk who considered all the outward observances of the Rule optional. This *disputatio* finds its place in Book Three of *The Mirror of Charity*, but the work as a whole is composed of notes collected over a period of ten years.

Let us come back to the *Life of Aelred* and take up the story when he is master of novices on his return from Rome. The only section of *The Mirror of Charity* that might perhaps date from this period (given by Walter Daniel as the date of the entire work) is the dialogue with the novice found in Book Two. Since we have there a propaganda interview, it is characteristic that the physical austerities arouse the novice's enthusiasm. The novice master, moreover, puts a damper on this lyricism, attributing it to lack of experience.

There is, however, in the *Life of Aelred* a detailed account of the difficulties he encountered with a novice who had come from the secular clergy.[46] Unstable by nature, the clerk soon admitted his desire to leave and, in spite of Aelred's rebukes, went out of the enclosure by the gate. After wandering around the woods surrounding the monastery, he 'miraculously' found himself in front of the same gate, which he now entered. This caused the novice master great joy, and he said nothing of the affair to the abbot. The real reasons for this flight are described later on,[47] when the same temptation again assailed the same monk, this time at the new monastery of Revesby, whither he had accompanied Aelred, the founding abbot, in 1143.

'My inconstancy', said the distressed monk, 'is not equal to the burden of the Order. Everything here and in my nature are opposed to each other... I am crushed down by the length of the Vigils, I often succumb to the manual labor. The food cleaves to my mouth, more bitter than wormwood. The rough clothing cuts through my skin

---

46 *Vita* XV; 24–25.
47 *Vita* XXII; 30–32.

and flesh down to my very bones...[My will] longs for the delights of the world.'[48]

With friendliness, the novice master told him he would go to the limit of what was permitted to make life easier for him. Meeting with a refusal, Aelred went on a hunger strike. This time the monk did not succeed in crossing the threshold of the open gate. An invisible barrier prevented him from passing through it.

We find the same monk once again in the *Life of Ailred*.[49] He had been sent with Walter Daniel's father, who was also a monk of Rievaulx, to the abbey of Hoyland, which had just passed with the Congregation of Savigny to Cîteaux. This little group's mission was to initiate the new Cistercians in regular observances. Aelred, since 1147 abbot of Rievaulx, foresaw the 'missionaries'' return in a dream. Given a premonition of the death of the unstable monk, he was told to be at the gate at the moment they returned. The reason was as follows: instead of entering, the monk asked to see his abbot. When the abbot told him that he was soon going to enter into glory, the monk misunderstood the meaning of his words and retorted: 'What, shall I enter again on that death without end which the cloistered always endure? No,...by your leave, I go at once to visit my kindred for a month to enjoy with them, for just a little while, the good things of this present world, and so return to you again.' Aelred succeeded in dissuading him, and the monk died in his arms six days later, saved at last. If the case of this monk occupies a considerable place in Aelred's biography, and if he shows up at three different periods of Aelred's life, he serves to bring out both the harshness of the cistercian observance and Aelred's compassion for the weak and for those who were accepted nowhere but at Rievaulx. He lost only one monk, Walter Daniel tells us.[50]

---

48 *Vita* XXII; 30.
49 *Vita* XXVIII; 35–36.
50 *Vita* XXXI; 40.

We find the same objection to which *The Mirror of Charity* replies already mentioned in a more specific way in the *Life* of Saint Waldef. In 1143, while prior of the Canons at Kirkham, Waldef had gone to Rome, called there by the pope at the same time as abbot William of Rievaulx.[51] On his return, Waldef asked to become a Cistercian and entered Wardon, a daughter-house of Rievaulx. But Count Simon, the lord of the county, felt humiliated by the wretched condition of this new Cistercian and threatened his abbey with maltreatment. So it was that Waldef went to Rievaulx in spite of the recriminations of the Canons of Kirkham who were in the vicinity. In the end they would oblige him to leave for the abbey at Melrose, Rievaulx's foundation in Scotland, where he eventually became abbot.

From the beginning of his novitiate Waldef, too, found quite painful the harshness of the observances, which weighed on him intolerably. The same list of burdensome things occurs: the insipid food and drink, the rough clothing, the exhausting manual work, the interminable vigils and psalmody, and the rest of the all too austere discipline. *Totius ordinis tenor nimis austerus*—the word *tenor* makes us think of the first lines of the *Exordium Parvum*. Waldef painted a picture for himself— or the devil painted it for him—of the life among Canons Regular where, he told himself, institutions 'although lighter, are at least closer to discretion, and consequently more apt to save souls'.[52]

Here we have in all its insidiousness the objection which had already made such an impression on Saint Bernard. Had he not reproached the cistercian pamphleteers of his day for their self-righteousness by asking them who observed the Rule: the most humble monk or the most tired; the monk who was the strictest or the monk who best observed discretion?[53]

---

51 John of Hexham, in *Priory of Hexham*, 142. Cited by Powicke in his introduction to the *Vita Ailredi*, lxxii.
52 *Vita S. Waltheni Abbatis* 3.34; *Acta Sanctorum* August 1: 258.
53 *Apo* VII.13–14 (CF 1:50).

The continuation of Waldef's story reveals the same claustrophobic complex we found in the preceding case. Left alone in the novitiate one day, worn out by a temptation to leave, he prostrated himself on the threshold, his legs and the lower part of his body outside the door and the upper part of his body inside. In tears he begged God for a sign so he might know whether he should remain a monk or return to the Canons. In a 'miraculous' way, he found himself transported to the place where he usually did his *lectio divina*. We should note that *lectio* was the least difficult of the observances for those who, like Waldef, had come from the ranks of the Canons or the black monks.

From then on, everything in the Order that had seemed burdensome and impossible seemed light to him, because the 'Lord's yoke is easy and his burden light'.[54] This was one of the great texts on which Aelred was to base his apology for cistercian discipline, which for him constituted one of the aspects of the school of charity.

The Mirror of Charity is situated in the Order's upward surge in England at this period. It is the first literary work of Aelred of Rievaulx. The responsibility entrusted to him by Bernard strongly stimulated the monk who came to be called 'The Bernard of the North'. Amply overflowing the limits of the controversy, this work gives us a solid theology of the cistercian life, very finely conceived and skillfully put together in spite of the fact that it was made up from variously inserted notes. The basis of the argument is scriptural. Aelred firmly establishes the value of the observance and its severity on a purely evangelical foundation. Here we find in all their fullness the demands of Aelred's formula: 'Our Order is the cross of Christ'.[55] Only love makes this yoke light. But, in turn, 'only the cross engenders love'.[56]

---

54 Mt 11:29
55 *Palm*; PL 195:263D, cf. *Spec car* II.1.3,45.
56 *Oner* 5(6); PL 195:381C.

Aelred never put aside this fundamental teaching, but never again did he attain the mastery and enthusiasm he reveals in his first work. Even his treatise on *Spiritual Friendship*[57] and his *Dialogue on the Soul*,[58] which date from the end of his life, are simply more fully developed chapters of this synthesis. A christian justification of the monastic life is not easy from a doctrinal point of view. It seems to us that Aelred's scriptural argumentation is remarkable enough to be considered unique, both in its scope and in its precision. The *Mirror* itself, moreover, is scripture. In addition, Aelred put into it his whole experience of conversion, his knowledge of Saint Augustine, and everything he had learned from his brothers, who were direct-line disciples of Bernard of Clairvaux.

At the centre of his monastic doctrine of charity, Aelred, following Bernard and the fathers, placed the restoration of the image of God in the human person. But since the divine nature is essentially love, as Scripture tells us, it is by conforming himself (that is, by reforming himself first of all) to this God-love that man rediscovers himself in rediscovering God, with whom he possesses a native affinity that has been deformed by sin. This reordering of our love draws us near God, makes us cleave to him and, by that very fact, brings us into conformity with him and makes us partakers of the divine nature. It deifies us. Cistercian anthropology gives great importance to the *affectus* of love which draws the other faculties of the soul along after it by its dynamic nature. This re-orientation is presented in the form of conversion and monastic profession which is free, willed, and gratuitous, and should remain so. This *ordo voluntarius* constitutes the unique character of the monastic life, its *intentio*, its meaning.[59]

---

57 *Spir Amic* CCCM I,279–350.
58 *Anima* CCCM I, 683–754. (ET in CF 22).
59 *Spec car* III.**36**.96–97.

By the practice of charity in all its forms man regains his original capacity for love, which has been diminished by self desire: *amorem cupiditas coangustat.*[60]

> [There exists within me] a place, and it is love, which has a capacity for you, great as you are. Someone who loves you grasps you, and he grasps you in the measure that he loves you, for you are charity.... It is then by loving you that I shall seek you, O Lord.[61]

For Aelred, to 'seek God' and thus to 'grasp him'[62] means 'love'. With great insight, he describes the experience of the loss of God. Human love has not only become narrowed, but has gone astray by losing sight of its true object. When the human person lost his relationship with his archetype, he lost his own identity at the same time. *Curiositas*—that is to say, a wrongly-oriented perverse seeking for divine likeness—continues to lead him astray and causes him to lose this identity. By this perverted, egoistic love he has lost himself by losing God, and he wanders among creatures in search of some being to love who will not deceive him. Finding only what is equal or inferior to himself, he becomes all the more unlike God to the degree to which he conforms himself to the world of creatures. Yet the imprint of divine love remains within him, and the whole work of salvation, that is to say, of the monastic life, is to liberate the soul for its thrust towards its object by setting it free from the passions which imprison it within itself. The search undertaken by liberated love is rooted in the soil of experience. If we wish to transpose this twelfth-century monastic and cistercian style into contemporary words, we have the best chance of recapturing its movement,

---

60 *Spec car* I.**4**.13 (181–182).
61 *Spec car* I.**1**.2 (24–26); 3 (38).
62 *comprehendere.* Cf. Bernard, *Csi* V (CF 37:139f.) and Thomas Aquinas, *De beatitudine* Ia IIae, q. IV, a.#3, conclusion: *Necesse est ad beatitudinem ista tria concurrere: scilicet visionem, quae est cognitio perfecta intelligibilis finis; comprehensionem, quae importat praesentiam finis; delectationem, vel fruitionem, quae importat quietationem rei amantis in amato.*

method, and results in the terminology of existential phenomenology. In his research on communion, Gabriel Marcel sometimes comes astonishingly close to our authors.[63]

In any case, we must be careful when we read Aelred's philosophical terms, which appear already to be those of pre-scholastic philosophy (in Book Three of the *Mirror*, for example). We should not read a thomistic meaning into them. This is particularly true when Aelred is dealing with such fundamental notions as the relationship of the created being with its Creator. Much more from the perspective of formal cause— 'in-forming' beings from the interior—than of efficient cause or even exemplary cause does Aelred consider God and the workings of grace. Rather than an analogy of being (finite-Infinite) in the intellectual order, cistercian authors found in the Greek Fathers a language of the univocal character of being wherein the universe is ordered in a hierarchy of degrees, but all beings are given their form directly by the divine Absolute according to their respective capacities. Symbolism also finds room for free play in this type of metaphysics. From this perspective of the formal cause we can better understand the whole process of the reformation of man to the image of the *forma* which is Christ.[64]

We must also take into account the flourishing courtly love of Aelred's day. This phenomenon, a real modification of human sentiment, had an indisputable influence on language, and not only on the language but also on the concept of love in the twelfth century. A kind of 'spiritualization' of courtly love occurs in our 'spiritual' authors. Their doctrine of love is nevertheless founded on concepts and vocabulary of the New Testament, and especially on that of the Gospel and the first Epistle of Saint John. Since it was not by his footsteps but by an inclination of his heart that man in his pride withdrew from

---

63 Gabriel Marcel, *Creative Fidelity* (New York: Farrar, Straus and Giroux, 1964) 167; *Mystery of Being* II: *Faith and Reality* (South Bend, Indiana: Regnery/Gateway, Inc., 1951) 85–86; *Pour une sagesse tragique* (Paris: Plon, 1968) 206, 211–212.

64 *Adv*; ed. C.H. Talbot, *Sermones inediti B. Aelredi Aldsatis Rievallensis* (Rome, 1952), p.34.

the sovereign good and corrupted the image of God within himself, then it seems that it must be by a motion of the heart that man, humbly approaching God once again, finds in himself once again the image of the One who created him. 'Be renewed in your heart, and put on the new man created according to God'.[65]

> But how will this renewal come about except by the new precept of charity, of which the Saviour says: I give you a new commandment.[66] Then, if the mind puts on this charity perfectly, charity will straightway reform the other two, namely, memory and knowledge, which we said were equally disfigured. A summary of this one precept, then, is presented to us in a very salutary way; it contains the divesting of the old man, the renewal of his mind and the reforming of the divine image.[67]

Here the restoration of the divine image is clearly attributed to fraternal charity; it is situated in the area of *praxis*, as Aelred brings out in a sermon:

> We must not lose sight of the fact that in the formation and the reformation of beings charity is active *in motu*; when the creature attains perfection in contemplation and love of God, it is said to 'abide' *(stare)*.[68]

This experience of love is not simply that of the soul's efforts in its struggle against the passions. It is at the same time the experience of grace. 'Conformation', conformity to God in Christ, pertains to the moral order certainly more than to the intellectual order in any case, but from the first movement of conversion it is 'mystical', in the ancient sense of the word as

---
65 Eph 4:24
66 Jn 13:34
67 *Spec car* I.**8**.24
68 *Adv, Sermones inediti*, p. 35.

we find it defined in Dom Anselm Stolz's work, *La Théologie de la Mystique:*

> When the Christian listens to what God inspires in him, separates himself from the distractions of the exterior world, applies himself to the divine life that he bears within himself, and deepens this to the point of experiencing it, he is a mystic.[69]

More augustinian than Bernard, Aelred describes the progress of charity as an increase of peace, by the three sabbaths: the human being enters progressively into divine contemplation, which is conformity of wills. In the first degree the converted conscience, freed from the anguish of sin, becomes recollected (*colligitur in se).* Serene, and renewed in its own sight, it can love itself in complete tranquillity. The monk enters the second sabbath when he opens out to others (*extenditur extra se).*[70] His capacity to love grows larger by the very practice of love. The brotherly affection which develops in community relationships enlarges and increases one's capacity to love. So it is that the school of charity orders all the elements of monastic life toward the only goal proper to them: charity. Just as in Saint Bernard, the second degree in Aelred's journey of return to God is the obligatory passageway, the decisive trial which frees the monk from the principal obstacle to love: egoism or self-centeredness. But this love of others, this fraternal peace, is possible only for someone who is himself inwardly at peace. These two degrees, then, work together. Love of self and love of neighbor represent a purification, a catharsis, of the heart by which it frees itself from tensions and divisions and recovers its unity. This is the peace which the Spirit has poured into our hearts, restoring to the heart its unlimited capacity for loving its ultimate and primordial object: God himself, Infinite Love (*rapitur supra se).*[71]

---

69 Dom Anselm Stolz, *La Théologie de la Mystique* (Chevetogne [Belgium], 1947) 260.

70 *Spec car* III.**6**.19 (359).

71 *Spec car* III.**6**.17–19 (318–360).

Ordering the sabbaths in three successive degrees or three concentric circles is not simply a pedagogical systematization. Aelred himself added two corrections which complete his presentation. First, there is interaction among the three loves. On this point Aelred is more specific than Saint Bernard. Secondly, there is an alternation of the three loves, following the dispositions of the heart and the circumstances of life.

The great liberty of sentiments and actions brought out by Aelred's teaching on the three sabbaths reveals the equilibrium of the cistercian life which was no doubt responsible for its original success. In an area where many ancient and modern spiritual authors speak of tensions and conflicts, this tranquil and optimistic assurance of the bond between nature and grace in different relationships frees the soul from its paralyzing situation by integrating coherently the various elements of an existence which is both changeable and complex.

To this second degree of charity, that of fraternal and human relationships, we should join two of Aelred's doctrinal developments: conformity to the humanity of Christ by meditation and action, and spiritual friendship. It is as a brother, a friend, and a model of brotherly charity that Jesus presents himself to us, to help us to love ourselves and others. With striking sobriety Aelred tells us that Saint John's affirmation that 'the Word was made flesh and dwelt among us'[72] gives us assurance of, and the means of access to, this divine love which is patient even in suffering and death, and is open to every human being, even to someone who may be our enemy.[73]

Aelred's allegory of Noah's ark, which represents our heart, simultaneously expresses charity's universality and the human way of practising it, which does not exclude preferences and attractions.[74]

---

72 Jn 1:14
73 *Spec car* III.**5**.13–14.
74 *Spec car* III.**38**.103–106 (2000–2054)

Conformity with Christ's heart unites us with him onto-logically, but an affection attentive to his human deeds and actions will most effectively help us imitate him interiorly.

There is a 'sacramental' doctrine of the humanity of Christ in which all the actions and all the words of Jesus are signs to be experienced in their transforming efficacy when we meditate upon them and imitate them in both our intention and our action. And so friendship is seen as sacramentalized by Jesus' affection for his favorite disciple. To forestall probable criti-cism against his teaching on spiritual and monastic friendship, given at the end of *The Mirror of Charity*, Aelred declared that Jesus had transformed friendship by assuming it.[75]

Monastic friendship is one form, the most noble, of charity (*sacratissimum genus*). Aelred made a coherent and more complete presentation of it in his treatise on *Spiritual Friend-ship*, which remains unique in christian and monastic litera-ture. Just like community relationships, spiritual friendship is a way toward liberation of the divine love which is in us and seeks its full and definitive object in God. Five times in the treatise Aelred affirms that friendship leads to God; it consists much more in mutual aid and support than in sentiments of affinity, although it finds its source and strength in attraction. In a true and deep friendship one experiences a conformity of sentiments and wills which is, in fact, never attained else-where with such perfection. This experience is enlightening and stimulating in itself, because it cannot help but give birth to a desire for a fullness which can be found only in the infinite love whose reflection it is and of which it has a savor. Love cannot be divided. It exists in its entirety in each of its forms. It has no other end but itself. A person easily rises from human to divine friendship because they both share the same nature and are close to one another; there is only a difference of degree.[76]

---

75 *Spec car* III.**39**.110 (2119–2134).
76 Cf. *Spir amic* III.87.

Friendship moves, however, not only in one direction. Herein lies the reply to the possible objection against friendship that it is used as a means of reaching something else, and because of this is not sincere. The experience of divine love makes human love perfect and sustains it by its grace; 'From the charm of fraternal affection we rise right up to the summit of divine Love, and on the same ladder of charity, we now rise and now descend to rest in the joys of fraternal love.'[77]

For Aelred, friendship remained the ideal form of fraternal charity, the form to which he would wish to liken every community relationship.[78] Spiritual friendship also remains the perfection toward which charity tends. In beatitude there will be a friendship without shade of change. In spiritual friendship, as in devotion to the humanity of Christ, the beauty of the image of God appears once more to the eyes of our faith. We can rise to things of the spirit only with the aid of things perceptible to our senses. Because of our experience of an easy and total conformity of sentiments and will, friendship for a brother makes us perceive what total, free, and chosen cleaving to the divine will is.

If Aelred's monastic teaching appears to us to be very close to life, this is because his life was that of a monk who was happy to be one and desirous of communicating his experience and his enthusiasm.

Like Saint Bernard, Aelred was drawn into affairs of Church and kingdom, but he was more successful than Bernard in avoiding entanglement. By nature he had less inclination toward them. Direct influence in monastic circles was more in keeping with his taste for friendship and for more personal and permanent relationships. The loss of his correspondence, consisting of some three-hundred letters, prevents us from knowing the extent of his social and political influence,

---

77 *Spir amic* III.127.

78 On the subject of the relationship between fraternal charity and spiritual friendship, see Charles Dumont, 'Personalism in Community according to Aelred of Rievaulx', *Cistercian Studies* 12 (1977)250–71, esp. 264–66.

although several allusions in his works let us guess at it. But he was first and foremost an abbot and a spiritual educator. While abbot of Revesby in Lincolnshire (1143–1147), he had two friends who must surely have held in high esteem his zeal for the monastic life: two Gilberts, whom both ancient and modern historians often confuse. The first, Gilbert of Sempringham, founded the Order of Gilbertines which spread rapidly in Lincolnshire and England. Aelred was Gilbert's advisor for the organization of his double monasteries and admired the Order's contemplative fervor. He must therefore have found all the more lamentable a certain scandal which he was obliged to look into.[79] The other friend was Gilbert, abbot of Hoyland, whom Aelred met when he was first abbot in Lincolnshire.[80]

In a way unusual among cistercian spiritual writers, Aelred also had a career as an historian. Besides the works we have already mentioned, he drew up a *Genealogy of the Kings of England* which was the first example of a 'Mirror of Kings' in the twelfth century.[81] The work was meant particularly for the edification of the young King Henry II, who came to the throne on 25 October 1154, and to emphasize the unbroken line by which he was attached to the ancient English dynasty. In addition, Aelred was invited by the abbot of Westminster to write a *Life of King Edward the Confessor.*[82] The only original aspect of this work is Aelred's interpretation of a dream Edward had. In a prefatory letter presenting his work to Henry II, Aelred assured the king that Edward had prophesied on his deathbed that it would be he, Henry, who would be the cornerstone uniting in himself the English and Norman heritages.

---

79 *De sanctimoniali de Watton*, PL 195:789–796.

80 On whether Gilbert of Hoyland (Swineshead) sojourned at Rievaulx, see Lawrence C. Braceland, SJ, *Gilbert of Hoyland: Sermons on the Song of Songs*, I, CF 14 (1978) 6. See also, Charles Dumont's review of this work in 'Bulletin de Spiritualité', n° 749, *Collectanea OCR* (1979).

81 PL 195:711–738.

82 PL 195:739–790.

The work which he, as well as his contemporaries, considered his most important literary writing was certainly his continuous commentary on Chapters thirteen to sixteen of Isaiah. This passage on the oracles on Babylon and Moab constituted, according to Father A.Condamin, a masterpiece 'able to bear comparison with the finest writings of classical antiquity without appearing at a disadvantage'.[83] The allegorical, moral, and spiritual commentary according to the four senses of Scripture covers thirty-one sermons. They are dedicated to the bishop of London, yet another Gilbert: Gilbert Foliot. In a sermon for Advent, Aelred had rapidly interpreted the eleven oracles of Isaiah found in chapters thirteen-sixteen.[84] Since this sermon pleased the monks, particularly because of its moral lessons,Aelred says, they asked him to develop this theme in an extended commentary.[85]

There, among many other things, we find once again the teaching of *The Mirror of Charity*. The burdens (hence the title: *De oneribus*) of the curses thrust at the Babylonians, the Philistines, and the Moabites often represent the intolerable weight of austerities to the monk who no longer possesses the zest and strength which come from charity. On the other hand, charity is preserved by discipline, which dispels the illusions of affective spiritual emotions and spiritual pride. In this work Aelred gives free rein to all his talent, verve, and ingenuity, just as Bernard and Gilbert of Hoyland did in their commentaries on the Song of Songs. Here, too, with simplicity and profundity he very often reveals himself as a mystic.

The fifty published sermons for the liturgical seasons are perhaps more easily accessible to us and here too we find his whole doctrine. The Fathers had a very consistent doctrinal synthesis that was complete and organically unified, although not at all systematic in the scholastic or modern sense of the

---

83 A. Condamin, *Le Livre d'Isaïe* (Paris: Lecoffre, 1905) 107.

84 PL 184:817–828.

85 See Charles Dumont, 'Autour des sermons *De Oneribus* d'Aelred de Rievaulx', *Collectanea OCR* 19 (1957) 114–121.

word. For them, the liturgy was the proclamation and representation (*re-citare, re-presentare*) of the mysteries revealed in
Scripture.[86]

We would like to be able to attribute the hymn *Dulcis Jesu
Memoria* to Aelred. In an abundantly-documented study,
Dom André Wilmart did not see fit to identify him as its
author, but in his opinion no likelier candidate than Aelred
presented himself.[87] It seems to me, however, that it is possible to reply affirmatively to the requirements set down by
Wilmart: first of all, he stated that the author must have been a
disciple of Saint Bernard. Who more than Aelred deserves this
name? As to the concepts and terms which Wilmart expected
to find in the literary work of the presumed author, let us point
out that the *memoria-praesentia* theme occurs frequently in
Aelred's writings, especially when he speaks of the mystery of
the liturgy. In his lamentation on the death of his friend Simon,
he speaks with emotion of his *Dulcis memoria tui*, and further
on, he cries out: *quaerit affectus dulcem eius praesentiam*.[88]
Here, however, I would like to make a connection which I am
astonished not to have seen in writings of any historian up till
now. From his friend Reginald of Durham, we know that
Aelred wrote hymns. In his *Libellus de admirandis Beati
Cuthberti virtutibus*, Reginald stated that during one of
Aelred's trips to Cîteaux, he had composed a hymn in honor
of Saint Cuthbert.[89] He had enough time to finish this hymn
after the Chapter, while waiting two weeks for weather favorable enough to permit the English abbots to cross the Channel. We do not find the hymn *Dulcis Jesu memoria*, signed, in
any manuscript of course. Unfortunately, that was not the
custom of those times. But since Aelred was the kind of author

---

86 *Ann*; PL 195:251B, *OS 2*; PL 195:340B.

87 André Wilmart, *Le* Jubilus *dit de St Bernard* (Rome, 1944), 225.

88 *Spec car* I.34.99 (1696) and 106 (1802).

89 Cf. Powicke, Introduction to the *Vita*, xxxviii, note 1: 'Reginald of
Durham, *De admirandis Beati Cuthberti virtutibus* (ed. Surtees Soc., 1835)
176–7, for the *'prosa rithmico modulamine in Beati Cuthberti honore
componenda'* by Ailred on his journey to and from Cîteaux'.

he was, and since he was skillful in several literary *genres*, he deserves to have us credit him with this poetic masterpiece.

The Last Years and Death of Abbot Aelred

During the last ten years of his life Aelred was afflicted with illnesses, particularly arthritis. We are told this by Walter Daniel, who was his infirmarian and therefore had a continuous relationship with his abbot during those years. He was dispensed from attending the Office, but he did not live in the infirmary. Instead, he had a little cabin built for himself where he received as many as twenty or thirty brothers each day, speaking with them about Scripture and the observances of the Order (*de spiritali iocundidate scripturarum et ordinis disciplinis*). [90] We have seen how closely these two subjects are bound together and how the exterior and interior practices of the monastery were a reply to the evangelical call to renunciation and union with God. Thus, in an original way, the abbot continued his task as educator.

We are obliged to read between the lines penned by this awkward and loquacious hagiographer and suppose that, almost without his being conscious of it, Walter Daniel was indeed transmitting Aelred's teaching. In the ten-page account of Saint Aelred's death—a sixth of the *Vita*—there are several very suggestive expressions.

At the very poignant moment when a brother was reading him the passion narrative, in which Aelred joined by moving his lips or smiling, all the brothers around him began to weep so profusely that they could no longer see one another. But they shared the sentiments of their father, the same in all and all in each: *eadem in omnibus et omnia ex singulis.*[91] Here Walter Daniel was echoing the familiar formula Aelred used to

---

90 *Vita* XXXI; p.40
91 *Vita* LVI; p.61.

signal the fraternal relationship within the community, a relationship which was for him eminently personal.[92]

In his preface to the *Life*, Walter Daniel also points out that he wanted to reveal the holiness of 'the one who begot [him] in the life of Saint Benedict through the Gospel of God'.[93] This is a repetition, but as usual a clumsy one, of what Aelred had said about Saint Benedict, who has begotten us in Christ Jesus by the Gospel.[94] Aelred exercised this evangelical paternity with an art which only humility and love can provide. All pretension and self-sufficiency must be excluded from it, and on the part of the master as well as of the disciple a continual reference must be maintained to the interior Master who teaches both of them. These lines of Gabriel Marcel speak of this:

It is according to the model of paternity that the relationship between the living God and a person who is faithful

---

92 The expression from the *Vita* LVI quoted above in note 91 should be added to those given in my article 'Personalism in Community' in *Cistercian Studies* 12 (1977:4) 250–271, especially 254–260.

93 *Vita* I; p.2: *Qui me genuit per evangelium Dei ad vitam Sancti Benedicti.*

94 *Ben* I; PL 195:239A: Cf. *Vita* XXXI; p.40: 'He did not treat them with the pedantic imbecility habitual in some silly abbots who, if a monk takes a brother's hand in his own, or says anything that they do not like, demand his cowl, strip and expel him'. Among the faults contrary to renunciation, Cassian mentions: 'si alterius tenuerit manum...' (if anyone holds another's hand...). But only more serious faults, which are enumerated in the following paragraph, are punished by dismissal (*De institutis coenobiorum* IV.16.2). SCh 109 (1965) 142.

We find an example of a dictatorial abbot in this passage from the Life of Saint Waldef:

O how many abbots act differently [than Waldef]! While doing so many reprehensible things they not only do not tolerate that their subjects point these out to them, but if they are so unfortunate as to say the slightest word which displeases them, they show implacable hostility towards them, and do everything to brush them aside. I remember having heard an abbot say repeatedly to monks who expressed to him an opinion different from his own, 'You speak that way to me? Do you not know that I have the power to crucify you?' (*Vita S. Waltheni abbatis* 3:41; *Acta Sanctorum*, Aug.1:260).

should be conceived. We could also say that human paternity is modeled on divine paternity and not vice versa, but here it is a question of paternity in all its richness. To clarify our ideas it is necessary simply to compare the father in the parable of the prodigal son to the *pater familias* of the Romans. In the parable, paternity appears in what I would call its supra-juridical fullness. And it is there that it shows itself to be divine in comparison with the simple relationships coming from power or law, or with the simple bond of the flesh which the history of human societies tends to bring out.[95]

Paternalism and authoritarianism—so feared today, but not more so than in the past—are attributed to the passion to dominate in those who hold authority. In itself, this passion is not connected with any one form of government more than another. It comes from the heart. In this connection, let us reread a passage from Aelred's *Pastoral Prayer.*

> You know, gentle Jesus, how much I love them, and that I have given them my heart, and that all my tenderness is bestowed upon them. You know, my Lord, that it is not in a spirit of severity or domination that I command them, that I desire to be useful to them in charity rather than to lord over them, that humility urges me to be subject to them and affection to be in their midst as one of them.[96]

Conscious of his responsibility to be the bond of spiritual union between souls, he said a little further along:

> that under the action of your Spirit, gentle Lord, they may have peace in themselves, among themselves, and with me.[97]

---

95 Gabriel Marcel, *The Mystery of Being* II: 'Faith and Reality' (The Gifford Lectures, 1950) (Harville Press, 1951). Chapter 8.

96 *Orat past,*8.

97 *Orat past,* 8.

This expression, moreover, reminds us of his teaching on the three sabbaths.

Let us conclude with an incident related by Gilbert of Hoyland. It is so true to life that it seems to reflect a personal remembrance. In Sermon 41 on the Song of Songs, Gilbert delivered a eulogy of Aelred immediately after learning of his death. All the rest of the sermon, and not simply the brief passage where he speaks directly of his friend, is consecrated to him, particularly the whole last part where Gilbert speaks of friendship. In this passage, he describes what we today would call 'the art of listening':

In a body drained and withered, 'his soul was fed as with marrow and fat'. Therefore 'with exultant lips his mouth will ever praise the Lord'[98], for his 'lips are a distilling honeycomb.'[99] For wholly changed into lips[100] by his modest countenance and the tranquil bearing of his whole body, he betrayed the calm affections of his spirit. He was lucid in interpretation, not hasty in speech. He questioned modestly, replied more modestly, tolerating the troublesome, himself troublesome to no one. Acutely intelligent, deliberate in statement, he bore annoyance with equanimity.

I remember how often, when someone in his audience rudely interrupted the course of his instruction, he stopped speaking until the other had fully exhausted his breath; when the gushing torrent of untimely speech had ebbed away, he would resume his interrupted discourse with the same calmness with which he had waited, for he both spoke and kept silent as the occasion demanded.[101]

---

98 Ps 62:6
99 Sg 4:11
100 *totus conversus in labiis...*
101 2 T 4:2

Quick to listen, slow to speak, but not slow to anger.[102]
How is he to be described as slow to anger? I would
rather say he was not in the race![103]

The art of speaking and silence which enabled him to write
useful things for monks is but the art of the spiritual master.
The past no longer exists; there is only the present in which
we now live. Tradition has a meaning only if there are monks
to hear it today and respond to it. Because Aelred knew how
to speak and write, he speaks to us still and we can still read
him. We can repeat about him what he said about Saint
Benedict at the beginning of the First Sermon:[104] that we love
to enliven our spiritual ardor by putting before our minds the
memory of his life and his teaching, because it is also by the
ministry of his words and his example that the joy and grace of
being monks, just as he was a monk, come to us from God.

THE MIRROR OF CHARITY

Among the great number of works entitled 'Mirror' during
the Middle Ages, a distinction can be made between those
which present a teaching aimed at the enrichment of knowledge and those shedding light on life's moral aspect.[105] *The*

---

102 Jm 1:19

103 Gilbert of Hoyland, SC 41.4; PL 184:216–18; trans. by L.C. Braceland, *Gilbert of Hoyland: Sermons on the Song of Songs*, III, CF 26 (1979) 495–96. Aelred died on January 12, 1167. The date is clearly given by Walter Daniel. In the preceding sermon Gilbert of Hoyland had alluded to the feast of Saint Lawrence (10 August). The coincidence has raised a problem. It is imposs- ible that Gilbert received the news only after so long a delay. The allusion to Saint Lawrence occurs in Sermon 40, to which Sermon 41 is not connected by so much as the formula *hesterna die*, which itself was often used as a conventual commonplace. Let us also add that Gilbert composed only seven sermons in the five remaining years of his life.

104 PL 195:239A

105 Other details may be found in the article 'Miroir' in the *Dictionnaire de Spiritualité*, 10. The *Speculum caritatis* is mentioned there in column 1293. But it asserts in error that the *Speculum spiritualis amicitae* is a compilation.

Mirror of Charity belongs to the second category, but since charity is the very life of God, its object is the spiritual life: life in the Spirit. How should we understand the metaphor of the mirror here? It is not a matter of man looking at himself as in a mirror. Although Aelred quotes the Letter of Saint James seven times, he does not mention the passage about man looking at himself in a mirror.[106] Nor is it a matter of the theme of which Gregory of Nyssa was fond,[107] and which we find in a beautiful passage of Sermon 25 of Isaac of Stella,[108] for example: the theme of the pure soul which reflects the image of God. What Aelred gives us in this treatise is a picture of authentic charity, with which each person is invited to compare his life and the intentions which motivate him.

The first of these mirrors seems to be the one Saint Augustine composed at the end of his life in the work entitled *De Scriptura sacra speculum*. There he recopied passages drawn from the entire Bible, following the manner of the *testimonia* of ancient catechetics, 'so that someone who already believes and wants to obey God may see, as if in a mirror, whether he has made some progress in his *mores*, and see all that he still lacks.[109] Saint Gregory the Great also wrote: 'Holy Scripture is offered to the eyes of our soul like a mirror. In it, we can see our interior countenance. There we see our ugliness and our beauty. There we become conscious of our advancement. There, of our total lack of progress.'[110]

---

106 Jm 1:23

107 Cf. Gregory of Nyssa, *De vita Moysis*, PG 44:340A–B; *Commentarium in Cantica*, PG 44:824C, 833A–C, 868C; *De beatitudinibus*, PG 44:1269C, 1272A–C.

108 Sermon 25.15; PL 194:1774C.

109 PL 34:889. See also, the end of his Rule (*S. Augustini Regula ad servos Dei*;PL 32:1384): *Ut vos in hoc libello tamquam in speculo possitis inspicere.*

110 *Moralia in Job* II.1; SCh 32 (1952) 180. We could also quote Cassian, who concludes the discourse of Abba Serapion on the eight principal vices with the words: 'After he had projected so much light on them [i.e. the passions of the heart], it seemed that we had them present in some way before our eyes, as in a mirror *(Conference* 5; SCh 42 [1955] 217).

In keeping with what Saint Bernard had asked of him, Aelred presented a theology of charity: its nature is the object of Book One; how cistercian life helps one attain it is Book Two; and finally, Book Three, by a detailed psychological analysis, deals with the discernment of the movements of the heart in order to direct them to their ultimate end in the diverse situations and human relationships where charity is expressed.

The Mirror of Charity is basically apologetic, in the sense that it was written with the very specific intention of replying to criticism mentioned by Bernard in his letter, and taken seriously by him because it raised doubt about the value of cistercian life as he saw it.

It seems that what Bernard had originally, and especially, asked Aelred to do was to speak of the difficulty which religious who had transferred to the cistercian observance were having in adapting to its severity. This is what he pointed out at the beginning of his letter. To be sure, in his *Apology* he had already (in 1125) encountered this difficulty when he reproached the Cistercians for their arrogance toward the black monks. He had clearly stated the superiority of the interior life over ascetical practices, while remarking that one cannot enter into the life of the spirit and maintain it except by corporal discipline. Nevertheless, discretion in this area was to take precedence over severity.[111]

Now, however, these complaints were being aimed at the observance itself, and in a very direct way within the Order, because charity was now considered fettered by the severity of corporal exercises which were accused of paralyzing or restraining charity's full flowering. Thus the very order of the cistercian life itself was said to be becoming inoperative, and the whole equilibrium falsified because the goal could not be attained.

Aelred's reply is simple, perhaps a bit too simple, because he accuses those who were making such complaints of not

---

111 *Apo* VII.13–14. (CF 1:50–51).

understanding the true nature of charity. Charity is not a matter of sentiments and affective emotions, which are most frequently illusory, but rather consists of an effective accord of the will with God's will in the observance of the commandments. What makes the monastic yoke heavy is precisely a lack of generosity towards the cross of Christ, whose burden is light for anyone who takes it up out of love. Throughout the treatise Aelred comes back to these arguments. He does not, however, limit himself to this negative attitude. In Book One he elaborates a theology of divine charity, to whose image human love should conform or be reformed, and he follows the same approach in the treatise on *Spiritual Friendship*. In contrast, by an account of his own life, he shows the unhappiness of the man who, having lost God, has lost himself. And this first book ends with a eulogy for his deceased friend Simon which is, as it were, proof that it is possible for true charity, very human charity, to exist in a cloister.

In Book Two he distinguishes love of God from the illusions of religious sensibility, and shows by means of a dialogue with his novice how traditional cistercian discipline, in its very strictness, effectively leads, by the cross of Christ, to the true charity of union with God and brotherly love. It is interesting to note that in Book Two we twice find mention of a mirror (*speculum*). The first appears after a series of twenty-five New Testament texts (*testimonia*) by which 'one may contemplate as in a mirror the countenance of his soul more carefully'.[112] The second, at the end of the book, after Aelred has given a commentary on triple concupiscence, repeats Aelred's point that if anyone looks attentively on the countenance of his soul he will find there, as in a mirror, not only any deformity in him but, in the light of truth, he will also recognize the hidden causes of his deformity. And so he will not blame them on the harshness of the Lord's yoke—which is not harsh at all—but on his own perversity.[113]

---

112 *Spec car* II.**14**.35 (640–42).
113 Cf. *Spec car* II.**26**.78 (1457–62).

In Book Three, Aelred develops his doctrine of the three sabbaths, and comes back to Bernard's three degrees of truth in the form of three degrees of peace: with oneself, with others, and in God—which are three degrees of charity. He then makes a detailed analysis of the psychology of love and, lastly, gives principles for practical application following circumstances, situations, and persons. At the end of this book we find his definition of the monastic life as the *ordo voluntarius*, that is to say, a free gift of self in love. This development is interrupted by the insertion of a *disputatio* in which he defends the specific character of the benedictine life by basing it on the observances proper to the Rule of Saint Benedict.

The Mirror of Charity, then, is Scripture, for God who is love reveals himself there. From the very first line of his treatise Aelred implies this, quoting psalm 103: *Extendisti, Domine, sicut pellem coelum tuum* (You have unrolled your heavens, O Lord, like a scroll). It is not impossible that the parchment on which he had begun to write had suggested this allusion to him. But it is to Book Thirteen, Chapter Fifteen, of the *Confessions* of Saint Augustine that we must refer to understand the significance of this image:

> Who then, if not you, our God, has created above us a firmament of authority in your divine Scripture? 'The heavens will be unrolled like a scroll'...and now it is extended over us like a skin.... You clothed men with tunics of skins when sin had made them mortal.[114] And so you have stretched out, like a skin, the firmament of your book which you have placed over us through the ministry of mortal men, your words always in harmony.... Now it is in the enigma of the clouds and on the mirror of heaven (*per speculum coeli*[115]) that your word appears to us.[116]

---

114 Cf. Gen 3:21

115 Cf. 1 Cor 13:12

116 These first fifteen lines form a fabric of scriptural allusions, the significance of which is no longer perceptible to us. The spiritual waters

In a sermon on the Beatitudes, which he set in parallel with the days of creation, Aelred has given us the same interpretation of the heavens of Scripture:

Blessed are the poor in spirit, for theirs is the kingdom of heaven.[117] Knowing herself now, the humble soul begins to know God in a religious way (*per pietatem*). By order of the Lord, a firmament called heaven is made for her, the one about which the prophet said: 'Unrolling the heavens like a scroll'[118] by this signifying Scripture. Let her therefore lift her eyes toward this firmament and let her there learn about God. Jesus made this reproach to the Jews: 'You are in error, knowing neither the Scriptures nor the power of God'.[119] It is Christ, in fact, who is the power of God, the wisdom of God. Let anyone who does not wish to be ignorant of Christ, the power of God, apply himself to understanding the Scriptures. Someone who is slow to speak and prompt to listen,[120] so that he

---

above the firmament let the rain of grace fall on the dry soil of the heart. A phrase which is scarcely understandable without its augustinian interpretation introduces the mystery of the incarnation: 'and this heavenly bread appears, which feeds the angels and nourishes the suckling child (*quem parvulus sugit*)' (*Spec car I.***1**.1 [11–12], see Ps 77:24–25: 'to nourish them he made manna rain down and man ate the bread of angels'). For Saint Augustine, the bread of angels is the Word, and the Word became flesh so that the little ones might be nourished by it (*Enarr in Ps* 33.1.4, and 6; *in Ps* 30.1.9; *in Ps.* 130.9. See G. Madec, 'Panis angelorum (selon les Pères de l'Eglise surtout S.Augustin)', *Forma Futuri*, Studi in onore M. Pelligrino (Turin, 1975) 824. The realistic image *Christus crucifixus et lac sugentibus* (*In Ioh. tract.* 98.6) is taken up by Aelred in *Rule for a Recluse*, 26: 'A representation of our Saviour hanging on the cross...will bring before your mind his passion for you to imitate, his outspread arms...and his naked breasts will feed you with the milk of sweetness'. (English translation, CF 2: p.73). See also, Augustine, *Confessions* VII.18.1: 'The Word was made flesh so that the food too strong for our weakness might become milk for our infancy'.

117 Mt 5:3
118 Ps 103(104):2
119 Mt 22:29
120 Jm 1:19

may learn with humility, gives witness of his meekness. It is thanks to this virtue [humility] that the firmament of the Scriptures appears best to us, as if on the second day of our restoration. It separates the upper waters from the lower, that is to say, the knowledge of the angels from that of human beings, because the latter is by far inferior to the former. On this day evening begins for us, that is, when we become conscious of our ignorance, but it tends toward the morning enlightened by divine grace. And this is already a step toward the promised land of the living, the land where we will abide forever. 'Blessed are the meek, for they will possess the land'[121].

A passage from Hans Urs von Balthasar's *Prayer* summarizes the objective of *The Mirror of Charity* quite well:

Man must, in fact, hand himself over to the divine physician, in all humility, naked and unprotected, and expose himself like a sensitive photographic plate to the objective image of himself contained in the Word of God.... And it is love that enables him, in contemplating the cross, to see in it an exact reflection of his immeasurable guilt.... 'What wilt thou have me to do?' asks the man thus subdued; and the answer is a demand for love, love lived in daily life among men, but proceeding from a deep heartfelt contrition before God.[122]

---

121 Mt 5:4. Sermon *OS* 3; PL 195:350C–D

122 von Balthasar, *Prayer* (New York: Paulist, 1971), part II: 'The Object of Contemplation', chapter four: 'The Word as Judgment and Salvation'. A kind of intersubjectivity should also be noted, when Aelred wrote: 'In this mirror of charity, one's likeness to charity will appear only to one who abides in charity, just as no one sees his face reflected in a mirror unless he is in the light' (Aelred's preface, 3 [116–119]). 'Because if the Word of God is simply a doctrine for you', says Kierkegaard, 'an impersonal thing, objective, it is not a mirror.... And if you observe an impersonal attitude toward the Word of God, one could not say that you look at yourself in its mirror, because this act requires a person; a wall can be reflected in a mirror, but it cannot look at itself. No, when you read the Word, you should constantly say to yourself: it is to me that it is addressed; it means me.' Soren Kierkegaard, *Pour un examen de conscience* (1852), quoted from the French, *Oeuvres complètes*, vol.18 (Paris: Ed. de l'Orante, 1966) 100 (XII.382).

For Aelred, to seek God meant to love, because one grasps God only in the measure that one loves.[123] But love means:

> to share in the sufferings of Christ, which means to submit to regular discipline, to mortify the flesh by abstinence, vigils, and toil, to submit one's will to another's judgement, to prefer nothing to obedience, and—to sum up many things in a few words—to follow to the limit our profession which we have made according to the Rule of Saint Benedict. This is to share in the sufferings of Christ, as our Lawgiver bore witness when he said: 'And so, persevering in the monastery until the end, let us share in the sufferings of Christ by patience, that we may deserve to share in his kingdom'.[124]

Having discovered in the cross of Christ the expression of his love, the monk responds to it by taking the cross on his shoulders with love. This makes the burden light. The practice of monastic observances thus becomes the safeguard of this love, and the love he expresses in this way in his whole life gives him the grace to be in the peace of the Truth which makes him free.

The Date of Composition of The Mirror of Charity

The redaction of *The Mirror of Charity* is generally placed during the years when Aelred was novice master: 1142–1143. What Walter Daniel says is taken as the basis for this; then it is assumed that Saint Bernard's suggestion was made to Aelred when he visited Clairvaux in March 1142. Finally, in the text itself, at the beginning of Book Two, Aelred alludes to his charge as master of novices. If we study this data more closely, however, we perceive that it is less conclusive than first appears.

---

123 *Spec car* I.**1**.2 (24–25).
124 *Spec car* II.**6**.15 (284–295), citing RB Prologue.

Let us first look at what Walter Daniel says in his *Vita*. Abbot William made Aelred a member of his council at an unspecified date. He sent him to Rome, where he was received by the pope to whom he explained the matter of the election of the archbishop of York.[125] When he returned, the abbot made him novice master (Chapter XIV). At this period (*illo tempore*) a secular priest was taken into the novitiate where Aelred taught as master (Chapter XV).

He constructed a cistern underneath the novitiate where he secretly plunged in icy water(Chapter XVI). Then occurs the passage of the *Vita* which concerns our treatise:

> During this same time (*per idem tempus*) he began to write to various personages letters most lucid in sense and distinguished in style. He also wrote what in my judgement is the best of his works, the *Speculum caritatis*, as he called it, in three books, which contains as good a picture of the love of God and one's neighbor as a man can see of himself in a mirror. (Chapter XVII)

When he returned from Rome, therefore, he was put in charge of the novitiate, but it was about this time that he began to correspond with various people and also wrote *The Mirror of Charity*. The vague expressions *eodem tempore...per idem tempus* are also found in the same order at the beginning of chapters twenty two and twenty three. In chapter thirty two, Daniel says that during the last ten years of his life Aelred composed many memorable works, but that previously (*ante tamen hoc tempus*) he had composed the *Genealogy of the Kings of England* and also (*Eciam ante illud*

---

125 *Vita*, XIV, 23: *tanta gracia receptus est a domino papa, tam strenue negocium expressit et consummavit.... F.M.Powicke has translated this last verb, *consummavit*, as 'brought to conclusion', whereas it means 'made a summary of the case'. The matter, in fact, was far from being concluded, for in the following year abbots, not simple monks, were convoked. In addition, Archbishop William would be confirmed by the papal legate on 26 September 1143. Only in 1147 would he be deposed, by Eugene III, and he took possession of the see once again when Henry Murdach died in 1153. In the end he was canonized.

tempus) the treatise on the Gospel, *Jesus at the Age of Twelve*. Consequently we are left with only an approximate date.

We might also ask if Aelred left Rievaulx for Revesby at the time of its foundation (spring 1143). Actually, the passage where Walter Daniel gives an account of the foundation of Revesby is extremely embellished with metaphors and rhetoric. This style often reveals a certain degree of embarrassment on the part of the edifying hagiographer: it seems that Aelred had been elected—which is not normal procedure in a foundation—and that he went to join the founders (*Veniens igitur cum illis illuc...* Chapter XIX).

Saint Bernard's *Letter*, found at the beginning of the work, alludes to the request he had addressed to Aelred to write at least something (*ut mihi pauca quaedam scriberes*) to reply to the complaints of those monks who found life in the Order too hard. It is generally assumed that this task was given to Aelred when he stopped at Clairvaux on his way to Rome.[126] But nothing obliges us to believe that this was the only possible occasion. Saint Bernard could very well have given him this order later, for example, by his abbot or by letter. Furthermore, this letter presupposes a reply from Aelred, whose excuses are mentioned by Bernard. With the time that such correspondence would have taken, it could be supposed that at least several additional months would have been required for the redaction.

Finally, the allusions to the master of novices found at the beginning of Book Two and in the dialogue with the novice, which is the most essential part of this Book,[127] can very well

---

126 This has been affirmed too categorically by Dom David Knowles: 'It can scarcely be doubted that he met Bernard as he passed through France, and that it was at this meeting that the abbot of Clairvaux first made the request that Ailred should write on Charity—a request which he repeated shortly with such compelling force' (*The Monastic Order in England* [Cambridge: CUP, 1949] 244).

127 This instance of internal criticism is brought out by Powicke in his Introduction to the edition of the *Vita Ailredi* (p.lvi): 'Internal evidence shows that he wrote this analysis of the religious life while he was actually teaching novices'.

be limited to this particular part of the work. It would therefore have been composed after Books One and Three. Consequently, we must put aside the idea that *The Mirror of Charity*
was composed during the year 1142–1143.

The Procedure for Composing The Mirror of Charity

If we are no longer obliged to restrict the composition of
The Mirror of Charity to the course of one single year, there
still remains for us the task of examining whether this work
came before or after 1142. We might suppose, as some persons have done, that Walter Daniel was speaking of a first
draft which was further developed and edited during the years
which followed.[128]

Saint Bernard's allusion to the *dispensator*[129] of spiritual
teaching would certainly seem more acceptable if it referred
to the abbot of Revesby.

It seems to me more plausible to place the definite redaction during this year, possibly continued during the several
years which followed. That is to say, at this time a certain

---

128 In his excellent book, *Aelred of Rievaulx: A Study* (London: SPCK,
1969, 1981 – Kalamazoo: Cistercian Publications, 1981) Aelred Squire wrote
the following in the chapter consecrated to *The Mirror of Charity* (pp.25–
26): 'Bernard probably knew what Aelred himself confesses in his own
preface...that records of Aelred's daily meditations already existed in some
written form.... Nevertheless, it is difficult to believe that so large a work can
have emerged in its finished state during the few months of 1142–43, while
Aelred was novice-master as, according to Walter Daniel, it did. It must be to
the substantial draft that Walter Daniel refers'. The matter is less improbable
when one sees how far the different sections which make up the *Mirror*
were already composed, and simply needed to be put together and placed
in order. This opinion is based on the importance Father Squire attributes to
a manuscript dating from the end of the thirteenth century or the beginning
of the fourteenth (Oxford, Bodleian Library, MS Asmole 1285), which presents a version of the text quite different from the one given in the other
manuscripts and which contains a quotation from Hugh of Saint Victor not
found in any of the others. See Squire, 'The composition of the *Speculum
caritatis*', *Cîteaux* 14 (1963) 135–46, 219–233. This manuscript seems to me
to be a copy reworked later in language more current to the period.
129 Letter, 3 (39).

number of works which *had been written* during the ten preceding years were given form and put into order.

We should point out that Aelred did not wait for Bernard's prodding to reflect and jot down his thoughts. He himself says this in the epilogue of his treatise: 'I thought it necessary for me to bind together by the chains of these meditations the wanderings and useless digressions of my mind which frolics hither and yon.'[130] He also gathered material from the letters he liked to write to his friend Hugh, his prior who was no longer at Rievaulx (but perhaps at a foundation).[131] Among these pieces which he 'inserted' (as he frequently repeats) in the treatise, there is notably what has been called since Dom Wilmart's study of it 'A Short Treatise on the Scope and Goal of Monastic Profession'.[132] It is evident that Chapter Thirty-five was inserted into Book Three *after* the redaction of the development on the three orders of human life (Chapters 32–36). It is easy to see that this insertion brusquely interrupts the flow of the development. And it is quite probably for this reason that a thirteenth-century manuscript placed it at the end of Book Three, as would anyone today who wanted to present the doctrine logically.

---

130 *Spec car* III.**40**.113 (2188–89).

131 Preface 4; 120–25. The same concern with exercising control over his thoughts in a practical way is expressed in the Prologue to Aelred's treatise on *Spiritual Friendship* (*Spir amic*, Prol 8;43–46): *Si quis autem superfluum aut inutile putat esse quod scripsimus parcat infelicitati meae, quae fluxum cogitationum mearum huius meditationis me compulit occupatione restringere.*

In the first sermon *De oneribus*, Aelred tells his monks that he is going to comment on Isaiah in a new way, because if seculars can be content with listening to Scripture and the ancient commentaries, the same does not apply to monks who are accustomed to them and must struggle against their vain and useless thoughts: *At vobis, charissimi, qui mundi huius renuntiastis operibus... cum immundis spiritibus ac propriis cogitationibus iniistis certamen, alia in Scripturarum meditatione ratio... inutiles et inanes cordis excursus, in id quod utile est revocentur....* (*De oneribus* 1(2) PL 195:364BC).

132 Dom Wilmart published the text with this title in the *Revue d'Ascétique et Mystique* 23 (1947) 259–73. The short treatise, or the *disputatio*, which is inserted as Chapter Thirty-five of Book Three of *The Mirror of*

A simple perusal of the *capitula*, that is to say, the titles of the Chapters which constitute a part of the authentic work, is enough to permit us to distinguish the 'insertions'. These are, moreover, sometimes indicated: Book Two, Chapter 17, for example, is called 'The questions of a certain novice, and the answers, are inserted'[133]; Chapter 21: 'From those things which have been inserted here *(quae inserta sunt)*...we can ascertain....'[134] In his Prefatory Letter, Aelred says that he inserted certain developments *(ipsa eadem ubi congruere videbantur inserens)*[135]

In addition to these explicit references, it is easy to distinguish other texts, previously drawn up, which, by being

---

Charity, is found in the manuscript indicated above, note 128, but taken out of Book Three and placed at the end of the treatise. Since in this manuscript terms used in the text of the *Mirror* to refer to monastic profession *secundum regulam sancti Benedicti* have been replaced by *secundum regulam beati Augustini*, Wilmart believed that this refutation was addressed to a canon regular. But the entire context belies such an interpretation, for the subject of the dispute is the observance of the Rule of Saint Benedict. He suggested that the canons followed the benedictine rule. If this were actually so, composition seems to me to have been impossible at this period and in the milieu where this controversy came up. There are several texts which affirm clearly that the canons followed the Rule of Saint Augustine:

– *illi canonici...viverent secundum regulam sancti Augustini* (*Chronicle of Byland*, in Dugdale, *Monasticon Anglicanum* 5:351)

– *Hic Willelmus canonicus primo fuit militans sub regula sancti patris Augustini inter clericos regulares* (*Chronicle of Fountains*,45; Dugdale, 303)

– *Canonicus regularis effectus ita disciplinate ac religiose se habuit, ut liquido ceteris claresceret, exhibitum in eius moribus et vita, quod scriptum invenerat in Regula clericorum, a B. Augustino tradita* (*Vita S. Waltheni*, *AA SS* August 1:255)

Dom Wilmart saw well the difficulty of considering the *Disputatio* as representing the original text, which supposedly would have been copied directly by the author of this manuscript as it is followed by an *explicit liber speculi caritatis*. It was therefore very logically transferred to the end of the treatise. As for whether the *Disputatio* is anterior or posterior to the composition of Book Three of *The Mirror of Charity*, it could have been anterior or contemporary, but the idea of inserting it into the *Mirror* came to Aelred only after the passage of the three orders of life had been drawn up (Book Three.32–36).

133 *Spec car* II.**17**.title (755–56)
134 *Spec car* II.**21**.title (1165–66).
135 Letter, 4 (125–126).

placed one after the other, make up the whole of the treatise. This is, moreover, one of the reasons why Aelred says in the Prefatory Letter that even though he has divided the work according to three subjects (the nature of charity or its excellence; the reply to the objections of those who complain; the discernment required in the practice of charity) he will speak of each of the three subjects in each Book.

The following are several passages which can be taken independently:

In Book One, Chapter 6, *Disputatio contra insipientem*,[136] clearly cuts into the development on recourse to Christ crucified begun in Chapter 5 and continued in Chapter 6. Chapters 10–15 are a digression on grace and free choice. Chapters 25–27, the first treatment of triple concupiscence, are introduced as follows: 'We are obliged to insert in this work a blemish, as it were, the pleasure of the flesh',[137] but he halts in his description and suppresses development of the subject, thinking of Saint Bernard, for whom he says he has destined his work, and fearing to shock his modesty (*Supprimo multa...verens nimirum pudicissimos oculos tuos, mi amantissime et desideratissime cui praesens opusculum destinavi...*)[138] And he continues by saying: 'I seem to imagine you blushing at what I have written' (*ad haec quae scripta sunt*).[139]

Aelred then gives, in Chapter 28 (79–82), an account of his own conversion. To this he adds a direct allusion to those who complain about the yoke of the observance (83 and 85–89). Paragraph 84 is a meditation on psalm 50:6: 'Against you alone have I sinned'. After this, he comes back to his subject: 'But to return to what I was saying before...'[140] Book One ends with an insertion artificially presented as interrupting the

---

136 *Spec car* I.**6**.title (244).
137 *Spec car* I.**26**.72 (1132).
138 *Spec car* I.**26**.76 (1202–1205).
139 *Spec car* I.**26**.76 (1205–1211).
140 *Spec car* I.**29**.85 (1394).

sequence of the treatise, the eulogy or lamentation on the death of his friend Simon.[141]

Book Two embarks on a comparison between the yoke of concupiscence and that of charity, in the form of a treatise on the three divine visitations. This gives Aelred a chance to justify by Scripture the austerity of the cistercian observance. In Chapter 6, Saint Paul, 'the valiant athlete' of Christ, is quoted along with Saint Benedict.[142] In Chapter 14, twenty-five New Testament texts are proposed under the title *divina testimonia*.[143]

Chapters 17 to 20 constitute a dialogue with his novice, and are meant to prove the excellence of the observance in comparison with its goal, charity. After this long digression, Aelred says: 'It has perhaps not been useless that we have inserted these remarks'.[144] As a conclusion, he develops the three-fold concupiscence as a source of temptation for the monk. After concupiscence of the ears (Chapter 23) and concupiscence of the eyes (Chapter 24), Chapter 25 and 26 are entitled: 'Pride of life'; 'The desire to dominate'. This picture forms a mirror in which a person may judge himself,[145] and thus see under which burden he labors: that of the passions or that of Christ's yoke.

Book Three begins with a description of the three sabbaths insofar as they signify three different aspects of rest for the soul in the different objects of its love: self, neighbor, and God. This theme had already been introduced in Chapters 18–21 of Book One. Next comes the analysis of the motions of love and charity. This constitutes the essential part of Book Three. In style and systematization it is more scholastic than the first two books. Once the principles have been

---

141 *Spec car* I.**34**.98–114.
142 *Spec car* II.**6**.15 (207; 285–295).
143 Cf. I.**13**.39 (581): *Prophetica, simul et apostolica testimonia.*
144 *Spec car* II.**21**.64 (1167): *Hactenus haec forte non inutiliter inseruimus.*
145 *Spec car* II.**26**.78 (1457–60).

established, it gives practical pointers for applying them to the life of each person. After having said that there are not two people for whom the same counsels can be given,[146] Aelred here distinguishes three orders or types of life: 1) the natural order, or order common to all Christians; 2) the order of what is necessary, that is to say, the 'penitential' order (taking 'penitential' in two ways: to do penance for one's past sins and to struggle against the passions in a life of conversion); 3) the voluntary order, that is to say, the freely-chosen order of the monastic life.[147] But Chapter 35 is inserted into the development of the voluntary order. It is the *Disputatio* which replied to letters of a monk who defends a 'broad' position on commitment by profession according to the Rule of Saint Benedict. According to him, the exterior observances do not make up part of the substance of the monastic condition, which, he says, simply binds a person to the practice of christian virtues. Although Aelred objects that this short treatise does not concern the subject—the voluntary order—it fits in very well, and Aelred must have known it. *Porro licet ad materiam non omnimodis pertinere videatur....*[148]

The Literary Genre of the Two Prefatory Letters

The imperative and authoritative tone of the Letter in which Bernard orders Aelred to write *The Mirror of Charity* is surprising. In his recent study of Saint Bernard, Jean Leclercq saw in it 'the clearest example' of insistence and unconscious repetition which is 'the indication of a deep though unexpressed state of soul.' The aggressiveness which flows freely in the first part of the Letter is softened in the second, according to Leclercq, 'as if once his repressed sentiments had been voiced, Bernard calmed down'. Leclercq also notes that 'he

---

146 *Spec car* III.**31**.75 (1399–1407).
147 *Spec car* III.**32–34**.
148 *Spec car* III.**35**.82 (1569).

did not put any form of salutation at the beginning of his letter, as writers of letters ordinarily do.'[149]

An analysis of the procedure employed in composing the treatise permits a different interpretation of these unusual features. Dom Wilmart had already pointed out the last words of Aelred's prefatory letter, where he tells Bernard that to save time he could simply glance at the titles of the chapters to see what interests him.

> From these last words we may gather that Aelred was not submitting his treatise for revision or correction. He was sending him a copy and, at the same time, really publishing his finished work before having received approval. This proves that in spite of his protests and excuses, which we may believe to be sincere, he was conscious of having written a serious work. So there is about this whole prefatory letter a bit more literary artifice than we had previously estimated.[150]

Furthermore, Aelred generally addresses the reader directly: 'Perhaps the reader will here ask us to explain this moderation of life.'[151]

The same literary artifice should be recognized in Saint Bernard's Letter. To ancient writers, the prologue was of great importance. Dom Leclercq has studied Bernard's prologues in a very penetrating and learned way. 'This prologue is simply the beginning [of the treatise]. It is really a foreword, conforming to all the requirements of the literary form. He announces

---

149 Jean Leclercq, *Nouveau visage de Bernard de Clairvaux*. Approches psycho-historiques (Paris:Cerf, 1976) 41. English translation by Marie Bernard Saïd, *A Second Look at Saint Bernard* (Kalamazoo, 1990) 28.

150 André Wilmart, 'L'instigateur du *Speculum caritatis* d'Aelred Abbé de Rievaulx', *Revue Ascétique et Mystique* 14 (1933) 377. In note 12 on that page, Wilmart has clearly shown (and confirmed by an addendum on page 429 of the same volume) that the *Compendium Speculum Caritatis* which was believed to be a first draft of the treatise is simply a compilation, probably made at Clairvaux and passed on from there to Clarmarais.

151 *Spec car* III.**31**.75 (1399–1400).

the subject of the book, the circumstances in which it was composed, and the intentions of the author.'[152] What Leclercq said here about the prologue to Saint Bernard's first work holds equally true for Aelred's first work, but Aelred quite simply had Saint Bernard write it. The exaggeration in the tone of command may be explained by the abbot of Clairvaux's intention to protect the young monk by his authority. At the same time, he approves the doctrine of the treatise as a reflection of his own thought, which is equivalent to saying that he approved it as the authentic theology of the cistercian life.

Neither Aelred's letter nor Bernard's ends with a complimentary closing. This cannot be explained by impatience. We should also note that Bernard uses the familiar grammatical form when addressing Aelred, whereas Aelred respectfully uses the more formal. It should not be forgotten that as Father Immediate, the abbot of Clairvaux was the superior of the monks of Rievaulx. Saint Bernard, perhaps a bit more than other abbots, considered all the monks of his filiation as his own sons. He ended a letter to Robert, abbot of Dunes, with these words: 'We greet all your sons and ours and we ask them to pray for us.'[153]

It is not impossible that Bernard knew of Aelred's work before his letter was drawn up. How, in fact, could he have given him the title and precise object of each of the three books if he had not even known that he was editing them? Furthermore, in Bernard's letter there is an allusion to Aelred's despair and temptation to suicide, which he mentioned in Book One.[154] Like Saint Bernard, Aelred took precautions and waited to be asked before writing for publication. It was not

---

152 Jean Leclercq, *Recueil d'études sur saint Bernard et ses écrits 3* (Rome, 1969) 17 = Chapter I: 'Aspects littéraires de l'oeuvre de saint Bernard', 1: 'Les prologues de saint Bernard et sa psychologie d'auteur'.

153 *Ep.* 324, in *Sancti Bernardi Opera* (Romae: Editiones Cistercienses, 1977) vol.8: 261, line 14.

154 *Ep. 5 (52–53)* : ...*de prostibulo mortis et coeno turpitudinis eripuit desperatum*, and *Spec car* I.**28**.79 (1307).

simply fear of failing or, on the contrary, humility, but also the knowledge that it would be contradictory for a monk who claimed to be dedicated to silence and separation from the world, a monk who had fled the schools, to start teaching beyond the limits of his cloister.

In his other treatises, as well as in this one, Aelred insisted that he had been asked to write and that he had finally decided to do so. This is quite clear in the case of the *Rule of Life for a Recluse* which he sent to his sister in the form of a letter. At the beginning of this treatise he reminds the reader that his sister had insistently asked him for this rule of life and that she had been doing so for a number of years. At the end he repeated that she now had what she had asked for. And the epilogue to the letter is almost identical to that of *The Mirror of Charity*.

The meditation entitled *Jesus at the Age of Twelve* also begins with a reminder of Yves' request that Aelred write something on this page of the Gospel, and he concluded by telling him: 'My very dear friend, now you have what you asked for....'[155]

As to the treatise on *Spiritual Friendship*, we have seen that in his prologue Aelred justified himself for having written these dialogues by saying that he did so to master the wanderings of his mind. It is clear that he said in this prologue that the form of dialogue or colloquium is a literary one—quite aside from the question of what colloquia and conversations otherwise were. And the discussion at the beginning of Book Two was a way for Aelred to join that to what had preceded, while here again insisting, indirectly, that he had been asked to publish the treatise. Walter Daniel's request, *quid de his quoque stilo tradideris*[156] corresponds to what Bernard mentions in his letter, that is, to put in writing (*stylo adnotare*) what he had noted down during his meditations.[157]

---

155 *Jesu* 3.32; CCCM I:278.
156 *Spir amic* II.4 (29). CCCM 1:303.
157 Bernard, *Ep.* 6 (64–66)

Let us point out also that the series of sermons on the burdens of Isaiah is presented by Aelred as a reply to his monks' request after a first successful sermon. When these sermons were published he had them prefaced by a letter to Gilbert Foliot, bishop of London. In this letter we find all the same precautions, the request for protection, the attenuating circumstances of his audacity and so on.[158]

There is no reason to be astonished by these literary procedures. On the contrary. They are imposed as rules of composition and it would be pretentious to attempt to deny them. Form, moreover, in architecture as in the Cistercian way of life, is more liberating than constraining. Finally, what young author would not feel encouraged when a renowned author offered him an introduction to his first book?

C.D.

Abbaye, Scourmont

Translated by Elizabeth Connor, OCSO

---

158 PL 195:361–364.

A LETTER OF BERNARD

ABBOT OF CLAIRVAUX,

TO ABBOT AELRED

1. Humility is indeed the very greatest virtue of the saints, provided it is genuine and discreet. Humility must neither be founded partially on falsehood, nor furthered by the sacrilege of disobedience. I asked you, my brother, rather, I ordered you, no, rather, I adjured you with God's name as witness, to write a little something for me in reply to the complaints of certain [monks] who are struggling from more remiss to stricter ways. I do not condemn or blame your making excuses, but I do reproach you for obstinancy. It may have been humility to excuse yourself, but is it really humility not to obey? Is it humility not to consent? On the contrary, *to rebel is like the sin of sorcery, and to refuse to consent is like the crime of idolatry.*[1] [1*]

2. You cry out that your shoulders, weak as a woman's, should never be made to bear a heavy weight, and that one is more prudent not to submit to the burden proposed than to fall under the load once you have submitted to it. What I command, then, may be heavy, it may be arduous, it may be impossible. But even so, you have no excuse. I persist in my opinion; I repeat my command. What are you going to do? Does not he whose Rule you have vowed to follow say: 'Let the junior know that this is best for him, and trusting in God's help let him obey'.[2] You did as much as you should have, but

1 1 S 15:23
2 RB 68

no more. You did as much as you could. You pointed out the reasons for your inability, saying that you are little skilled in letters—almost illiterate,[2*] in fact— and that you have come to the desert not from the schools but from the kitchens where subsisting peasant-like and rustic amid cliffs and mountains you sweat with axe and maul for your daily bread, where one learns to be silent rather than to speak,[3] where the buskin of orators[3*] is not allowed beneath the garb of poor fishermen.

3. I accept your excuses very gratefully, but I feel that they fan still more, rather than extinguish, the spark of my desire, because it should be tastier to me if you produce something you have learned in the school, not of some grammarian, but of the Holy Spirit, and because perhaps you bear a treasure in an earthen vessel that the excellence may be God's doing and not yours.[4] And how pleasing it is that by some presage of the future you have been transferred from the kitchen to the desert. Perhaps in the royal household serving bodily fare was entrusted to you for a time so that one day in the house of our King you might provide spiritual nourishment for spiritual persons,[5] and refresh the hungry with the nourishment of God's Word.[6]

4. But I do not dread the steep mountains or the rugged cliffs or the deep valleys, for in these days the mountains drip with sweetness and the hills with milk and honey;[7] the valleys abound in grain;[8] honey is drawn from the rock and oil from the hardest stone;[9] and on the cliffs and mountains are pastures of Christ's sheep.[10] And so I think that with your maul you will hew out for yourself from these cliffs something which you would not have gotten by the keenness of your

---

3 Cf. RB 6
4 Cf. 2 Cor 4:7
5 Cf. 1 Cor 2:13
6 Cf. 1 Cor 10:3–4
7 Jl 3:18
8 Ps 64:14(65:13)
9 Dt 32:13
10 Ps 99(100):3 Ezk 34:14

talented mind from the bookshelves of the schoolmasters, and at times you will in the heat of midday, in the shade of the trees, have sensed something you would never have learned in the schools.

5. Give glory then, not to yourself, not to yourself, but to his name.[11] The gracious and merciful Lord, mindful of his wonders,[12] not only snatched a desperate man from the swamp of misery and the miry bog,[13] from the ill-famed house of death and the mud of depravity, but to encourage sinners more fully to hope also gave sight to a blind man,[14] instructed an ignorant man[15] and taught an unskilled man. Therefore, since everyone who knows you knows that what you will accomplish is not yours, why blush, why be upset, why pretend? Why, at an order from the voice of him who gave, do you refuse to pay back what he gave? Do you dread the mark of presumption or the envy of others? As if anyone has ever written anything worthwhile without being envied! Or as if you could be accused of presumption, when as a monk you have deferred to your abbot!

6. I command you, then, in the name of Jesus Christ and in the Spirit of our God, to the extent that these things have been remarked to you in prolonged meditation, not to put off jotting [something] down on the excellence of charity, its fruit and its proper ordering. Thus in this work of yours let us be able to see as in a mirror what charity is, how much sweetness there is in its possession, how much oppression is felt in self-centeredness,[16] which is its opposite, how affliction of the outer man does not, as some think, decrease, but rather increases the very sweetness of charity, and finally what kind of discretion should be shown in its practice. Yet to spare your

---

11 Ps 113(115):1
12 110:4(111:3)
13 Ps 39:3(40:2)
14 Ps 145(146):8
15 Cf. Pr 14:33
16 *cupiditas*

modesty, let this letter be placed at the beginning of the work, so that whatever in the *Mirror of Charity* (for we are giving the book this title) may displease the reader may be attributed not to you, who are deferring to me, but to me, who obliged you against your will.

Farewell in Christ, dear brother.

NOTES

1 Bernard, *Pre* XI,26 (CF 1:125)

2. *pene illiteratum.* Cf. Aelred's Preface,2. See also *illiteratum*, in *Ep. ad Gilbertum* (Foliot), PL 195:361; *Oner* Sermon 1(2) PL 195:365C: *Neque enim meritis id ascribendum meis, cum peccator sim; nec scholasticis quidem disciplinis, cum pene, ut scitis, illiteratus sim.*

3. Augustine, *Conf* VII,9,14: 'But those who raise themselves up on the high boots (*cothurno*) of some supposedly more sublime doctrine do not hear him when he says: 'Learn of me because I am meek...' Saying they are wise, they become foolish' (i.e., the neoplatonist philsophers). The *cothurnus* was a type of thick-soled buskin used by Greek and Roman tragic actors to make them appear taller. By adding layers to the wooden soles, the principal actors' height was sometimes increased ten per cent. Cf. also Aelred, *In synodo* (*Sermones inediti*, Talbot), p.156; *Non sum sapiens, non sum legisperitus, sed homo fere sine litteris, piscatori quam oratori similior;* Ambrose, *De Abraham* II,2,70. PL 14:515A. Augustine, *De moribus Ecclesiae catholicae et de moribus manichaeorum.* I,30,68. PL 32:1339.

THE MIRROR OF CHARITY

1. Genuine and discreet humility is indeed the virtue of the saints, whereas mine and that of others like me is a lack of virtue. Of this kind the prophet said: *Notice my humility and rescue me.*[17] He was not asking to be rescued from a virtue, nor was he boasting about his humility. Rather, in his dejection he was imploring aid. So that I may not seem to conceal how wretched my humility is—if only it were genuine humility and discreet virtue!— by some stubborn disobedience, I yield to the request, the order, the adjuration of one so worthy, because it is worthy; although [I obey] less worthily because it involves me. And so I undertake an impossible, inescapable task worthy of criticism: impossible because of my faintheartedness, inescapable because of your command, and deserving of the criticism of anyone who looks at it closely.

2. Who would rightfully tolerate someone who from the start promises to write about the more excellent way of charity[18] as if with Apostolic authority! Someone who is not only inexperienced in writing—illiterate, if you will—and tongue-tied as well, not yet capable of lapping milk properly![19] How can someone who is a tiny part of things or, in fact, no part at all, hold forth on the eminence of charity, someone disorderly

---

17 Ps 118(119):153
18 Cf. 1 Cor 12:31
19 Cf. 1 Cor 3:2; Cf. Heb. 5:12

on its proper order, someone sterile on its fruit. How can someone tasteless and insipid draw out its sweetness, someone overwhelmed by self-centeredness raise himself up against it. Finally, who am I to explain how charity is increased by harrowing the flesh , and its discerning practice? By your leave, I tell you that, contrary to what you think, when I came from the kitchens to the desert, I changed my place but not my station.

3. But you will say: you should not make excuses. I know, my lord, I know. Yet, although one is not permitted to make excuses, one is bound to accuse oneself, so that a less indulgent reader coming along may not feel obliged to continue further, if at the beginning he sees something which may justifiably offend him. Still, because you have unhesitatingly shown me the holy attachment[20] of charity, how much confidence I have about writing this and accepting the criticisms which could deservedly be brought against me? And so, with little hope of accomplishing what you ordered about charity, with that maul of mine you joked about I have put together what I could to complete this mirror, discovering this absolute certainty: that although hope and all else will disappear, charity remains forever.[21] He who has not bestowed talent has, however, furnished grace. In this mirror of charity the image of charity will be reflected to no one except the person who abides in love,[22] just as no one sees his face reflected in a mirror unless he is in the light.[23]

4. So then, with the goal of undertaking the present work, I have selected material intended for it, some from my own

---

20 *affectus*. This rich and untranslatable term has been rendered as attachment, following Aelred's own definition: '*Affectus* is a kind of spontaneous, pleasant inclination of the spirit towards someone.' Spec car III, **11**.31. See the discussion of Thomas X. Davis, in *The Mirror of Faith*, Appendix (CF 15:93–95).
21 1 Cor 13:8,13
22 Jn 15:9–10
23 Augustine, *De Trin* VIII,8,12.

meditations, some as if mine, yet even more mine, because I dictated them from time to time to be communicated to my very reverend prior, Hugh,[24] who is closer to me than I am to myself. Then, inserting these different notes where they seemed to fit in best, I divided the whole work into three parts. Although I mention all [the subjects] in each of the books, still, in the first book my painstaking intention was to recommend especially the excellence of charity, not only because of its worth but also because of the blameworthiness of its opposite, self-centeredness; in the second book, to reply to the inappropriate complaints of certain people; and in the third, to show how charity should be practised.

5. If something corresponding to our goal has resulted from my sweat it is due to the grace of the Bestower and your prayer. If it has turned out otherwise, may I who have no talent for or practice in writing be pardoned. That the great length of this work may not frighten you, busy as you are, first look through the chapter titles listed below and, having examined them, decide which you should read and which skip.

HERE ENDS THE PROLOGUE

---

24 In his introduction to the *Life of Ailred*, Powicke says that Hugh had left Rievaulx, so Aelred had sent his meditations to him. 'We must suppose that Hugh returned the meditations with his comments' (Powicke, p. lix-lx). Compare *Spec car* I.34.109, where Aelred speaks of Hugh's absence at the moment of Simon's death.

HERE BEGIN THE TITLES
OF THE CHAPTERS OF BOOK ONE

1. Nothing is more deserved than a creature's love for its Creator.

2. The nature, form, and usefulness which all creatures have in common.

3. Created in the image of his Creator, the human person[1] is capable of happiness.[2]

4. By love, in which there is a fuller taste of happiness itself, man withdrew from God and so, made wretched, disfigured yet did not destroy, the image of God in himself.

5. God's image was renewed in man after our Saviour's coming, yet we must expect the perfection of this renewal not here and now but in the future.

6. A refutation of the fool who says in his heart: *There is no God*.

7. The human person withdraws from God by an attachment of the mind.[3]

8. By the attachment of charity, God's image in the human person may be restored.

9. Our love is divided against itself by the opposing cravings of charity and self-centeredness.

10. Free choice occupies a mid-point in the soul but is not equally capable of good and evil.

11. Grace does not take away free choice.

12 Free choice is taken away from neither the saved nor the damned, and grace works only in free choice.

13. The reason why [free choice] is not equally capable of good and evil.

14. A difference exists between the grace which the first humans had in paradise and that which the elect have in this

---

1 *homo*
2 *beatitudo*
3 *mentis affectus*

world; ill will is justly imputed to humankind, although the faculty of free choice is not sufficient for good will to prevail.

15. Even the condemnation of little children is very just.

16. Charity does not fall short of perfection.

17. Spiritual circumcision is included in charity.

18. In charity should be sought the true and spiritual sabbath.

19. The seventh should be preferred to other days, for on this day God's charity is commended.

20. Why six is the number commended in God's work, seven in his rest.

21. A trace of divine charity is visible in all creatures, therefore all tend towards a sabbath, that is, towards rest.

22. A rational creature rests only once he obtains happiness; he hopes for happiness, but unhappily avoids the path by which he may arrive at it.

23. The prerogative of the rational creature, which naturally craves rest not found in the health of the body or wealth of the world.

24. Among the rich, the elect differ from the reprobate.

25. Rest should not be sought in worldly friendship.

26. Rest cannot be found either in bodily pleasure or worldly power.

27. Charity is that easy yoke, beneath which is found real rest, like a real sabbath.

28. An illustration from [Aelred's] life and conversion.

29. How wrong they are who complain about the harshness of the Lord's yoke, since any labor we experience comes from what remains of self-centredness and any respite from the infusion of charity.

30. Those who complain about the weight of the Lord's burden are oppressed instead by the world's burden.

31. The great perfection of charity: what distinguishes it from other virtues and how other virtues without charity are not virtues.

32. The works of the six days may be applied to the other virtues, but the seventh day of rest may be assigned to charity.

33. In this life other virtues are servants of charity but after this life they are absorbed into the fullness of charity.

34. Consideration of the threefold concupiscence is delayed because of a friend's death, and this first book ends with his eulogy.

HERE BEGIN THE TITLES
OF THE CHAPTERS OF BOOK TWO

18. In what we should believe love of God consists.

19. [In reply] to the novice's questions, the fruit of the various types of compunction is explained.

20. The novice is convinced that when he supposed he loved God more, he loved him less. Those who profit from shedding tears is also shown.

21. From those things which have been inserted here, we can ascertain what charity, and what self-centeredness, do in someone making progress.

22. What great joy exists in contempt for, and conquest of, yearnings.

23. The vain pleasure of the ears.

24. Concupiscence of the eyes is found in outward and inward curiosity and afflicts those who have been converted to a more perfect way.

25. A treatise about pride of life; it deals first with vanity.

26. The desire to dominate.

HERE BEGIN THE TITLES
OF THE CHAPTERS OF BOOK THREE

1. The law about distinguishing sabbaths is presented.

2. The distinction beween these sabbaths is to be sought in threefold love. Also the bond which exists among these three distinct loves.

3. How the spiritual sabbath is experienced in love of self.

4. The kind of sabbath attained by brotherly love, and how the six years which precede the seventh are connected with charity.

5. How each of these loves is preserved by the love of God.

6. How the perfect sabbath is found in God's love, and how the fiftieth year may be compared to this love.

7. What love, charity, and self-centeredness are.

8. The right and perverse use of love depends on the choice, the development and the fruit.[4]

9. What we ought to choose for enjoyment.

10. Our love is moved to action and desire; and it is moved to each of them sometimes by attachment and sometimes by reason.

11. What attachment is, and how many types of attachment there are. That spiritual attachment may be understood in two ways is also shown.

12. Rational and irrational attachments.

13. Dutiful attachment.

14. Natural attachment.

15. Two different ways of understanding physical attachment.

16. What our view of these attachments should be.

17. How the mind is moved by reason to love God and neighbor.

---

4 *fruitio*

18. The distinction between the twin loves between which wavers the spirit [*animus*] of anyone making progress.

19. By twin comparisons is explained why a kind and pleasant person, although less perfect, may be loved with more agreeable attachment than someone who is austere but more perfect. The love of either of these persons is shown not to be dangerous.

20. The three loves: from attachment, from reason, and from both together.

21. A review of what has been said; and how true love of God is recognized.

22. What considerations should be entertained in love of neighbor.

23. Which attachments are unacceptable, and how far spiritual attachment, which is from God, should be pursued.

24. Rational attachment and the extent to which it should be pursued.

25. The extent to which we should be wary of, or allow, dutiful attachment.

26. The measure to be kept in natural attachment; what it means to love 'in God' and 'for God's sake'.

27. Physical attachment; that it should be neither utterly rejected nor completely allowed.

28. An examination of the origin of the attachments and also their development and end, and examples of how one kind of attachment leads to another.

29. Various attachments very often struggle in the same mind; which is to be given preference is made clear by examples.

30. What utility is to be sought in attachments.

31. By which acts we should tend towards God, and by which we should have concern for ourselves and our neighbor.

32. Beginning to treat moderation of human life, [Aelred] shows what sobriety should be observed in the natural order.

33. The measure of satisfaction and amendment in the necessary order is described.

HERE BEGINS THE WORK ENTITLED

THE MIRROR OF CHARITY

BOOK I

Chapter 1: Nothing is more deserved than a creature's love for its Creator.

*Y*ou have unrolled your heavens like a scroll[1]*, O Lord,[1] in which you set stars to shine for us in this night, when beasts of the forest prowl, lion cubs roar for prey and seek us as their food.[2] You cover the heights of heaven with waters [3] from which by hidden cascades you send rain down on the soil of our hearts that it may produce plentiful harvests of grain and wine and oil,[4] that we may not seek our bread in futile toil, but seeking may find, and finding may feed and may taste how sweet you are, O Lord. My soul, a soul parched, a soul sterile and fruitless, thirsts to be drenched with these gentle drops of dew that it may behold the heavenly bread which nourishes angels and suckles infants,[2]* that with my inward palate I may relish every delight and yearn no longer for the fleshpots abandoned in Egypt, where at Pharaoh's command, even after the straw was taken away, I furnished the bricks exacted.[5]

---

1 Ps 103 (104):2. Psalms are cited by the Vulgate enumeration, with the Hebrew variants in parentheses.
2 Ps 103 (104):21, 1 P 5:8
3 Ps 103 (104):3
4 Ps 4:8(7)
5 Cf. Ex 5:7

2. Let your voice sound in my ears, good Jesus,[6] so that my heart may learn how to love you, my mind[7] [3*] how to love you, the inmost being[8] of my soul[9] how to love you. Let the inmost core of my heart embrace you, my one and only true good, my dear and delightful joy. But, my God, what is love?[10] Unless I am mistaken, love is a wonderful delight of the spirit:[11] all the more attractive because more chaste; all the more gentle, because more guileless; and all the more enjoyable because more ample. It is the heart's palate which tastes that you are sweet, the heart's eye which sees that you are good. And it is the place capable [of receiving] you, great as you are. Someone who loves you grasps you. The more one loves the more one grasps, because you yourself are love, for you are charity. This is the abundance of your house, by which your beloved will become so inebriated [12] that, quitting themselves, they will pass into you. And how else, O Lord, but by loving you and this with all their being?[4*]

I pray you, Lord, let but a drop of your surpassing sweetness fall upon my soul, that by it the bread of her bitterness may become sweet. In experiencing a drop of this[5*] may she have a foretaste of what to desire, what to long for, what to sigh for here on her pilgrimage. In her hunger let her have a foretaste, in her thirst let her drink. *For those who eat you will still hunger and those who drink you will still thirst*[13] Yet they shall be filled *when your glory appears*[14] and when will be manifest *the abundance of your sweetness* which you reserve for those who fear you[15] and disclose only to those who love you.

---

6 Sg 2:14
7 *Mens*, translated throughout as 'mind'.
8 *viscera*
9 *anima*
10 *amor*
11 *animus*
12 Ps 35: 9 (36:8)
13 Sir 24:21(29)
14 Ps 16(17):15
15 Ps 30:20 (31:19)

3. Meanwhile I shall seek you, O Lord, [6]* seek you by loving you. Someone who advances on his way loving you, O Lord, surely seeks you, and someone who loves you perfectly, O Lord, is someone who has already found you. And what is more equitable than that your creature should love you, since from you it received the ability to love you? Creatures without reason or without sensation cannot love you; that is not their way.[16] Of course they also have their own way, their beauty and their order, not that thereby they are or can be happy by loving you, but that thereby, thanks to you, by their goodness, form, and order they may advance the glory of those creatures who can be happy because they can love you.

Chapter 2: The nature, form and usefulness which all creatures have in common.

4. Now our God, whose being is supreme and unchangeable, whose being is ever the same (as David says: *You are ever the same*[17]) has allotted to all his creatures these three gifts in common: nature, form, and usefulness;[7]* a nature by which all are good, a form by which all are beautiful, and usefulness by which all in good order may serve some purpose.[8]* He who is responsible for their being is also responsible for their being good, beautiful, and well-ordered. They all exist, because they are from him who is supreme and unchangeable being. All are beautiful because they are from him who is supremely and unchangeably beautiful. All are good, because they are from him who is supremely and unchangeably good. All are well-ordered, because they are from him who is supremely and unchangeably wise. They are therefore good by nature, beautiful in form, and well-ordered that they may give splendor to the universe itself.

---

16 *modus*
17 Ps 101:28 (102:27)

5. *God saw all things he had made*, it says, *and they were very good.*[18] In as far as they exist, then, they are good. In as far as each part is in harmony with its entirety, they are beautiful. In as far as each thing in the universe keeps its proper place, time, and measure, all are in excellent order. Thus everything has a fitting place in which to exist: for example, angels have heaven, irrational beings have earth, and humans have paradise, which is midway. In the same way, each has its specific time and duration: for example, in the beauty of the universe itself one being, like the angelic nature, begins all at once but never ends; others, like human beings, although they by no means all begin together, nevertheless, once begun will by no means cease to exist; yet others, like irrational beings, do not begin together, and at some time or other cease to exist.

6. Furthermore, so that we may not seem to have omitted the way in which each creature subsists and how all are allotted a way suited to each, what is more suitable for a rational creature than happiness, provided he is righteous, or what is more suitable than misery, if he is wicked? For irrational and insensate creatures, since they can be neither happy nor miserable, what way is more fitting than that they assist the salvation of the righteous and increase the misery of the impious? Most truly does a wise man say: *water, fire, and iron, milk, bread, and honey, a cluster of grapes, oil, and clothing;*[19] as all of these turn to good for the saints,[20] so they turn to evil for the impious and sinner. Let no one complain that he now shares a place in common with beasts; although previously set in honour, he did not understand and was therefore compared to beasts of burden and became like them,[21] and not in place alone. For when the divine likeness, though not the divine image, was destroyed in the rational

---

18 Gn 1:31
19 Sir 39:31(26)
20 Rm 8:28
21 Ps 48:21 (49:20)

mind, who could easily tell how much its likeness to irrational beasts was increased. But more on this topic later.

7. We must now turn our attention to the Creator's wisdom and proclaim it. Although he is not the Creator or Abettor of evils, nevertheless he rules over these evils with the utmost prudence. Why, then, should my most gentle and at the same time most mighty Lord not allow evil to exist, since evil cannot overthrow his eternal plan in the slightest way? What, moreover, could make his own power appear more manifest, his wisdom more awesome, his mercy more tender, than that he can omnipotently bring good out of evil, wisely keep in order what has been set in order, and mercifully confer happiness on the miserable?

Chapter 3: Created in the image of his Creator, the human person is capable of happiness.

8. In creating the universe, then, God gave man not only being and not only some good or beautiful or well-ordered being, as he did other creatures, but in addition he granted that he be happy. But as no creature has being of itself nor is any beautiful or good of itself but from God who is the supreme Being, supremely Good and Beautiful and therefore the Goodness of all things good, the Beauty of all things beautiful, and the Cause of all existent things, so a creature is not happy of itself but from the One who is supremely happy and therefore the Happiness of all the blessed. 9*

9. Only a rational creature is capable of this happiness. Made in the image of its Creator, this creature is fitted to cling to him whose image it is, because this is the rational creature's sole good; as holy David says: *for me to cling to God is good.*[22] Obviously this clinging is not of the flesh but of the spirit, since the author of all natures inserted in this creature three things that allow it to share his eternity, participate in his

---

22 Ps 72 (73):28

wisdom, and taste his sweetness. By these three I mean memory, understanding, and love or will.[10]* Memory is capable [of sharing] his Eternity, understanding his Wisdom, and love his Sweetness. By these three man was fashioned in the image of the Trinity; his memory held fast to God without forgetfulness, his understanding recognized him without error, and his love embraced him without the self-centered desire for anything else. And so man was happy.

Chapter 4: By love, in which there is a fuller taste of happiness itself, man withdrew from God and so, made wretched, disfigured, yet did not destroy, the image of God in himself.

10. Although happiness is achieved in or through all three, still the taste of happiness is proper to the third. How very miserable it would be to be delighted with what is worst, where indeed there is neither delight nor any happiness. Again, where there is no love,[23] there is no delight. Finally, the greater the love[24] for the highest good, the greater the delight and the greater the happiness. Though memory may bring forth many things, and knowledge grasp deep things, unless the will itself turns to what is presented or grasped, there is still no delight.

11. Our first parent was endowed with free will and aided by God's grace. By a lasting love of this same God, he could have delighted everlastingly in the memory and knowledge of God and been everlastingly happy. But he could also divert his love to something less, and so by withdrawing from God's love begin to grow cold and deliver himself up to misery. Now for a rational creature, just as there is no other happiness than to cling to God, so its misery is to withdraw from God. But *set*

---

23 *amor*
24 *dilectio*

in honor, man did not understand.[25] Understand what? Perhaps what someone said as he entered God's sanctuary and understood truths not only about the present but also about the last day: *those who withdraw from you will perish; you destroyed all adulterous betrayers.*[26] He did not understand that those who by pride betray God stumble into foolishness and that anyone who by theft usurps the likeness of God is rightly garbed in the unlikeness [characteristic] of beasts.[27]

12. By abusing free choice, then, he diverted his love from that changeless good and, blinded by his own self-centeredness, he directed his love to what was inferior. Thus withdrawing from the true good and deviating toward what of itself was not good, where he anticipated gain he found loss, and by perversely loving himself he lost both himself and God.[11*] Thus it very justly came about that someone who sought the likeness of God in defiance of God, the more he wanted to become similar [to God] out of curiosity, the more dissimilar he became through self-centeredness. Therefore, the image of God became disfigured in man without becoming wholly destroyed. Consequently man has memory but it is subject to forgetfulness, understanding but it is open to error and, none the less, love but it is prone to self-centeredness.

13. In this trinity within the rational soul there still persists an imprint, however faint, of the blessed Trinity. It was stamped on the very substance of the soul, for the soul remembers itself, knows itself, and loves itself; the soul loves, knows, and remembers the very memory of itself; remembers, knows, and loves the very knowledge of itself; and likewise loves, remembers, and knows its own love of itself. The soul then mirrors the Unity in its substance, and the Trinity in the three words we have woven together. Accordingly, the psalmist says: *surely man passes by in an image, but is troubled in*

---

25 Ps 48:21 (49:20)
26 Ps 72 (73):27
27 Ps 48:21 (49:20)

vain.[28] By these words holy David suggests briefly but quite explicitly that the human soul does not lack the image by nature, and that its disfigurement comes from sin. Indeed, forgetfulness distorts memory, error clouds knowledge, and self-centeredness stifles love.[12*]

Chapter 5. God's image was renewed in man after our Saviour's coming, yet we must expect the perfection of this renewal not here and now but in the future.

14. Once, through Jesus Christ the Mediator between God and men,[29] the debt had at last been paid for which human nature was being held liable, and the contract destroyed, by the terms of which our ancient enemy with menacing pride held us bound,[30] and once the principalities and powers had been despoiled,[31] to whom divine justice had submitted us, and once finally God the Father has been appeased by that unique Victim on the cross, then memory is restored by the text of sacred Scripture, understanding by the mystery of faith, and love by the daily increase of charity. The restoration of the image will be complete if no forgetfulness falsifies memory, if no error clouds our knowledge, and no self-centeredness claims our love. But where will that be, and when? This peace, this tranquillity, this felicity may be hoped for in our fatherland, where there is no opportunity for forgetfulness among those living in eternity, nor any creeping in of error among those enjoying the truth, nor any impulse of self-centeredness among those absorbed in divine charity. O charity eternal and true! O eternity true and beloved! O truth beloved and eternal! O Trinity, eternal, true, and beloved! There, there is rest, there peace, there happy tranquillity! There is tranquil happiness, there happy and tranquil joyfulness.[13*]

---

28 Ps 38:7 (39:6)
29 1 Tm 2:5
30 Col 2:14
31 Col 2:15

15. What are you doing, O human soul, what are you doing? Why are you seized by so many distractions? One thing alone is necessary.[32] Why so many? Whatever you seek in the many exists in the one. If you long for excellence, knowledge, delight, abundance, all is there, there to perfection and nowhere else but there. Can real excellence exist in this *swamp of misery and miry bog?*[33] Or perfect knowledge in this realm of the *shadow of death?*[34] Or real delight in *this place of horror and vast solitude* [35] or genuine abundance amid so many hardships? Again, in this world, what excellence exists which fear does not overthrow? How great is man's knowledge when he does not even grasp himself? If you delight in the flesh, so do *the horse and the mule which have no understanding.*[36] If you delight in glory or wealth, you will not take it all with you when you die, nor will your glory go with you. [37] Real excellence exists where there is nothing higher to strive for, real knowledge exists where nothing remains unknown. That delight is real which is not lessened by boredom and that abundance is real which is never exhausted. Woe to us, Lord, because we have withdrawn from you! *Alas for me, that my stay has been prolonged.*[38] *When shall I come and appear before your face?* [39] *Who will give me the wings of a dove that I may fly away and be at rest?*[40]

16. Meanwhile let my soul grow wings, Lord Jesus; I ask, let my soul grow wings in the nest of your discipline.[14*] Let it rest *in the clefts of the rock, in the hollow of the wall.*[41] Let my soul meanwhile embrace you crucified and take a draught of your

---

32 Lk 10:42
33 Ps 39(40):2
34 Cf. Ps 22 (23):4
35 Deut 32:10
36 Ps 31 (32):9
37 Ps 48:18 (49:17)
38 Ps 119:5 (120:6)
39 Ps 41:3 (42:2)
40 Ps 54:7 (55:6)
41 Sg 2:14

precious blood. Let this sweet meditation meanwhile fill my memory, lest forgetfulness wholly darken it. Let me meanwhile *judge that I know nothing but my Lord, and him crucified,*[42] lest empty error lure my knowledge from the firm ground of faith. May your wondrous love[43] claim all my love[44] for itself, lest worldly self-centeredness engulf it. What then? Do I hope for this for myself alone? Fulfill, I ask you, Lord, fulfill that prophecy: *all the ends of the earth will remember and turn back to the Lord.*[45] They will *remember*, it says. It means that in a rational mind the memory of God is concealed, not utterly buried, so that it is not so much something newly engrafted as an old [truth] restored. For unless human reason did not gleam naturally even just a little, in some way, with the memory of God, I think there would be no reason why even the fool would say in his heart, *there is no God.*[46] 15*

Chapter 6: Refutation of the fool who says in his heart: there is no God.

17. Whoever you are, foolish enough to claim in your heart *there is no God*, tell me if you consider anyone wise. Yourself perhaps? Let us suppose so. Yet are you so wise that you could not become unwise? Or if you are unwise, are you so unwise that you could not become wise? Should you deny either of these, I would say, not that you are unwise, but that you are not alive. Now if you have become unwise, do you think it was through loss of wisdom? But you can also become wise. But whence, I ask, if not from wisdom? Even if you are unwise, wisdom still does exist. Yes, you say, but in a wise man. But what man exists who cannot become unwise? If all men were to become unwise, therefore, wisdom would nonetheless exist, otherwise they could not become wise

---

42 1 Co 2:2
43 *dilectio*
44 *amor*
45 Ps 21:28 (22:27)
46 Ps 13 (14):1

again. Yes, among angels, you say. But that great throng of unwise angels shows that despite their nature even angels can become unwise, for they are equal to the others by nature, but unequal by grace. No creature, then, is wise of itself. How then, if not by wisdom? And where does the unwise find the wisdom to become wise again? If he finds it, surely wisdom exists, which is found by the unwise that he may become wise. Otherwise how is that found which does not exist, unless it has previously begun to exist?

18. Not in that way do I find wisdom, you say, but I make myself wise by meditation and [ascetic] exercises. Then do you make yourself wise? And do you make your own wisdom yourself? Why not? I presupposed you were unwise and suddenly you have become so wise that you are even competent to create wisdom for yourself! Or is this being slightly wise, creating a wise man? But if anyone claimed he could make a fool wise, who would not laugh at hearing him? Whence then comes wisdom for the fool? Perhaps from some wise man. And whence is he wise? Perhaps he made himself wise. But before he made himself wise, what was he but unwise? Then the previously mentioned absurd conclusion follows, that a fool made a wise man.

19. If you say that an angel can make someone wise, then whence comes the angel's wisdom? If the angel likewise made himself wise, the previous absurd conclusion follows no less. It remains, then, that the wisdom which makes others wise is not itself made [wise]. Wisdom cannot be unwise, because it cannot be folly, as death cannot be life—although Christ's death is our life—as light cannot be darkness—although we were *once darkness but [are] now light in the Lord.*[47] Nor was John the light, but *he bore witness to the light. That was the true light which enlightens every person who comes into this world.*[48] That is true wisdom, which passes into holy souls so they also may be wise. Is this not enough for you, O fool?

---

47 Eph 5:8
48 Jn 1:7–9

20. I ask again: do you know you exist? Who does not know that, you answer. Surely not even an academic! Have you always existed? Then whence did you receive your existence? Did you make yourself? But how could you, who were nothing, make something so great? Where then did you get your being? From some other man? Then where did he get his? From an angel? Then where did [the angel] get his? We conclude, therefore, that the being from which everything else has its being was not created, just as the wisdom from which all others derive wisdom was not created. So turn a deaf ear to this or that about wisdom and to this or that about being. Let Wisdom itself and Being itself speak to your heart and no longer will you say in your heart, *there is no God*, because in it you will plainly see that you could not even exist to say in your heart, *there is no God*, unless God also existed.

21. I ask again: do you wish to be and to be wise? I assume you will not deny it. Then connect these three: to be, to be wise, to will. Return to your heart, then, you dissembler.[49] Consider what unity and what equality exist in these three. When you discover that these three do exist in you but do not exist from you, think of the eternal essence, the eternal wisdom, and the eternal will of the eternal wisdom and essence, and do not say in your heart, *there is no God*, but rather remember and with all the ends of the earth turn back to the Lord your God.[50]

Chapter 7: The human person withdraws from God by an attachment of the mind.

22. *Your knowledge is too excellent for me, O Lord, you are exalted far above my reach.*[51] Meanwhile, I shall embrace

---

49 Is 46:8
50 Cf. Ps 21:28 (22:27)
51 Ps 138 (139):6

you, Lord Jesus. I, small, shall embrace you small; I, weak, you weak; I, a man, you, a man. For even you, O Lord, were *poor, riding on a donkey, on a colt, the foal of a donkey.*[52] So I shall therefore embrace you, O Lord. All my greatness is but small to you, all my strength is weak to you, all my wisdom is foolish to you. I shall run *towards the scents of your ointments, O Lord.*[53] Are you surprised that I call *ointments*, things which heal the sick, strengthen the weak, and gladden the sorrowing? Awakened by the fragrance of your ointments and refreshed by their perfume, I shall follow you, Lord Jesus. I shall follow you, Lord, although not upon the mountains of spices, where your spouse found you,[54] surely in the garden where your flesh, O Lord, was sown. There you leap, here you sleep. Here, yes, here, you sleep, Lord, here you slumber, here you keep a gentle sabbath in sabbath rest. May my flesh be buried with you, Lord, that what I live in the flesh I may live not in myself but in you who gave yourself up for me.[55] Let my flesh with you be anointed, O Lord, with the myrrh of modesty, that sin may no longer reign in my mortal body,[56] and that I may not become like a beast of burden rotting in its own dung.[57]

23. Whence have you come into the garden? Whence, if not from the cross? If only I, too, might take up your cross, O Lord, and follow you. But how should I follow you?

You ask: 'how did you withdraw from me?' Not by the stride of my foot, I think, Lord, but by the attachment of my mind.[16*] Unwilling to keep my soul's substance for you, I took it for myself, and wishing to possess myself without you, I lost both you and myself. See what a burden I have become to myself![58] I became a place of gloom and misery for myself, a place of

---

52 Zc 9:9. Jn 12:15
53 Sg 1:3
54 Sg 8:14
55 Gal 2:20
56 Rm 6:12
57 Jl 1:17
58 Jb 7:20

horror and a region of destitution. *I shall arise, therefore, and go to my Father and say to him: Father, I have sinned against heaven and against you.*[59]

Chapter 8. God's image in the human person may be restored by the attachment of charity.

24. It is obvious, if I am not mistaken, that just as human pride, by departing from the supreme good not by a footstride but by the mind's attachment, and becoming decrepit in itself disfigured God's image in itself, so human humility, by approaching God by his spirit's attachment is restored to the image of his Creator. Hence the apostle says: *be renewed in the spirit of your mind, and put on the new man who was created according to God.*[60] But how will this renewal come about except by the new precept of charity, of which the Saviour says: *I give you a new commandment.*[61] Then, if the mind puts on this charity perfectly, charity will straightway reform the other two, namely, memory and knowledge, which we said were equally disfigured. A summary of this one precept, then, is presented to us in a very salutary way; it contains the divesting of the old man, the renewal of his mind and the reforming of the divine image.[62]

25. Our love, infected by the venom of self-centeredness and wretchedly ensnared in the birdlime of pleasure, was by its own weight being dragged down ever lower from vice to vice. But when charity, flowing in from above, by its warmth melts our inborn sloth, our love lifts itself to higher levels, sheds its oldness for newness, and is given the silvered pinions of a dove,[63] to fly to that pure and sublime Goodness to

---

59 Lk 15:18
60 Eph 4:23–24
61 Jn 13:34
62 Cf. Eph 4:23–24
63 Ps 67:14 (68:13)

which it owes its birth,[17*] as blessed Paul proclaimed quite openly to the Athenians.

26. For when Paul had subtly discoursed on many things about God, and from the writings of philosophers very insistently proved the existence of the one God in whom *we live and move and have our being,*[64] he said, among other things: *we are indeed his offspring,* and he repeated: *then since we are the offspring of God.*[65] Let no one think that the apostle said *we are God's offspring* to prove we are of the same nature or substance as God. Were that so, we could never be changeable or corruptible or miserable. Nor are we like his only-begotten Son who, born of God's substance, is proved equal in all things to the Father himself. But [Paul] insists, or rather does not deny, that *we are God's offspring*, because the rational soul, created to God's image, is known to be able to share in God's wisdom and happiness. Therefore charity raises our soul up to that for which it was created; but self-centeredness degrades it to what it was sinking towards of its own accord.

Chapter 9. Our love is divided against itself, by the opposing cravings of charity and self-centeredness.

27. Since only that power of the soul which is more usually called love is capable both of charity and of self-centeredness, this love is obviously divided against itself, as if by opposing appetites caused by the new infusion of charity and the remnants of a decrepit self-centeredness. About this the apostle says: *I do not do what I will,*[66] and again: *The flesh lusts against the spirit and the spirit against the flesh. These are so mutually opposed that you do not do the very things you will.*[67] Understand that, contrary to what the corrupt

---

64 Ac 17:28
65 Ac 17:28–29
66 Rm 7:15
67 Gal 5:17

Manichaeans foolishly say, by the terms *spirit* and *flesh*, the apostle in no way describes two opposing natures in one man. By the word *spirit*, he expressed rather the renewal of the mind caused by the infusion of charity: *for the love of God has been poured into our hearts by the Holy Spirit who has been given to us*;[68] by the word *flesh*, he suggests the wretched slavery of the soul caused by the remnants of decrepitude; he affirms that an unending conflict rises in the one mind between an old familiar state and a new and unfamiliar one.

Chapter 10. Free choice occupies a mid-point in the soul, but is not equally capable of good and evil.

28. Between these two—the concupiscence the apostle calls *of the flesh* not because every evil concupiscence is *of the flesh* (since devils, though without any flesh, have no lack of evil concupiscence), but because this comes not from God but from man, who without ambiguity is called *flesh* in Scripture—between this concupiscence, very aptly called self-centeredness, and [the desire] of the spirit which we quite properly call charity (surely not our spirit but the Spirit of God, for *the charity of God has been poured into our hearts by the Holy Spirit who has been given to us*[69])—between these two, I repeat, what is called free choice in man somehow occupies a mid-point, so that to whichever the soul turns, it doubtlessly acts by free choice. No one would be so foolish as to dare to attribute to man, on the basis of free choice, an equal aptitude for good and evil, since we are not *sufficient of ourselves to claim anything as coming from ourselves, because our sufficiency is from God,*[70] since *God is at work* in us both to will and to work for his good purpose,*[71] and finally since *it*

---

68 Rm 5:5
69 Rm 5:5
70 2 Co 3:5
71 Ph 2:13

depends not on man's will or striving, but on God's mercy.[72]
What follows? In all these texts is it denied that free choice
exists in man? Far from it.

29. Free choice is indeed the soul's force or nature, or
whatever other term can be found for that power in man
whereby, not without the judgement of reason,he consents to
anything whatever. It is not the actual consent to this or that,
to good or evil, but that [power] by which one consents. Just
as sight is one thing and vision is another, for sight is one of
the five senses in the body and vision the activity of that sense,
so we distinguish between consent and that [power] by which
one consents. Consent is indeed an action of the soul, but free
choice is a natural power of the soul, by which it gives
consent, possessing implanted within itself a judgement by
which it chooses the object of consent. But because consent is
made by the will, and judgement by reason, both together, the
will and reason, constitute free choice. The reason presents, as
it were, things good and bad, just and unjust, or things in
between; the will gives consent, and only by the will is consent given, no matter what consent is given to.

30. Where there is a will, there also is freedom. Free choice,
then, as we said, seems to consist of these two, liberty of the
will and the choice of reason. You see, therefore, that whatever the source of man's good will, this does not coerce his
free choice, since neither in good nor in bad will does he lose
his will, and because of this, he does not lose his freedom; nor
indeed does he lose his reason, nor therefore his judgement.
What follows? *Since God is at work* in us *to will,*[73] have we
then lost our *will?* Or because it is God's doing that we use our
reason well, do we therefore not use our reason? Or because
anything good we perform comes to us from God, do we
therefore not perform that good? Or since we are not *sufficient
of ourselves to claim anything as coming from ourselves, since*

---

72 Rm 9:16
73 Ph 2:13

our sufficiency is from God,[74] does our sufficiency therefore not exist? Although it is by the grace of God that we do all these things, we do them, and we do them not without our will or without our reason, and hence we do them not without free choice.

Chapter 11. Grace does not take away free choice.

31. God accomplishes nothing of this kind in such creatures as cattle, which lack will and reason and hence free choice. Hence they themselves perform nothing of this kind. Any good God accomplishes through us or by us without our will is God's alone and not ours. But anything he accomplishes along with our will is both his and ours. *If I do a thing willingly,* says Paul, *I have a reward, but if not of my own will, I am entrusted with a stewardship.*[75] Therefore, that the work God accomplishes in or through us may also belong to us, he sways our will to give consent, and thus thanks to his grace the reward become ours. If I do the deed willingly, I receive a reward. But that I may be willing to do a good work, it is God who causes even my willing.[76] Then arousing the will itself to seek, to ask, to knock, he gives grace upon grace to complete what the good will chooses.

32. Finally, because the reward of good works is eternal life, by granting that, God sets a crown on his own gifts which he willed to be our merits. See all this in Paul who says: *I was a blasphemer, a persecutor and reviler*[77]—here is a will, but an ill will, and here are merits, but the worst of merits—*but I received mercy that I might have faith.*[78] See his good will, but look at its source. Not because some good in me came first,

---

74 2 Co 3:5
75 1 Co 9:17
76 Cf. Rm 9:16
77 1 Tm 1:13
78 1 Tm 1:13; Cf. 1 Co 7:25

but because his mercy anticipated me. *I obtained mercy indeed, that I might be faithful.* *Specifically,* as blessed Augustine says, *anyone can go to church, hear the word of God, receive the sacrament of Christ unwillingly, but no one can believe except willingly.*[79] Listen to [Paul] about works: *I worked harder than any of them.* [80] In this, Paul, do you have something you did not receive? On the contrary, I did receive. Surely *I worked harder than any of them, yet not I.*[81]

33. How can both be true: *I…and not I? Not I,* because not by me, not by my efforts or by my wisdom or finally by my merits, but *by the grace of God.*[82] What follows? Does God act to take away your free choice, destroy the will and withdraw the judgement of reason? Far from it! I said, *not I,* because *by the grace of God;* but still I,because *the grace of God with me.* How is it *with me?* By acting so that I would consent to his activity and thus co-operate, and willingly co-operate, lest if he should act by me or through me but against my will I would be unable to exclaim: *I have fought the good fight, I have finished the course, I have kept the faith.*[83] Free choice, then, is not sufficient for any good work, but in it or with it or through it God accomplishes many good works. In it, when by a hidden inspiration he awakens [our choice] for some good work; with it, when by our consent he joins our free choice to himself; through it, when with God's co-operation one advances through the other. *There is reserved for me a crown of righteousness,* says [Paul]. What is this crown if not eternal life? *There is reserved for me a crown of righteousness which the Lord will bestow on me on that day.*[84]

34. *Will bestow,* he says. Therefore because it is bestowed, eternal life is a reward. It is a reward, obviously, because a good work has preceded; *I have fought the good fight.* But

---

79 *In Ioh. tract.* 26.2; cf. *Ep. Ioh.* 3.1 & 5.
80 1 Co 15:10
81 1 Co 15:10
82 1 Co 15:10
83 2 Tm 4:7
84 2 Tm 4:8

where does this work come from? *Not I, but the grace of God with me*. The merits belong to us, the grace belongs to God. For these merits he awards eternal life, grace for grace. He will make settlement with each according to his works.[85] But only those works are honored with the reward of heaven which are first conferred by his largess. That eternal life is a grace, listen to him again: *For the wages of sin is death, but the grace of God is life eternal.*[86] Eternal life is a grace, I tell you, and a twofold grace: a grace because given for grace; a grace because glory outweighs our merits. *For the sufferings of the present life are not comparable to the future glory which will be revealed in us.*[87]

Chapter 12. Free choice is taken away from neither the saved nor the damned, and grace works only in free choice.

35. But in that glory shall we be without the will to consent to such a great good or the reason to appreciate such a good? Of course not. We shall not be without free choice, not that by it we shall be able to do any evil but that by it we may remain capable of that good. Since beasts are devoid of reason and will, they can be neither liable to damnation nor capable of salvation. But infants in whom grace is not greater but more obvious, in whom no merits exist even gratuitously, although through the weakness which follows the punishment of sin they live and die without free choice, once divested of the flesh which envelopes and confines them, they surely should never be thought to share either in eternal happiness or deserved condemnation without their rational will.

36. Whatever the number of [children] saved, grace is more apparent in as much as they lack the free choice to which

---

85 Cf. Mt 16:27, Rm 2:6
86 Rm 6:23
87 Rm 8:18

merits could be attributed. Further, that grace by which both merits and rewards are conferred seems to me quite bountiful. Hence we should boast of nothing, when nothing is ours. For what distinguishes you, man? Free choice? Yes, clearly, but [that distinguishes you] from beasts of burden, not from the unjust. Even the unjust have free choice, for without it they could not even be unjust. Prescinding from original sin,which for a different reason binds without exception even the unwilling, no one can be just or unjust except through the will and hence through free choice. But only grace arouses the will to justice; the will casts itself down into injustice.

37. Further, wherever there is a will, there also is freedom. For, wherever one is voluntarily, there one is not forced to be by necessity. Somehow, then, the will has an innate freedom, because it cannot be subject to any determinism.[88] Do you wish to hear about a freedom even amid injustice? Listen to the apostle: *when you were slaves of sin, you were the freemen of justice.*[89] Do you see that even in the slavery of sin the will does not lack freedom? But in the freedom of an unjust will is there lacking the judgement of reason whereby it discerns what it wants from what it does not want and judges what is advantageous, or good or pleasurable for it, even what it wants maliciously? Of course not! If either [the will or judgement] were lacking, perhaps one could want only the pleasurable, or like a beast of burden sense [only] by the flesh, but not give or refuse consent to the pleasurable by the judgement of reason that is characteristic of free choice. That a person can abuse reason even for evil is proved by these prophetic words: *they know how to do wrong.*[90] Even in the pains of hell there is no lack of free choice, through which the damned voluntarily, that is, freely, object to the woes they suffer, and no lack of the judgement of reason by which they accuse and

---

88 *necessitas*
89 Rm 6:20
90 Jr 4:22

judge themselves, because they suffer such woes through their own fault.

38. Unless I am wrong, the reason is obvious: because grace does not destroy free choice nor does free choice lessen grace. How would grace take away free choice, when grace can act only within free choice? The grace we are discussing acts neither in brute beasts nor in senseless beings, but only in creatures capable of hearing a command or a prohibition: do this and do that, don't do this and don't do that. Such commands are undoubtedly spoken only to creatures in whom there exists the free choice of willing this or that. The grace of God acts that they may will the good, not by destroying free choice so that they may not will anything at all, but by influencing them to will the good. Consequently, when you do something good, do not think you perform these acts through your own powers, but on the other hand do not make the deed independent of your will, since the deed must not be called good unless it is also voluntary.

Chapter 13. The reason why free choice is not equally capable of both good and evil.

39. Someone will say: I agree now to what has been sufficiently proved: that God's grace can so *accomplish all things in all persons* [91] without detracting from freedom of choice. But who knows whether that is so? What is the reason why a person is not self-sufficient for good, while he needs no help for evil? Who is there who needs greater proofs than these: the catholic faith agrees with this statement; the daily experience of anyone progressing well proves it; the evidence of both prophets and apostles together affirms it; and a still greater witness than these, the very mouth of Truth confirms this statement: *you can do nothing without me.*[92] Moreover, for

---

91 1 Co 12:6
92 Jn 15:5

eyes purified by this faith, reason cannot be lacking, understanding will assist, and truth will shed its light.

40. Let anyone who can, see. Let anyone who cannot see, believe. Let anyone who sees, rejoice, but humbly. Let anyone who does not see, believe but perseveringly, because *unless you believe, you will not understand.*[93] Let him see, I say, that since every creature was made from nothing and made changeable, by the natural impetus of its own mutability it always sinks towards that from which it was made, that is, towards nothing. It is very easy to see that everything changeable by nature needs something unchangeable to avert change. Of course nothing changeable has unchangeableness in itself or it would certainly not be changeable. How much less does it confer [unchangeableness] on something else. But if a creature, not protected by some support, may change, would anyone not readily see that, more naturally and specifically—by an inevitable impulse, so to speak—it is changed into what it was made from? Accordingly, that it may not sink to the bottom by its own changeableness, that it may hold changeableness in check where it is, and that it may rise to higher levels under happier auspices, it always needs the grace of the One by whose power it was created.

Chapter 14. A difference exists between the grace which the first humans had in paradise and that which the elect have in this world; ill will is justly imputed to humankind, although the faculty of free choice is not sufficient for good will to prevail.

41. Although no weakness hampered either an angel in heaven or man in paradise, allowing any evil to dominate them, still because each by nature was changeable, this grace was necessary for both. Certainly, had this grace not been conferred, each would have had an excuse for sinning. But

---

93 Is 7:9 LXX (Cf. *Anima* 2.53; CCCM 1:726).

because good will had been conferred on them by creative grace, and because the faculty for persevering in good will would have been added by assisting grace, if they had wished, their changeable nature cannot be used as an excuse. Divine goodness would not have failed to support and promote that nature, if their own wickedness had not betrayed it. But I dare not hazard an opinion about whether at some time, even now, such a grace may be conferred on the reprobate in order that good will may be inspired in them, too, or whether a grace may be added by which, if they wished, the faculty for perseverance would not fail them.

42. Because greater misery hangs over the elect than over the first humans in paradise, surely greater grace is also conferred on them. The greater the weaknesses afflicting them, the more abundantly the faculty to resist is offered them. As we said already, we know that the power to persevere was granted to the first humans, if they wished, and that perseverance itself was granted to the elect. But what, you ask, is the fault of a man if he did not possess good will, which he can neither acquire by his own efforts nor, once acquired, retain by his own efforts? What kind of foundation for good will is one that is made worse by his fault? Why should that inability not be very justly imputed to him, which the Creator did not impose on him but to which he submitted of his own accord? Now if perhaps it does not seem fair that he be blamed for it, if he does not now have the good will which indeed he could not have if he had not received it, is it unjust to blame him for losing what he had received and unjust to impute to him the bad will by which, under no compulsion, he sinned?

Chapter 15. Even the condemnation of little children is very just.

43. Reason, you say, very justly condemns to these [punishments] the reprobate who, capable of reason, lacked neither

the judgement to choose nor the will to consent; yet why sentence to condemnation little children whom neither creation made evil nor self-will made unjust? Why indeed? Do you consider it unjust that fire should devour a useless and unfruitful tree trunk? Think, I ask you, of the entire human race as a dry trunk, fruitless and blighted to the roots because infected by the venom of the ancient serpent; this is very justly consigned to the flames, destined for the fire, sentenced to condemnation. What follows? You show your ingratitude, useless trunk, that some twigs pruned from your dead roots are snatched from the blaze to be grafted onto a fruitful trunk like shoots and restored to their original beauty!

44. Behold that green wood, the tree of life, the tree *whose leaf does not wither and which prospers in all it does.*[94] In his own tenderest side, which he purposely permitted to be opened on the cross, he made a place for branches pruned by his compassion from the condemned root, so that, engrafted and planted and made one with him—not by their own power, which is nothing, but by sharing his spirit—they might revive and grow green. Then having received the *abundant rainfall which God reserves for his heritage,*[95] with the warming sun of divine charity and the returning new sap of heavenly grace, they might bear spiritual fruit to be stored in heaven's barns. But I have been abandoned, says a worthless branch. Of course you have been abandoned. Why do you complain? *Is your eye evil because I am good?*[96]

45. I gave to many what I owed to none. In return, are you grudging, are you envious? In return, are you hostile, do you spread calumny? But since an equal condemnation engulfs both children, you ask, why is one chosen but the other rejected? Hear why! Because, said [the Lord], *I have loved Jacob, but hated Esau.*[97] Unjustly! you shout. *Does the pot say*

---

94 Ps 1:3
95 Ps 67:10 (68:9)
96 Mt 20:15
97 Ml 1:2–3, Rm 9:13

to the potter who made it: why did you make me this way?
Does the potter not have the right to make from the same clay
one pot for special honorable use and another for ignominy?[98]
If then from the vessels a man makes he designates those he
chooses for honorable use or exposes to ignominy those he
chooses, and no one charges him with being unjust, are you
going to make false accusations if, from among all the vessels
exposed very justly to ignominy, God takes or leaves whichever he pleases? Or if he should restore either to its original
honor or expose to deserved condemnation whichever he
pleases? If, in distinguishing among vessels fashioned from the
same clay, I say, the potter's own will is his justice, how then is
the will of the Omnipotent, who created all things from nothing, not much more than supreme justice, in distinguishing,
setting in order, taking or leaving, saving or condemning all
things?

46. Therefore, God pities whom he wills and shows mercy
to whomever he pleases.[99] He makes obdurate whom he wills
by very justly abandoning him, or makes gentle whom he
wills by his ever tender mercy. He does whatever he wills but
does nothing unjust, because between justice and injustice his
will alone distinguishes, for his will is nothing less than Equity
itself. His will depends on no other law of justice, but certainly
the law of justice depends on his will. We have said all this, so
that the condemnation of little children may not seem unjust.
So do not be haughty, man, *but stand in awe. If God does not
spare the branches,* whose condition is like yours and whose
merit equal, *perhaps he may not spare you.*[100]

47. *Notice, therefore, the severity and the goodness of God:
severity* to those who are abandoned, *but goodness towards
you, if indeed you abide in goodness. Otherwise you also will
be forsaken.*[101] Again, that you may be, not forsaken, but

---

98 Rm 9:20–21
99 Rom 9:18
100 Rm 11:20–21
101 Rm 11:22

rather distinguished from those forsaken, be not overconfi-
dent[102] in yourself, do not despair of God's goodness, do not
be careless about good works, do not be sluggish in praying
with the prophet: *distinguish my cause from an ungodly
people.*[103] Indeed, that you may abide in this goodness, do not
flatter yourself on your strength, but presume on him to whom
the prophet likewise cried: *you, O Lord, will save us and
guard us forever from this generation,*[104] from that generation
about which he added in the next verse: *the wicked prowl
round about.*[105] These, like Sampson, with the locks of their
virtues shorn and the eyes of knowledge and reason gouged
out, are relegated to the millstone,[106] so that abandoning the
shortcut of charity, they may follow the round about way of
self-centeredness.[18*]

Chapter 16. Charity does not fall short of perfection.

48. What about you, my soul? Are you entangled enough,
turning in this circle? *Those who circle around me lift up their
head,* it says, *let their busy whispering recoil upon themselves.*[107] What is the reward of this busy-ness, I ask? Anything
more than the husks of swine? But with no satisfaction. If
perhaps there is, then what kind of satisfaction? How much
sweeter, more pleasing, more gratifying is the hunger of charity than the satisfaction of self-centeredness. But in terms of
happiness there is no comparison. The more stuffed one is
with self-centeredness, the more empty one is of truth and
hence the more miserable. Therefore, my soul, when you
overhear the *recriminations of the crowds who dally in this*

---

102 *praesumere*
103 Ps 42(43):1
104 Ps 11:8 (12:7)
105 Ps 11:9 (12:8)
106 Jdg 16:21
107 Ps 139 (140):10

circle, be *like a broken shard*,[108] so that by abandoning yourself and passing wholly to God,[19*] you may know how to live and die not for yourself but only for him who died and rose again for you.

49. O, who will allow me to be so inebriated with this saving cup, so steeped in amazement of mind, so lulled in sweetest languor, that loving the Lord my God with all my heart, with all my soul, and with all my strength,[109] I may seek always not my interests but those of Jesus Christ,[110] and *loving my neighbor as myself*[111] I may seek what is useful not for myself but for another. O word summing up and abbreviating with equity! O word of charity, word of love,[112] word of endearment,[113] word of total inner perfection! O summarizing word which can lack nothing, abbreviating word on which *depend the whole law and the prophets*.[114] O Judaean, why do you need so much ritual? Here circumcision, here sabbath, here saving victims, here fragrant sacrifice, here incense of the sweetest aroma. Hold fast to charity, and none of these will be missing. Omit charity, and none of these will do any good.[20*]

Chapter 17. Spiritual circumcision is included in charity.

50. This is obviously not the amputation of a physical member, but rather a true and perfect circumcision of the inner and outer man. This prunes sensual pleasure,[115] extinguishes lust,[116] holds gluttony in check,restrains anger, completely overturns envy and vanquishes pride, the parent of all

---

108 Ps 30:14 (31:13)
109 Mt 22:37
110 Cf Ph 2:21
111 Mt 22:39
112 *amor*
113 *dilectio*
114 Mt 22:40
115 *voluptas*
116 *libido*

vices. With spiritual sweetness, this soothes the gnawing pangs of sadness and heals the listlessness of nagging sloth. With the sharpest swordtip of generosity excising the pest of greed, it frees and protects the soul from the vice of idolatry. What, I ask, is more perfect that this circumcision, for it dismembers the vices, destroys the body of sin, strips off the hairy skins of our first parents and scours all the filth and corruption of ancient times. Indeed, fear does not constrict, wantonness does not defile, anger does not tear to pieces, and pride does not puff up a mind steeped in the sweetness of charity. No smoke of empty vainglory blows through it, no fury agitates it and no ambition goads its flanks. Avarice does not diminish it, nor sadness dishearten it, nor envy waste it away. *Charity is not jealous, does no wrong, is not arrogant or ambitious; it is not selfish, is not irritable, thinks no evil, does not rejoice at wrong.*[117] You see how this spiritual circumcision is the deathblow for all the vices. With a divine scalpel it purifies all the physical senses, it gouges out wantonness of the eyes, scrapes away prurience of the ears, drives away excessive sweetness from the sense of taste, peels off the impudence of the tongue, shuts out alluring perfumes from the nostrils, and extirpates dangerous softness from the sense of touch.

Chapter 18. In charity should be sought the true and spiritual sabbath.

51. Now the Judaean should recognize what kind of sabbath this is, if, poor little man, groaning under the burden of sin, caught in the snares of passion, having little or no taste of this sweetness, he can say something about it. If only I could be given the slightest respite from Pharaoh's taskmasters[118] to allow my soul to pause for at least half an hour in the silence

---

117 1 Co 13:4–6
118 Cf. *Spir amic* (CF 5:29)

of this sabbath, straightway *falling asleep in his presence*[119] *I would be silent and in my slumber rest with kings and consuls who build solitary retreats for themselves...and fill their palaces with silver.*[120] But whence such hope for a wretch? I shall seek, yes, I shall seek that sabbath, if perchance you heed the desire of a poor man, Lord, and that *after you draw me from the swamp of misery and the miry bog,*[121] you may allow me, even by the taste of a tiny drop, to experience *how bountiful is the goodness you have stored up for those who fear you,*[122] because you reveal yourself only to those who love you.

52. Those who love you, rest in you. There is true rest, true tranquillity, true peace, a true sabbath for the mind. But for you, O Judaean, what is the origin of the sabbath? That on the seventh day, you say, God rested from all his works. So then what? Did he not rest on the preceding six days? Surely no, you say, for during those six days he made heaven and earth, *and on the seventh day he rested.*[123] Because of this, then, you are commanded to be at leisure.[124] To be at leisure, I say, not to dance. If you only knew how to be at leisure and see [125] that Jesus himself is God, then certainly with the darkness of unbelief soon lifted to reveal his face, you would recognize the perfect observance of the sabbath in charity. No longer would you be much attached to the banquets of flesh for your sabbath of flesh but, entering the place of the wondrous tabernacle right up to the house of God, with the cry of a banqueter in his song of exultation and praise, in thanksgiving you would break into this song: *we will exult and rejoice in you, extolling your love above wine.*[126] But at the peak of your

---

119 Ps 4:9(8)
120 Jb 3:13–15
121 Ps 39:3(40:2)
122 Ps 30:20 (31:19)
123 Gn 2:2
124 *vacare*
125 Cf. Ps 45:11 (46:10)
126 Sg 1:3

joyfulness you would take up the song of Habakkuk: *but I shall rejoice in the Lord and exult in Jesus my God.*[127]

Chapter 19. The seventh should be preferred to other days, for on this day is God's charity commended.

53. Let us turn our attention briefly to why the seventh day takes precedence over others. Of course, it was a great day on which, at God's command, light, dispelling darkness, shone forth. Great also was the day on which the divine voice separated the upper from the lower waters by putting the firmament between them. Not less precious was the day on which, once the waters had been gathered together, at God's word dry land was clothed with grass, adorned with trees, decorated with flowers, and made fruitful with crops. Nor was that day inferior on which heaven was adorned with lights to distinguish the succession of days, the change of seasons, the course of the year and the order of the constellations. How outstanding, too, was the day on which the water, giving forth the race of living creatures, plunged some into its waves and sent others off into the air. No lack of wonders marked the sixth day, for then quadrupeds and serpents emerged from the earth, and at last man, fashioned from clay, was animated by the divine breath. None of these seems comparable to the seventh, on which was celebrated no creation of nature, but the rest of God himself and the perfection of all his creatures. You remember the text: *on the seventh day God finished his work and rested from all the work he performed.*[128] Great is this day, great this rest, great this sabbath.

54. O if only you understood! If I am not mistaken, this day is not brought to an end by the passing of our visible sun; it does not begin with sunrise or end with sunset. It has no 'morning', no 'evening'. Furthermore, about the first day—if

127 Hab 3:18
128 Gn 2:2

we should say the first, because Scripture does not call it the first day, but day one. Then why is the next day called the second, you ask, if day one is not the first? Notice that one is not said haphazardly of the second [day], nor again of the third, so that one day repeated six times, the number six is commended to us. But whatever that obscure passage means, the text does say: *there was evening and morning day one,*[129] and below: *there was evening and morning the second day,*[130] and so on for the others. The mutability of all creatures is meant by these words, I think, a decrease and an increase, a beginning and an end. Nothing of this sort about the seventh day. No evening, no morning, neither end nor beginning is ascribed to it. This day of God's rest, then, is not temporal but eternal. A moment ago you imagined for yourself a God toiling in time and, as it were, being fatigued and resting in time. This was not pondering on God, but fashioning an idol.

55. Since you have no idol in the temple at Jerusalem, beware of having one in your heart. God made nothing by working, because he spoke and it was done.[131] He did not rest fatigued on one day only, because the day of his rest is eternal. Therefore his rest is his eternity, because it is nothing other than his divinity. You had thought he was like you, needing to create something to please his eye, or for him to enjoy, finding repose in it. This is why his rest is not described as being in any creature, that you may know precisely that he needs none of them, is self-sufficient in everything, and created nothing to meet his own needs, but everything to satisfy his overflowing charity. Furthermore, he created all things that they might exist, he sustains all things which endure that they may endure, and he guides all things together to their appointed ends. He does this from no necessity, but only from his own ever gracious will. He *reaches mightily from one end of the earth to the other* by his ever present and omnipotent

---

129 Gn 1:5
130 Gn 1:8
131 Ps 32(33):9

majesty, but *he disposes all things gently,*[132] restful and resting in his own ever calm charity.

56. Charity alone is his changeless and eternal rest, his eternal and changeless tranquillity, his eternal and changeless Sabbath. Charity alone is the reason why he created what was to be created, guides what needs guidance, moves what needs moving, advances what needs to be advanced and perfects what needs perfection. Therefore where his rest is recorded, there most aptly is added the perfection of all things. [133] For his charity is his very will and also his very goodness, and all this is nothing but his being. Indeed for him this is to be always resting, that is, always existing, in his ever gracious charity, in his ever peaceful will and in his ever abounding goodness. Accordingly, as the changeableness of creation is signified in the succession of days and the alternations of morning and evening—by which all created things are recorded—so by this day, for which there is no addition or subtraction or succession, which is neither straitened by a beginning nor terminated by an end, is God's own eternity duly commemorated; in it his rest is aptly described, so that it not be thought he made any creature from need or with effort. But why is the number six there and the number seven here? Accept such explanation as we can give.

Chapter 20. Why six is the number commended in God's work, seven in his rest.[21*]

57. The number six surely seems to contain the greatest perfection. Its factors are one, two, and three. Indeed, six is the sum of all its factors, with no remainder. If you ask what part of six is one, two, or three, the answer is a sixth, a third, a half. Now there is no other number in six of which you can say that it is a factor of six. So all the factors of six are one, two,

---

132 Ws 8:1
133 Cf. Gn 2:1–2

and three. Add these and you will find neither more nor less than six. This number, then, was kept for the creation of the world, that among all creatures you might consider nothing superfluous, nothing imperfect.

Moreover, the number seven was reserved for God's rest. God's rest we called his charity. Rightly so. *The Father loves the Son,* [Scripture] says, *and shows him all that he does;*[134] and again: *as I keep my Father's commandments, so I remain in his good pleasure;*[135] and the Father testifies: *this is my beloved Son, in whom I am well pleased.*[136] This mutual delight[137] of Father and Son is the gentlest love, the pleasing embrace, and the most blessed charity by which the Father reposes in his Son and the Son in his Father. This imperturbable rest, genuine peace, eternal calm, incomparable goodness, and indivisible unity is surely the unity of both, or rather, that in which each possesses the unity, sweetness, kindness, and joy we call the Holy Spirit; and it is for this reason that he is believed to have assumed this title as properly his own, because it is clearly common to both.

58. Now although each of the two, Father and Son, is Spirit and each is holy, still he who proceeds from both, namely the consubstantial charity and unity of both, is properly called the Holy Spirit.[22*] Though he is one [person] and one [being] with the Father and the Son, still because of the sevenfold grace which is believed to flow from the fullness of that fountain, he is referred to in Scripture by the number seven. Hence also, according to Zechariah, *on one stone are discovered seven eyes,*[138] and according to the Apocalypse, seven spirits stand before the throne of God.[139] You see, then, how great is the excellence of charity, in which the Creator and Ruler of all things celebrates an unending and ineffable sabbath.

---

134 Jn 5:20
135 Jn 15:10
136 Mt 3:17, 17:5, 2 P 1:17
137 *dilectio*
138 Zc 3:9
139 Rv 1:4

Chapter 21. A trace of divine charity is visible in all creatures, therefore all tend towards a sabbath, that is, towards rest.

59. Moreover, if you more closely contemplate every creature, from the first to the last, from the highest to the lowest, from the loftiest angel to the lowliest worm, you will surely discover divine goodness—which we have called nothing other than divine charity—which contains, enfolds, and penetrates all things, not by pouring into a place, or being diffused in space, or by nimbly moving about, but by the steady, mysterious, and self-contained simplicity of its substantial presence. Charity joins the lowest to the highest, binds in harmonious peace contraries to contraries, cold to hot, wet to dry, smooth to rough, hard to soft, so that among all creatures there can be nothing adverse, nothing contradictory, nothing unbecoming, nothing disturbing, nothing to disfigure the beauty of the universe, but that all things should rest, as it were, in utterly tranquil peace, with the tranquillity of that order which charity ordained for the universe. Hence anything which bursts its bonds and goes beyond the order of divine goodness is soon caught up by the order of that supremely unconquered power, so that although in itself this thing may be restless and disordered, not only is it not a hindrance to the tranquillity of the unwise, but it is a great help, if only by comparison with it beautiful things are judged to be more beautiful and good things better.

60. Consequently, each and every group tends toward its own order, seeks its own place,[23*] and is restless outside its own order, but restful within [it]. If you throw a stone into the air, for example, does it not soon fall to the ground by its own weight, as if submitting to some force ? It will come to rest only where, on contact with something more solid, it neither tips to the side nor sinks yet lower. If you pour oil into other fluids, it resists submersion, immediately rises to the surface and rests nowhere until, on top of the others, it comes to the rest proper to its own order. What about plants or bushes? Do

they not seem to seek their own soil, some heavy, some light, some rich, some clayey, some sandy, where they may produce more abundant fruit?

61. If shrubs are set out or reset, planted or transplanted according to the order of their nature, they testify by their growth, as it were, that they aspire to[140] nothing more. Finally, if you carefully observe each and every group of bodies, you will notice, of course, that each is composed of its own parts, that various parts are joined by a bond of unity, that they maintain the order of their nature in which they rest as if by a kind of peace, so that if you wish to transfer a part from that mode in which each exists, the peace of the parts is somehow disturbed until, brought into the pattern you desire and with tranquillity regained, they again find rest. Moreover, with irrational animals, what a task it is to protect their safety, to avoid misfortune, to try to satisfy their physical appetites! When these are satisfied they are at rest, since they have appetites for nothing more. They can desire nothing more because they lack reason and knowledge.

Chapter 22. A rational creature rests only once he attains happiness;[24*] he hopes for happiness, but unhappily avoids the path by which he may arrive at it.

62. This privilege of rising above the physical senses to strive for higher things is reserved for you, O rational soul, in preference to other living things. You will never satisfy your desire until by a felicitous curiosity you reach what is highest and best, what nothing surpasses and nothing excels. Wherever you stand below that, however high or great or pleasant it may be adjudged, you will doubtlessly remain miserable. Miserable, because needy. Needy, because ahead lies what you seek; ahead lies what you are panting for; ahead lies that happiness towards the achievement of which a natural force

---

140 *affectare*

drives the rational soul. Wherefore, since the conscience of each and every individual testifies that all humans want to be happy and since this will can in no way be destroyed, obviously a rational creature can attain the rest desired by all humans only by attaining happiness.

63. Moreover, the blind perversity of miserable man is lamentable enough.Although he desires happiness ardently, not only does he not do those things by which he may obtain his desire but rather, with contrary disaffection,[141] takes steps to add to his misery. In my opinion, he would never do this, if a false image of happiness were not deceiving him, or a semblance of real misery frightening him off from happiness. Does anyone not see that poverty, grief, hunger, and thirst are no slight part of misery? Yet through them real misery is frequently averted and eternal happiness pursued. *Blessed are you poor,* said Jesus, *for yours is the kingdom of heaven.*[142] *Blessed are you who weep, for you shall be comforted.*[143] *Blessed are you who hunger now, for you shall be satisfied.*[144] Poverty, then, is rewarded with eternal riches, grief is changed to eternal joy, for the hungry eternal satisfaction is in store. No one doubts that all these, riches, joy, and satisfaction, are not lacking in happiness. But because an appearance of joy deludes any wicked person by some attachment of his will, his false delight disappears with the satisfaction of his desires, while in his misery he does not know what consolation there is for the elect even in oppression and what rejoicing in hope.

64. The wicked dreads an unhappy look appearing on the features, but under the hue of happiness grasps at real unhappiness, the false joy which does not escape real sorrow, preferring that to the misery which presages true happiness. He is like a sick person who earnestly hopes to recover but because of the immediate pain shuns an amputation or dreads

---

141 *Proniori affectu*
142 Mt 5:3, Lk 6:20
143 Mt 5:5
144 Lk 6:21

cauterization. Lured by immediate relief he demands the fomentations of an oil poultice, though his disease is a kind that rages more on this gentle treatment and does not abate without the pain of cautery or amputation. So man is miserable, or deceived, as long as he thinks that happiness is something it is not, or allured by the agreeableness of present things that fool him. He gets used to misery, and indeed never loses his longing for happiness; and, as if struggling unhappily in this circle, never rests. Now since God alone is superior, and an angel equal, to a rational soul, and all other things are considered inferior, what is closer to madness than to abandon the superior and to pine for rest in beings inferior to oneself?

Chapter 23. The prerogative of the rational creature, which naturally craves rest not found in health of the body or wealth of the world.

65. O wondrous creature, inferior only to the Creator, how much will you debase yourself? Do you love the world? But you yourself are superior to the world. Do you admire the sun? But you yourself are brighter than the sun. Do you philosophize about the harmony of the revolving heavens? But you are more sublime than the heavens. Do you examine the mysterious causes of creation? But no creature is a greater mystery than you. Do you doubt it, when you may pass judgement on all creatures, yet none of them on you? But if you wish to judge them, then do not love them. Do not love to judge them. Love him who set you over, not under, all creatures. He set you over them not that through them you might be happier, but that he might be the one through whom you would be superior, subjecting all things to you as a crowning honor and keeping himself for you as rewarding happiness. Why then do you pursue fleeting beauties, when your own beauty neither fades with age nor grows shabby with poverty, nor becomes wan with illness, nor is ruined even by death

itself? Seek what you seek, but not there. You are seeking, that nothing may elude your will and that thus you may find rest. Then seek this. Where, you ask? Not in health of the body, for if you love it so much you seek rest there, realize with what efforts you acquire it if you do not have it, and with what painful remedies painful diseases are driven out. If you enjoy good health, consider how much care is required to maintain it; and how many diseases, fevers, plagues, and finally deaths, lie in wait for it!

66. What next? Is [rest to be sought] in wealth? But what a task to acquire it, what anxiety to keep it, what dread lest it be lost, what grief if it slips away.²⁵* You increased your money only to increase your anxiety. You fear the powerful may extort it. You fear a thief may steal it. You fear a clerk may lose it. Who can say how often happens what the wise man describes: *riches were stored up to their owner's loss.*¹⁴⁵ The poor man, therefore, rests more easily. The traveller with empty pockets—as someone said—does not fear the robber's ambush. With his gate unbarred, the poor man sleeps safe from nocturnal burglars. The satirist's verse says the same: *The traveller with pockets empty whistles in the face of the highwayman.*¹⁴⁶

With an elegant smile a wise man mocks the gnawing anxieties of the rich, saying: *the surfeit of the rich will not let him sleep.*¹⁴⁷ Although it sometimes happens literally that a rich man, stuffed to indigestion and trying to sleep on a heavy stomach, is kept awake by his own flatulence, still the verse applies rather to the sleep of which the beloved boasts in the Canticle: *I slumber but my heart keeps vigil,*¹⁴⁸ and about which the psalmist says: *in peace I shall lie down and take my rest.*¹⁴⁹

---

145 Qo 5:12
146 Juvenal, *Sat.* 10.22
147 Qo 5:11
148 Sg 5:2
149 Ps 4:9(8)

67. Once the physical senses slumber and temporal cares are thrust from the inner recesses of the heart, this is the sleep in which a holy soul reposes in the sweetness of the Lord, *tastes and sees how sweet is the Lord and how happy is someone who hopes in him.*[150] But do not suppose that any rich man ever dozes off to sleep so easily, because, always ardently desiring wealth, the more he amasses the more he lusts with insatiable greed for what he has not. No wonder Solomon says: *The miser finds no satisfaction in money; someone who loves wealth gains from it no profit.*[151] He brings down on his head this curse of the prophet: *Woe to anyone who amasses what is not his,* and deriding his accumulation of coins, he adds immediately: *why does he weigh himself down with heavy clay?*[152]

Chapter 24. Among the rich, the elect differ from the reprobate.

68. Note that Solomon does not say, *someone who has wealth,* but *someone who loves wealth gains from it no profit.*[153] Now there are some elect who, even if they have wealth, do not love it, so do not seek rest in it. But heeding Paul's instruction to the rich *not to be haughty or to set their hope on uncertain riches,* they *give freely, share, and so save up a good capital sum for themselves that they may possess true life,*[154] and derive no little fruit from their riches, for certainly they will hear from the Lord: *come, blessed of my Father...for I was hungry and you gave me to eat* and so forth.[155]

---

150 Ps 33:9 (34:8)
151 Qo 5:9
152 Hab 2:6
153 Qo 5:9
154 1 Tm 6:17
155 Mt 25:34–35

69. Surely [the elect] do not labor to acquire riches, for they fear the apostle's warning: *those who want to be rich fall into the devil's snare.*[156] Futile anxiety to protect their wealth does not crucify them. They sing aloud the promise of the Lord who forbids anxiety and promises what is needed: *do not be anxious, asking, what shall we eat or what shall we drink.*[157] And a little later, *seek first the kingdom of God and his justice, and all this will be yours as well.*[158] Finally, they do not murmur at the loss [of riches], but instead they accept *with joy* even *the theft of their goods,* remembering *their possession of a better and enduring substance.*[159] But the contrary befalls the perverse. They think they can pacify the appetite of the rational soul, which only God can satisfy, with the cheapest abundance of worldly goods. But no matter how many goods they succeed in consuming, they do not free themselves in the least from their unhappy worries or ever get rid of their trouble. Worse still, in their futile blindness they pride themselves on their pursuit of such possessions. And if these are their present woes, how will they end?

70. Let us hear instead their last words, which Holy Scripture does not pass over: *they will speak to one another with remorse, it says, and groaning in anguish of spirit.*[160] [Wisdom] then quotes them: *we exhausted ourselves on the way of iniquity and destruction and walked along rough roads. But we disregarded the way of the Lord. What has pride profited us? What gain has bragging about our riches brought us? They all vanished like a shadow, like a messenger who runs on, like a ship that cuts through the billowing waters and in its wake leaves no trace to be discovered.*[161] *So we, too, scarcely born, immediately cease to be; we were not able to leave any trace*

---

156 1 Tm 6:9
157 Mt 6:31
158 Mt 6:33
159 Heb 10:34
160 Wis 5:3
161 Wis 5:7–10

of virtue to show. We have wasted ourselves in our wickedness. Those who sinned talk like this in hell, for the hope of the ungodly is like chaff swept away in the wind, like fine spray driven by the gale, like smoke dispersed by the wind, like the remembrance of a passing guest who stays but one day.[162] It seems then, that this rest and this sabbath must be sought elsewhere.

Chapter 25. Rest should not be sought in worldly friendship.

71. But what is more tranquil, you ask, than to love and be loved?[26*] If this is in God and for God I do not disapprove; on the contrary I entirely approve. But if this is according to the flesh or the world, realize how many acts of envy, suspicions, or stinging lashes of a jealous spirit banish peace of mind. If none of these occur, then death, which everyone is going to have to experience, will sever this unity and bring sorrow to the survivor and punishment to the departed. But we also know that in this life serious enmities have arisen among the dearest of friends. Of course, we shall write elsewhere about that endearment[163] which exists between good persons.

Chapter 26. Rest cannot be found either in bodily pleasure or in worldly power.

72. We are obliged to insert into this work a blemish, as it were. I mean a discussion about yearnings of the flesh. About this I would have been silent, did I not notice that many persons have divested themselves of their humanity, as it were, and clothed themselves in some brutish likeness until they suppose all the enjoyment of their life should be put in yearnings of the belly and what is under the belly. Lest anyone

---

162 Wis 5:9–10,13–14
163 *dilectio*

think, then, that rest for the mind is to be sought in these pleasures, I must say a few words about them.

What is more perverse than to place the good of a rational mind in the pit of the stomach, and to make what is noblest in man subject to an ignoble part of the flesh, especially since in them he realizes that he cannot distinguish himself from the dullest brutes. Eventually, hunger begets torment and satisfaction disgust.[164] For even if one should satisfy yearning, one inevitably exceeds the limits of necessity; if, however, one exceeds the limit of nature, it is impossible to avoid bodily pain. Again, just as nothing is more shameful, more foul, more embarrassing, more humiliating than to delight in the squalor of lust and to wallow in the mire of shamefulness like the filthiest pig, so surely nothing is more disturbing, nothing so void of peace and tranquillity. But what should be said of its repulsiveness, when its squalid corruption infects the flesh, enfeebles the mind, overthrows and destroys everything honest, decent, and vigorous in the soul.[165]

73. Although other vices are generally camouflaged under the cloak of virtue and so do not blush, but rather swell up with pride at being revealed to human eyes, only this [wantonness], when revealed, has such horror for itself that—especially at the moment it traps and claims the flesh as its victim—it eagerly flees from being seen. Yet [wantonness] through its own obscenity brought so much shame upon these members, modestly set in the human body by the all-wise Creator, that he who preferred to gaze on them rather than to cover them respectfully was punished by his father's undying curse, whereas the grace of perpetual blessing rewarded those in whom these naked members inspired an act of modesty.[166] But now that the cross of Jesus is everywhere triumphant and gleams victorious over wantonness, no wonder the filth of this passion has been revealed and exposed, even by that

---

164 2 M 9:6, Ezk 16:31
165 *animus*
166 Cf. Gn 9:25–26

demon-worshipping people among whom, thanks to a crafty ruse of demons, the disgraceful goings-on of false gods were worshipped as sacred rites and in their honor dances were performed in theaters; at times not even the lewd could escape feeling ashamed of Jove, the lewdest of all. Yes, even by these worshippers of adulterous gods adultery was punished and chastity praised above all. What then should be the conduct of those who worship the Virgin's Son and the Author of virginity?

74. Surely we must beware that it not befall anyone what the prophet said of certain people: *the beasts rotted in their own dung*.[167] In these words he expressed aptly enough the means and the end of this lewdest passion. He means to say that anyone engulfed by the Charybdis[27*] of debauchery[168] rots in the filth of his flesh as if wallowing in excrement, that you may not only consider him to be deprived of life or engulfed but also smell him, festering and reeking like an entombed cadaver with puss oozing from once-itching sores.

75. Inevitably, then, the mind in which this vile spirit is settled is hounded by the furies. Goaded by the fiery spurs of debauchery, loosening all reins of decency, drunk and disorderly, it is driven into every kind of disgraceful action. When the inferno of a passion once conceived is extinguished, it must be enkindled no less in another with greater intensity. In such yearning, then, it is quite absurd to look for rest for the rational mind, especially since we never read of a greater penalty being exacted by divine justice in this present life than when a person is given up to defilement by his own desires. As Scripture says: *my people did not listen to my voice and Israel did not heed me. So I left them to the desires of their hearts*.[169] The apostle speaks even more clearly of those who bartered the glory of God for idols: *therefore God surrendered them to the desires of their hearts, to impurity, so that they*

---

167 Jl 1:17
168 *luxuria*
169 Ps 80:12–13 (81:11–12)

dishonor their bodies with reproaches among themselves.[170]
Not that God, like an instigator of evil, drove them to shameful
actions, but that they, most deservedly abandoned by him,
could not avoid such wicked deeds.

76. I pass over in silence many arguments suggested to my
mind against this vile plague, through respect for your modest
eyes, my most loving and beloved friend, for whom I intend
this little work. At what I have written, I seem to imagine a
blush, that mark of modesty, spreading over your features and
the gentlest lowering of your eyes summoning me to be silent.
I know that your chaste breast, so filled with gentle charity
and so scented with the blossoms of modesty, breathes such a
heavenly and divine aroma that it would be burdensome even
to hear of the stench of this filth.

77. Now to pass to other failings, about pleasures of the
ears, the eyes, and other senses, about domination and
power, let us consult Solomon, that richest and most powerful
but wisest of kings, or rather in him let us listen very attentively to wisdom itself. First then, speaking for his own person
or the person of others, he said: *I said in my heart: I shall go
and abound in delights and enjoy good things;*[171] and again: *I
built palaces, I planted vines, I made gardens and orchards,
and planted in them trees of every kind.*[172] After much in this
vein, he added: *I owned slaves and handmaids and had a
very great household.*[173] *I amassed for myself silver and gold,
the treasures of kings and provinces.* When he remarked on
pleasure of the ears: *I acquired for myself men and women
singers,*[174] after a few words he added: *Whatever my eyes
desired I did not deny them; I did not prevent my heart from
enjoying every pleasure and my heart delighted in what I had
prepared.*[175] I ask, what is more comfortable, more attractive,

---

170 Rom 1:24
171 Qo 2:1
172 Qo 2:4–5
173 Qo 2:7
174 Qo 2:8
175 Qo 2:10

more enjoyable in this life? Yet listen, because nothing is more
vain. *When I turned to reflect upon all my works and labors,
at which I had vainly sweated,* said Solomon, *in everything I
saw vanity and affliction of spirit, for nothing under the sun
endures.*[176] So he advanced this general statement, saying: *I
have seen everything done under the sun and look! It is all
vanity and affliction of spirit.*[177] Let us add that statement of
our Saviour: *everyone who commits sin is the slave of sin.*[178]
Hence these three should be linked together: vanity, slavery,
and affliction of spirit. Where then is rest, where is the sabbath, especially since the Law says: *you shall do no servile
work on that day?*[179] Certainly *everyone who commits sin is
the slave of sin.* When will leisure from this servile work be
assured? When will the contagion of this slavery be avoided?
When will there be a real and perfect celebration of the
sabbath? Finally, is there on this earth a just man who does not
sin? Again, *I was shaped in iniquity,* says holy David, *and in
sin has my mother conceived me.*[180]

Chapter 27. Charity is that easy yoke, beneath which is found real rest, like a real sabbath.

78. Wherefore, let us heed the One who said: *If the Son frees
you, you will indeed be free.*[181] Let us heed him, I say, calling,
crying out and inviting the laborers to rest and a sabbath:
*come to me, all you who labor and are burdened, and I will
refresh you.*[182] Behold this refreshment, like the preparation
for a sabbath! Now let us heed the Sabbath himself: *Take my*

---

176 Qo 2:11
177 Qo 1:14
178 Jn 8:34
179 Lev 23:8
180 Ps 50 (51):5
181 Jn 8:36
182 Mt 11:28

yoke upon you and learn from me, because I am meek and humble of heart and you will find rest for your souls.[183] Look! Here is rest, tranquillity, and a sabbath. *And you will find rest for your souls, for my yoke is easy and my burden light.*[184] Yes, his yoke is easy and his burden light; therefore you will find rest for your souls. This yoke does not oppress but unites; this burden has wings, not weight. This yoke is charity. This burden is brotherly love.[185] [28*] Here one rests, here one celebrates a sabbath, here one is free from servile works. *Charity is not conceited...does not scheme evil.*[186] Love of neighbor works no evil. You see, O Judaean, where a Sabbath exists. If on it some sin creeping in should occur, not from charity but from weakness, the celebration of the sabbath does not end *because charity covers a multitude of sins.*[187] This leisure is rightly consecrated on the seventh day, *because God's love has been poured into our hearts by the Holy Spirit who has been given to us.*[188] Moreover, as we said above, the number seven signifies the Holy Spirit.

Chapter 28. An illustration from [Aelred's] life and conversion.

79. Look, gentle Lord, I have wandered the world and [perused] those things in the world, and [found that], as he who knew your secrets said, *whatever exists in the world is concupiscence of the flesh, or concupiscence of the eyes or pride of life.*[189] In these I sought rest for my unhappy soul, but everywhere [I found] labor and lament, sorrow and affliction of spirit.[29*] You cried out, my Lord, you cried out and called

---

183 Mt 11:29
184 Mt 11:29–30
185 *dilectio*
186 1 Cor 13:4–5
187 1 P 4:8
188 Rom 5:5
189 1 Jn 2:16

[me], you terrified me and shattered my deafness. You struck, you flogged, you conquered my obduracy. You sweetened, you savored, you banished my bitterness. I heard you calling, but how late! *Come to me, all you who labor and are heavy burdened.*[190] And I said: *you will stretch your right hand to this work of your hands.*[191] I was lying rotting and covered over, bound and captive, snagged in the birdlime of clinging iniquity, overwhelmed by the weight of inveterate habits. So I interrogated myself: who am I, where am I, what kind of person am I? I shuddered, my Lord, and trembled at my own effigy. I was terrified at the loathsome image of my unhappy soul. I was displeasing to myself, because you were becoming pleasing to me. I wanted to escape from myself and to escape into you, but was paralyzed in myself. *My old friends, trifles of trifles and vanities of vanities, held me fast*, as [Augustine] said.[192] The chain of my worst habits bound me, love of my kinsmen conquered me, the fetters of gracious company pressed upon me tightly; above all the knot of a certain friendship was dearer to me than all the delights of my life. I relished the others, the others were pleasing to me, but you more than any. Weighing these one by one, I recognized that sweetness was mixed with bitterness, sadness with joy, adversity with prosperity. The charming bond of friendship gratified me, though I always feared being hurt and inevitable separation some day in the future. I pondered the joy at their beginning, I observed their progress, and I foresaw their end. Now I saw that their beginnings could not escape blame, nor their midpoint an offense, nor their end condemnation. The specter of death was terrifying, because after death inevitable punishment awaited such a soul. Observing certain things about me, but ignorant of what was going on inside me, people kept saying: 'O how well things are going for him! Yes, how well!' They had no idea that things were going badly for

---

190 Mt 11:28
191 Jb 14:15
192 *Conf.* 8.11.26

me there, where alone they could go well. Very deep within me was my wound, crucifying, terrifying, and corrupting everything within me with an intolerable stench. Had you not quickly stretched out your hand to me, O Lord, unable to endure myself I might perhaps have resorted to the worst remedy of despair.

80. At last I began to surmise, as much as my inexperience allowed, or rather as much as you permitted, how much joy there is in your love, how much tranquillity with that joy and how much security with that tranquillity. Someone who loves you makes no mistake in his choice, for nothing is better than you. His hope is not cheated, since nothing is loved with greater reward. He need not fear exceeding the limit, since in loving you no limit is set. He does not dread death, the disrupter of worldly friendships, since life never dies. In loving you, he fears no offense, for none exists but the abandonment of love itself. No suspicion gets in the way, since you judge by the testimony of conscience itself. Here is joy, because fear is banished. Here is tranquillity, because anger is curbed. Here is security, because the world is scorned.

81. Meanwhile, you gradually began to become tasty to my palate, though it was not quite healed, and I kept saying: 'if only I might be healed!' I was swept towards you, only to fall back into myself again. Those things I used to experience pleasurably in the flesh kept me shackled, as it were, by force of habit, although what my spirit[193] proposed by force of reason pleased me more. I often said, even in the hearing of others, 'where now, I ask, are all the delights, pleasures, and joys we appreciated until this very moment? Now at last, at this moment in time what sensations remain of them? Whatever was joyous has vanished. Of all these, this alone remains: what pricks our conscience, strikes the fear of death into us, and condemns us to eternal punishment. I ask you, compare with all our riches, delights, and honors the one joy of the servants of Christ, that they do not fear death.'

---

193 *animus*

82. In saying these words I often felt worthless and sometimes wept with bitter contrition of soul. Anything I gazed at turned worthless to me, but habits of sensual pleasure oppressed [me]. But you who *hear the groans of the prisoners and free the children of the slain*,[194] broke my chains asunder. You who offer your paradise to harlots and publicans turned me, the worst of them all, back to yourself. See, under your yoke I breathe easily, and under your burden I am at rest, because *your yoke is easy and your burden light*.[195]

Chapter 29. How wrong they are who complain about the harshness of the Lord's yoke, since any labor we experience comes from what remains of self-centeredness and any respite [we enjoy comes] from the infusion of charity.

83. They are wrong, O Lord, wrong and deceived who, ignorant of themselves and not recognizing what they are experiencing, complain about the harshness of your yoke and the weight of your burden. What then, you say: do you never labor, you who seem to have bowed your necks to his yoke and bent your shoulders to his burden? I do, all too often. Yes, even today, I labored not a little. For when a thoughtless word escaped me a while ago, a very dear friend of mine took it so badly that he even betrayed the hurt on his face, and when I fell prostrate at his feet, was in no hurry to lift me up. My spirit[196] has still not sweated out that sorrow, as you know, Lord, not because I was left prostrate so long but because he was hurt and I caused this by a thoughtless word. Perhaps this idle word slipped out too easily because of the singular familiarity by which I was in the habit of speaking with him more frankly; according to the common adage: *An overly-familiar master makes for a foolish servant.*

---

194 Ps 101:21 (102:20)
195 Mt 11:30
196 *animus*

84. Now, O Lord, scrutinizer of my weakness, physician of my soul, only hope of my salvation, even in sinning against him, *I sinned against you alone.*[197] It was a sin not because I hurt him, but because you forbade me to hurt anyone. Anyone who sins, sins against you, Lord, and against you alone, because sin is either failing to do what you command or doing what you forbid. Homicide is a sin, Lord, because you said *you shall not kill.*[198] Consequently, when you sometimes said: 'Kill', failing to kill was not only a sin, but the greatest crime,[199] since you commanded it. Your law also condemns fraud, yet when the Israelites, pretending to borrow precious vessels and vestments at your command, plundered Egypt, they did not sin because they were obeying you. You say, nonetheless, *do not commit fornication;*[200] therefore fornication is a monstrous crime. Yet your prophet at your command did not hesitate *to take a harlot to beget children of harlotry,*[201] which he certainly would not have done had he united with her within wedlock, though one may doubt whether this is meant literally. *Against you alone, then, have I sinned.*

And Scripture does not readily use towards a human being this expression: *I have sinned against you [tibi],* although it does say *I have sinned towards you [in te].* The expression *against you* hints at something great; then what is the meaning of *against you alone have I sinned,* if not that my sin must be weighed by your decision, sentenced by your decision, and punished by your decision. Why then does the Judaean pick up a stone? *Against you alone have I sinned. Let him who is without sin among you,* said Jesus, *throw a stone at her first.*[202] Against him *alone have I sinned,* who has the right to judge about sin and to decide whether this is a sin. You, Lord.

---

197 Ps 50:6 (51:4)
198 Ex 20:13
199 Ex 3:22
200 Cf. Ex 20:14 and Hos 3:3
201 Hos 1:2
202 Jn 8:7

You forgive me for sinning because *against you alone have I sinned.* Yet since I have also sinned towards my friend, I shall still cast myself at his feet. Please inspire him also to forgive me, because I have hurt him, although, as you know, I did not then intend nor did I wish to hurt him.

85. But to return to what I was saying before, does this labor of mine come from the Lord's yoke or not rather from my own sickness? I sense clearly that his sweet yoke gives birth to whatever tranquillity, peace and joy I have, but whatever labor, fatigue or lethargy I have stems from the remnants of worldly concupiscence. Now under that yoke, which the prince of Babylon (I mean, of confusion) laid upon my hapless neck, my *strength grew weak, my bones* were crushed.[203] Although to a certain degree I was freed from captivity, nevertheless some weakness remained from the former oppression. Hence the serenity of the sweetness of which I now have some slight experience is often troubled, until he who atones for all my iniquities shall also heal all my infirmities and, by redeeming my life from ruin, in his mercy shall crown me with mercy and compassion, *when the corruptible becomes incorruptible and the mortal puts on immortality, and the prophecy which has been written is fulfilled: death is swallowed up in victory.*[204] Meantime I experience no little consolation from the gentleness of this yoke, and some struggle against my inveterate weakness.

Chapter 30. Those who complain about the weight of the Lord's burden are oppressed instead by the world's burden.

86. Accordingly, those who dispute about the harshness of this yoke perhaps have either not completely cast off the very heavy yoke of concupiscence of the world, or with greater

---

203 Ps 30:11 (31:10)
204 1 Cor 15:54, Is 25:8

confusion have taken up anew what was once cast off.[30*] Outwardly displaying the Lord's yoke, but inwardly bowing the shoulders of their mind under a load of worldly business, they ascribe to the weight of the Lord's burden[31*] the labors and sorrows to which they deliver themselves. Then disdaining the Lord's commands, which *are not burdensome*, as John says,[205] and *like dogs* feeding on *their own vomit*,[206] beneath the habit of those who practise abstinence they worship their bellies, under the garb of penitents they pant after worldly glory and honor, beneath the holy amice of the chaste they are defiled with lusts of the flesh, under the lamb's fleece they hide a wolfish spirit. Seething with insatiable avarice, *they add house to house and field to field*,[207] do not spare widows or pity orphans, but appropriate the patrimony of the poor. For these purposes inclined to lawsuits and disputes and ready to go to court, they are ennervated by endless cares, aflame with hatred, distracted with worrisome thoughts; because the yoke of the world, not of the Lord, is rough and the burden of the world is heavy. By contrast, *the Lord's yoke is easy and the Lord's burden light*.[208]

Chapter 31. The great perfection of charity; what distinguishes it from other virtues and how other virtues without charity are not virtues.

87. What is more pleasant, what more glorious, than through contempt of the world to perceive oneself loftier than the world, and by standing firmly on the peak of a good conscience to have the whole world at one's feet! To see nothing to crave, no one to fear, no one to envy, nothing of one's own which could be taken away by another, no evil

---

205 1 Jn 5:3
206 Pr 26:11
207 Is 5:8
208 Mt 11:30

which could be inflicted by another on oneself! And while one focuses the gaze of the mind on that *incorruptible, undefiled, and unfading inheritance stored in heaven,*[209] how consoling it is with some nobility of mind to despise worldly wealth as perishable, carnal enticements as defiled, worldly pomp as prone to fading away, and to exult in the words of the prophet: *all flesh is grass and all its glory like the flower of the field. The grass withers and the flower has fallen, but the Lord's word lasts forever.*[210] What then is sweeter or what more tranquil, I ask, than not to be agitated by the turbulent impulses of the flesh, not seared by the fires of provocations of the flesh, not stirred by any seductive sight, but to possess a body cooled by the dew of modesty and subject to the spirit, one which is no longer a seducer to pleasures of the flesh, but a very obedient aide to spiritual exercises? Finally, what is so close to divine tranquillity as not reacting to proffered insults, not being terrified by torture or persecution, keeping the same steadfastness of mind in prosperity and adversity, regarding with equal eye both friend and foe, [and] conforming oneself to the likeness of him *who makes his sun shine on both the good and the wicked and his rain fall on the just and the unjust?*[211]

88. All these exist together in charity, and all exist together only in charity. Likewise in charity true tranquillity and true gentleness exist because [charity] is the Lord's yoke, and if we bear this at the Lord's invitation we shall find rest for our souls, because his *yoke is easy and his burden light.*[212] In brief, *charity is patient and kind; it is not jealous or conceited or boastful, is not ambitious,* and so on.[213] For us, then, other virtues are like a carriage for someone weary, food for the traveller's journey, a lamp for those groping in darkness, and

---

209 1 P 1:4
210 Is 40:6–8, 1 P 1:24–25
211 Mt 5:45
212 Mt 11:30
213 1 Co 13:4–5

weapons for those waging battle. But charity, which permits other virtues to be virtues, must exist in all the virtues. It is most particularly rest for the weary, an inn for the traveller, full light at journey's end, and the perfect crown for the victor. For what is faith, but a carriage to carry us to our fatherland? What is hope, but food for the journey to support us in the miseries of this life? What are the four virtues—temperance, prudence, fortitude, and justice—, but the weapons with which we wage battle? But when death will be fully swallowed up in charity,[214] which will reach its perfection only in the vision of God, there will be no faith for those for whom this is here only begun in faith, because there is no need to believe in one who is seen and loved. Nor will hope exist because for someone who embraces God with the arms of charity there remains nothing to hope for.

89. Temperance fights against lusts, prudence against errors, fortitude against adversities, and justice against inequities. Yet in charity, chastity is perfect and so there is no lust for temperance to fight. In charity, knowledge is perfect and so there is no error for prudence to fight. In charity, there is true happiness and so no adversity exists for fortitude to conquer. In charity, everything is at peace and so there is no inequity against which justice must remain vigilant. But faith is not a virtue, if it does not act through love, nor hope a virtue, if what is hoped for is not loved.[32*] If you look into this more closely, what is temperance but love which no sensual pleasure entices? What is prudence, but love which no error seduces? What is fortitude but love bravely enduring adversity? What is justice, but love righting with due moderation the iniquities of this life. Charity, then, begins in faith, is exercised in the other virtues, and is perfected in itself.

---

214 Cf. 1 Co 15:54

Chapter 32. The works of the six days may be applied to the other virtues but the seventh day of rest may be assigned to charity.

90. Let faith be for us, then, like the first day on which we believers are separated from unbelievers, as light from darkness. Let hope be the second day: through it, dwelling in the heavens and through the merits of faith hoping only for things above the heavens,with God urging us on, we are distinguished from those who, relishing what is upon earth[215] and importuning God for only earthly things, flood and ebb like waters under the firmament of heaven. Let temperance dawn on us like the third day on which, while we mortify our bodies on earth and restrain within necessary limits concupiscences of the flesh like the most brackish waters, the parched and waterless soil of our hearts emerges, thirsting for the Lord God. At last, like the light of the fourth day, let prudence burst forth. By prudence let us distinguish, as between day and night, what we should and should not do. With its help let the light of wisdom shine like the splendor of the sun, and let the light of spiritual knowledge, which waxes in some of us or wanes in others, appear like the beauty of the moon. Through prudence also let the devout mind gaze at the examples of our forefathers as at clusters of stars, and through it mark division between days and years, months and hours.

91. Let prudence with balanced judgement discern, for example: how do those before the Law differ from those under the Law? how do they differ from others under grace? what is fitting for each group? what precepts, what times, what customs, what sacraments? Let fortitude be for us like the fifth day. On it let us endure the storms of the great, vast sea of this world. At God's working become spiritual fish, let us save our lives amid tempests and billows, and by raising heavenward like winged birds both the desires and attachments of our mind and setting our mind on things above,[216] with God's

---

215 Cf. Phil 3:19
216 Cf. Col 3:2

blessing let us bear many fruits of good deeds. Let justice declare for us the sixth day; on it let us, clothed again with the divine likeness, govern with noble authority the savage beasts of our vices, the reptiles of our earthly desires and the beasts of burden of our bodily impulses, working so that the body may be subject to the mind and the mind to God. Thus, as justice dictates, we may render to each his due. This is again a blessing not to animals or beasts of burden or reptiles, but for humankind. From this account, taken literally, we are clearly advised to harvest spiritual fruit, for we read that God's blessing was ascribed to the fish of the sea and the birds of the air, although we do not notice that the divine bounty granted this blessing to animals or beasts of burden or reptiles, even if they do increase and multiply, a gift which by the previous blessing God is seen to have conferred on birds and fish. Here is the text: *God blessed them, saying: increase and multiply and fill the waters of the sea and let the birds multiply upon earth.*[217] For animals and beasts of burden there is none of this. Of course, a blessing is deserved, multiplication is deserved, and a progeny through spiritual generation is deserved by virtues and holy attachments, which we consider comparable to birds and fish.

92. But just as by God's blessing animals and beasts of burden are subject to humankind created in God's image and likeness, so by God's command spiritual beasts, who deserve no progeny (of whom the psalmist says: *do not betray to beasts the soul which trusts you*[218]) are subjected to humankind restored to God's image and likeness by the merits of justice. There remains a seventh day, that is, the sabbath, on which all these works are consummated, true rest is entered into, and a limit and end is assigned to our toil. This is charity, the consummation of all virtues, the agreeable refreshment of holy souls, the virtuous harmony of our conduct. This is the root from which all good works spring so that they may be

---

217 Gen 1:22
218 Ps 73 (74):19

good, and in which all good works are perfected. This is the seventh day on which divine grace refreshes us, the seventh month in which, after the deluge of temptations, the arc of the heart gently comes to rest. Temperance protects it, prudence keeps watch over it, fortitude fights for it, and justice is its servant.

Chapter 33. In this life other virtues are servants of charity but after this life they are absorbed into the fullness of charity.

93. Whereas [charity] is the power of temperance to restrain and check the enticing impulses of the body or spirit,[219] so that the mind,[220] seduced, may not prefer the taste of harmful pleasure to the pleasantness of brotherly love, and whereas the watchful care of prudence distinguishes between what ought and ought not to be loved, so that self-centeredness cloaked in charity's colors may not mislead an incautious heart, and whereas the strength of fortitude confronts the foes of this world, for the simple reason that an oppressed spirit may rashly overstep the law of charity when things go less well than desired or when adversities combine to overwhelm it, then surely it is clear that these three should be counted under the title of virtues, if their usefulness is directed in every way to obtaining and preserving charity. Not considered a virtue, however, is that temperance by which the mind, though it hides or checks the itching of the flesh, in its greed for filthy lucre abuses the name of chastity, and fails to check so vicious a greed in the inner man. Nor should we consider a virtue that prudence by which anyone shrewd at trickery distinguishes not between what ought and ought not to be loved, but between temporal loss and gain and, abandoning the ideal of charity, strives by the ruination of others to acquire

---

219 *animus*
220 *mens*

for himself something gainful. Far be it from us to count Catiline's fortitude among the virtues; though by it he was able to bear all adversities in an incredible way, still by this fortitude he won no other reward but that of worldly power or surely of his own pleasure, and cheated himself of the reward due virtue. Similarly, however temperate someone eager for popular acclaim may seem to himself, and however prudent a miserly and cunning fellow may be esteemed by popular opinion, however unmoved by adversity some philosopher steeling himself by inhuman impassibility, our philosophers considered that anything which has not sprung from the root of charity should be separated from the fruits of virtue, for they saw clearly that anything in the structure which does not point in a straight line to that one measurement[33*] should be measured outside the framework of the spiritual ark.

94. Consequently, real temperance, real prudence, and real fortitude act in such a way that the rational mind, either allured, deceived, or oppressed respectively, may not overstep the norm of charity. Yes, when perfect charity shall bring its followers into the kingdom of tranquillity, when with the mortal nature of the flesh all lusts of the flesh shall be at last extinguished, when in contemplation of divine light all the darkness of error shall be dispersed, when, with genuine security replacing the troubles of this world, all the weapons of wartime shall be laid down, charity alone by its own agreeableness will refresh the conquerors. Then, indeed, the other virtues will flow back into the fullness of charity, so that in that blessedness, temperance, prudence, or fortitude may be considered nothing other than charity, so chaste as to be tempted by no allurements, so enlightened as to be distracted by no errors, so firm as to be quite unassailable in any adversity.

95. Promising us this state of tranquillity, the Lord says in a mystical text: *I shall remove evil beasts*[221] from the land, *and I*

---

221 Lv 26:6

shall make you *sleep securely.*[222] When the most atrocious beasts of the passions have been removed from our land, that is, from the flesh we bear, he will make us sleep in heavenly slumber. Absorbed in the immense sea of divine brightness, ineffably exalted above ourselves, we shall enjoy perfect freedom and shall see that the Lord himself is God. Celebrating that eternal sabbath of charity which the holy prophet Isaiah describes: *from month to month and from sabbath to sabbath,*[223] that is, from the sabbath on which—tasting some beginnings of charity, as far as the day's evil allows—we are given holiday from daily toil, we shall be introduced to that perfect sabbath when, without disturbing annoyance or disabling misery of the flesh, we will *love our Lord God with our whole soul,* our whole virtue *and all our strengh, and our neighbors as ourselves.*[224]

96. Moreover, that justice by which each one is given his due, as the apostle says: *Repay to each his due, taxes to whom taxes are due, respect to whom respect is due, honor to whom honor is due,*[225] I would have called an incentive to brotherly love, which begins by harming no one and grows by showing oneself without complaint against anyone. Through the charm of kindness, someone particularly wins to himself the minds of others who, by his quiet manner of life offends no one, obeys his elders, gets along with his peers, and is considerate of his juniors, by showing the first respect and reverence, the second honor and graciousness, and the third humble compassion. In money matters as well, justice prompts observers to the goodness of charity, because according to the apostle's previous precept, charity does not put off paying a debt until a troublesome creditor exacts it, but rather with cheerfulness anticipates his claim. If then, this virtue [justice] includes only the administration of temporalities, I do not fear

---

222 Hos 2:18
223 Is 66:23
224 Lk 10:27
225 Cf. Rm 13:7

its diminishing the tranquillity of that blessed state in which supreme justice confers rewards or punishments according to the merits of each. Some are struck with the irrevocable sentence of damnation and others are given the reward of eternal blessedness, so that there can be no variation in temporalities because eternity will exist on both sides.

97. But if you contemplate more deeply the rules of justice itself, no one gives to each his due better or more fully than someone who loves what ought to be loved as much as it ought to be loved. That is to say: God above oneself and one's neighbor as oneself; God only for himself; oneself and one's neighbor only for God. If I am not mistaken, you see that the perfection of justice depends on the perfection of charity, so that justice seems to be nothing but well ordered charity. The more one has made progress in it, the more one remains at rest.

Chapter 34. Consideration of the threefold concupiscence is delayed by a friend's death, and this first book ends with his eulogy.

98. Wherefore, the threefold concupiscence must be considered: *concupiscence of the flesh, concupiscence of the eyes, and the pride of life*, which the holy apostle describes as existing in the world,[226] so that the less pleasant things we endure beneath the Lord's yoke may perhaps not be a shoot from the poisoned root of these passions.

But grief prevents me from going further. The recent death of my dear Simon forcibly drives me instead to weep for him. Perhaps this was the cause of that fear which disturbed my mind at night.[227] Perhaps this was the cause of the nightmares which robbed me of needed rest; that is, that my most beloved friend was to be suddenly snatched from this earth. It is no

---

226 1 Jn 2:16
227 Cf. Ps 90(91):5

wonder my mind had so disturbing a premonition of his death, since it took joy with such delight in his life. See how the fear which I feared has now overtaken me, how what I dreaded has come to pass. Why do I pretend? Why am I silent? Very likely because that tribulation still hovers above me. Let what is concealed in my heart spring to my eyes and to my tongue. If only, if only, yes, if only the heart of a mourner might exude in teardrops and rivulets of words the sorrow born in its inner depths. *Have pity on me, have pity on me, if any of you are my friends, for the hand of the Lord has touched me!*[228] You are astonished that I am weeping; you are still more astonished that I go on living! For who would not be astonished that Aelred goes on living without Simon, except someone who does not know how sweet it was to live together, how sweet it would be to return together to the fatherland. So bear patiently with my tears, my sighs, the moaning of my heart, then.

99. And you, my beloved, although you have been brought *into the joy of the Lord,*[229] although you feast with delight at the table of the great father of our family and in the kingdom of the Father with your Jesus are happily inebriated *on that new fruit of the vine,*[230] still permit me to offer you my tears, to disclose my attachment to you and, if possible, to pour out my whole spirit[231] for you. Do not forbid these tears which your memory evokes, my beloved brother. Let not my sighing burden you, for it is prompted not by despair but by attachment. Do not restrain my tears, which flow not from lack of faith but from tenderness. If you remember where you have arrived, what you have escaped, where you have left your close friend, you will assuredly realize how justified is my grief, how worthy of tears my wound. *Let me alone, then, that I may assuage my sorrow.*[232] Mine, I say, mine, for your death

---

228 Jb 19:21
229 Mt 25:21
230 Mt 26:29
231 *animus*
232 Cf. Jb 10:20

is not to be wept over when it was preceded by a life so praiseworthy, so lovable, so pleasing to all, a life commended by your amazing conversion, your remarkable way of life, and your blessed perseverance.

100. Really, your conversion was amazing! Who would not be amazed, who would not marvel that a frail young boy, distinguished by birth, remarkably handsome, should have taken to such a life and in such a way! You took your leave, my gentle brother, *knowingly unknowing and wisely unwise.*[233] Like the first patriarch abandoning *your fatherland, your kin, and your father's home,*[234] you went by a route unknown to you, you arrived at a place you did not know. But he who was leading you knew, he who had already enkindled your young heart with the flame of his love to run *in the scent of his perfumes.*[235] *Fairest of all the sons of men,*[236] he went before you, *anointed with the oil of joy above his fellows,*[237] *anointed with the spirit of wisdom and understanding, the spirit of counsel and fortitude, with the spirit of knowledge and piety,*[238] and you continued to run *to the scent of his perfumes.* That spiritual *hart preceded you over rough and mountainous places,*[239] scattering on his path *the aromas of myrrh, frankincense, and all the perfume merchants' powders,*[240] and you continued to run *to the scent of his perfumes.* The boy Jesus preceded this boy, showing him the manger of his poverty, the resting place of his humility, the chamber of his charity decked with the blossoms of his grace, rich with the honey of his sweetness, strewn with the balsam of his consolation; and you continued to run *to the scent of his perfumes.* I do not know what great, what ineffable foretaste

---

233 Gregory the Great, *Dialogi liber 2*
234 Gn 12:1
235 Sg 1:3
236 Ps 44:3 (45:2)
237 Ps 44:8 (45:7)
238 Is 11:2
239 Sg 2:8–9
240 Sg 3:6

your mind had even then, that it believed a diet of hay should be fed to its frail body fainting from hunger, as if to a wearied beast of burden. The devout boy fled from the face of his father, but even more, to the face of his Father. He wanted *to forget his own people and his father's home*, that a King, the King's Son, *might desire his beauty,*[241] and that they might be *two in one spirit,*[242] as far as he who was his Son's Father by nature might become his son's Father by grace.

101. O wonderful devotion! O wonderful self-forgetfulness! It was not enough for this rival of the venerable patriarch Joseph who, leaving to the Egyptian woman the cloak by which he was held fast, slipped naked from the clutches of his captor,[243] but in addition this zealous pursuer of evangelical perfection took no thought for the morrow. With no provisions, undertaking a wearisome enough route, as his limbs grew more and more faint from fasting, he said: 'I heard that servants of Christ feed on grass. Why don't we, too?' Turning aside a bit from the path, he began to pluck some grass and said: 'O how delicious!'

102. O good lad, how did it taste to you? What is that grass, I ask, but faith, that hay but charity? He tasted Jesus in his heart, of course, and so the hay in his mouth. Whence, I ask, whence did these come to the lad? They are yours, Lord Jesus. You give and accept, provide and exact. Who gives you anything not your own? But if anyone wished to give you something which he had not accepted from you, you would not deign to accept it. Therefore, Lord Jesus, that boy accepted; he accepted from you and made return, he accepted and offered. He accepted and offered this devotion of his mind, this fervor of faith, this ardor of love.

103. All things belong to you, Lord. You consecrated the beginnings of his conversion by these marvels, you received afterwards the pleasing sacrifice of his devout life, and you

---

241 Ps 44 (45):11
242 Cf. 1 Co 6:17
243 Gn 39:12

have now mercifully transferred that most acceptable holocaust to your temple on high. There my Simon, my gentlest
friend but your poor [servant], Lord Jesus, rests in the bosom
of Abraham. There he rests transferred from death to life, from
labor to rest, from misery to blessedness.

104.See how I, who began to grieve, have found reason to
rejoice. Clearly I have found reason, but in you, my beloved
brother, not in myself. *Do not weep for me,* he said, *but for
yourselves and for your children.*[244] For you, beloved brother,
for you I rejoice, but for myself I feel keen sorrow. For you
one should rejoice, yet I should be wept over, because I can
live without Simon. What a marvel that I be said to be alive,
when such a great part of my life, so sweet a solace for my
pilgrimage, so unique an alleviation for my misery, has been
taken away from me. It is as if my body had been eviscerated
and my hapless soul rent to pieces. And am I said to be alive?
O wretched life, O grievous life, a life without Simon! The
patriarch Jacob wept for his son; Joseph wept for his father;
holy David wept for his dearest Jonathan. Simon, alone, was
all these to me: a son in age, a father in holiness, a friend in
charity. Weep, then, poor fellow, for your dearest father,
weep for your most loving son, weep for your gentlest friend.
Let waterfalls burst from your wretched forehead; *let your eyes
shed tears day and night.*[245] Weep, I say, not because he was
taken up, but because you were left. Who will allow me to die
with you, my father, my brother, my son? I would not wish
to die instead of you. This would be to consider not your
interests but my own. Holy David kept repeating this about
his son the parricide: *Absalom, my son, my son Absalom,
who will allow me to die instead of you?*[246] David did not say
that about his friend Jonathan, did he? Nor Joseph about his
father? It had to be said about the parricide, it had to be said
about the sinner, because *the death of sinners is worst of*

---

244 Lk 23:28
245 Jer 9:18
246 2 S 18:33

all.[247] It was pious to wish to die for an impious man, that he might live to repent, live to weep, live to receive God's mercy so that he might not perish forever.[248] But those who departed in peace were not afterwards to be recalled to this misery, nor to be subjected again to so many fears, so many sorrows.

105. Then again, *Rachel weeping for her children refused to be consoled.*[249] Why was she weeping? Attachment. But her attachment would be consoled, if her son were recalled from death, if the mother again enjoyed the sight of him. But Rachel did not wish this. Why? Because if the son were recalled from death, he would be cast precipitately from blessedness into misery. She wished not that her son be recalled to life, but that she be taken up to her son in eternal rest. Attachment demanded sons, but reason resisted attachment, so that [the sons] might not be recalled. Divine providence delayed taking her up. Therefore, *Rachel weeping for her children refused to be consoled.*

106. My case is the same. I grieve for my most beloved [friend], for the one-in-heart with me who has been snatched from me, and I rejoice that he is taken up to eternal tabernacles. My attachment seeks his sweet presence which nourished it delightfully, but my reason does not agree that this soul, beloved by me, once free from the flesh should again be subject to the miseries of the flesh. My soul along with his, a part of its own, longs to enjoy the embrace of Christ, but my weakness resists, my iniquity resists, and even divine providence resists this. Surely, the one who was ready *entered the marriage feast with the Bridegroom,*[250] but to me, wretch that I am, the door is still closed. If only, Lord Jesus, if only that door be opened one day. But I hope in your mercy, Lord, that someday it will be opened. I have sent my first fruits

---

247 Ps 33:22 (34:21)
248 Cf. Jb 4:20
249 Mt 2:18
250 Cf. Mt 25:10

on ahead, sent on my treasure, sent on no small part of myself. Let the rest of me follow on after you. *Where my treasure is, there let my heart be also.*[251]

107. Here now, O Lord, I shall follow his ways, that in you I may enjoy his company. I was able to do so, Lord, though at a slow pace, when my eyes observed his devout way of life, when the sight of his humility blunted my pride, when the thought of his tranquillity calmed my restlessness and when the bridle of his admirable seriousness checked my levity. I remember that often when my eyes were darting here and there, at one glimpse of him I was filled with such shame that, suddenly recovering myself, I checked all that levity by the strength of his seriousness and, pulling myself together, I began to employ myself in something useful. The authority of our Order forbade conversation; his appearance spoke to me, his walk spoke to me, his very silence spoke to me. His appearance was modest, his walk mature, his speaking serious and his silence without bitterness.

108. Finally, during this last year of his life, as if he were not unaware of his future vocation, with what tranquillity, what peace, what circumspection he completed his life! Oblivious to everything external, even to me, and enclosed within the confines of his own mind, he seemed to have portrayed quite exactly the man whom the holy prophet Jeremiah describes: *It is good for a man when he has borne the yoke from his youth. He will sit alone and be silent, because he has exalted himself above himself.*[252] Indeed, he shouldered the yoke of discipline in the flower of youth, Lord Jesus, choosing *that narrow way which leads to life;*[253] he chose *in the sweat of his brow to eat his bread*[254] and to submit his will to another's judgement. What is more, even from his youth he bore the heavy yoke of poor health, with which for eight years, even to the last, I

251 Mt 6:21
252 Lam 3:27
253 Mt 7:14
254 Gn 3:19

believe, with fatherly attachment you scourged him without remission. Therefore, finding almost nothing exterior in which to delight, he withdrew to the interior solitude of his mind, *sitting alone and being silent*, but not listless in his inactivity. He used to write or read, or devoted himself privately to meditation on the Scriptures, for which his senses were always keenly alert. He hardly ever spoke of necessities, even with the prior. He walked about *like a deaf man, not hearing, like a dumb man not opening his mouth, become like one not hearing and having no rebuke on his lips.*[255] Indeed if anyone, seizing the occasion, approached him, such gentleness soon marked his speech, such cheerfulness without any dissipation appeared on his face, that his moderation in speaking and his humility in listening disclosed how free of bitterness and how full of sweetness was his silence.

109. Look at what I have lost. Look at what I miss. Where have you gone, O model for my life, harmonizer of my conduct?[256] Where have you gone, where have you vanished? What shall I do? Where shall I turn? Whom now shall I propose to follow? How have you been torn from my embrace, withdrawn from my kisses, removed from before my eyes? I embraced you, dear brother, not in the flesh but in the heart. I used to kiss you not with a touch of the lips but with attachment of the mind. I loved you because you welcomed me into friendship from the very beginning of my conversion, showed yourself more familiar with me than with the others, linked me with your own Hugh in the inner depths of your soul. So great was your love for both of us, so similar your affection, so single your devotedness, that as I seem to have gathered from your words to me, your attachment preferred neither one to the other, though unbiased reason would have preferred him to me because of his holiness. Why then did you pass away while I was not there? Why did you not want me present at your departure, whom alone when I was present you thought

---

255 Ps 37:14–15 (38:13–14)
256 *compositio morum*; see I.92.

took the place of both? Perhaps you thought we should be spared this, that is, you and I, so that your departure would not cause affliction to my sight, and my grief would not sadden your joyful and tranquil departure even in the slightest way. Or, as I am inclined to believe, perhaps divine loving-kindness looked upon you alone, in order to transfer your calm and peaceful soul in all tranquillity from the miseries of this life to your longed-for fatherland, and almost without your knowing it to break the bond of your physical dwelling with such ease that not the slightest fear of death might trouble a soul so dear to him.

110. Finally, the person who was resting near your bed detected in you no sign of impending death. Rather, your cheerful mien and greater facility in speaking increased his hope of your recovery. When, gently reclining your head, you gave up your spirit, he believed that you had fallen asleep, not that you had passed away. For you, my beloved brother, for you it was meant to be that way, that you passed away with such tranquillity. By your very peaceful death you showed quite clearly that you were welcomed by ministers of peace. No wonder. You did not dread but rather desired that hour, for on the day before you left us, you said to the superior of our monastery when he visited you, that you hoped not to tarry longer in this life.

111. What then did you gain, bitter death? What did you gain? Of course, you invaded his tent, the site of his pilgrimage, but you broke the chain which tethered him. You destroyed the dwelling he enjoyed in the meantime, but you removed the load which oppressed him. *We know that if the earthly house we inhabit is destroyed,* said the apostle, *we have a building from God not made with hands, an eternal home in heaven.*[257] Now, therefore, his soul, friend of virtues, desirous of quietness, eager for wisdom, victorious over nature, has been divested of its enveloping flesh and, if I may

---

257 2 Co 5:1

say so, has flown off on freer wings to that pure and sublime Good to be gathered into the long desired embrace of Christ.

But, you object, the flesh once committed to the earth is reduced to ashes.

Yes, of course.

Then why rejoice?

The flesh is dead so that it may be brought to life, dissolved so that it may be renewed yet better. *Sown in weakness, it will rise in strength.*[258] *Sown in corruption, it will rise in incorruption.*[259] *Sown in dishonor, it will rise in glory.*[260] Lastly, *sown an animal body, it will rise a spiritual body.*[261] *O death, where is your victory? O death, where is your sting?*[262] Where you seem to have done something to him, you are shown to have been profitable to him. So you spewed all your poison over me. Seeking him, you inflicted dire wounds upon me. Me, what sorrow, what bitterness, what harshness I bore, because I lost my guide on the journey, the mentor for my way of life.

112. But why, O my soul, did you gaze so long without tears on his dear mortal remains? Why did you bid farewell without kisses to that body so dear to you? I grieved and moaned, poor wretch, and from my inmost being drew long sighs, but yet I did not weep. I realized that I should be grieving so hard that even when I was grieving exceedingly, I did not believe I was grieving at all. So I felt afterwards. My mind was so numb that even when his limbs were at last uncovered for washing, I did not believe he had passed on. I was astonished that he, whom I had clasped to myself with the bonds of sweetest love, suddenly had slipped from my hands. I was astonished that this soul which was one with mine could, without mine, cast off the shackles of his body. But my numbness at last gave

---

258 1 Co 15:43
259 1 Co 15:42
260 1 Co 15:43
261 1 Co 15:44
262 1 Co 15:55

way to attachment, gave way to grief, gave way to compassion. Now, O my eyes, what are you doing, what are you doing? I beg you, do not be sparing, do not pretend. Offer whatever you have, whatever you can, over the remains of my beloved. Why do I blush? Am I the only one to weep? Look at how many tears, how many sobs, how many sighs surround me! Are these tears reprehensible? Yet the tears you shed over the death of your friend excuse us, Lord, for they express our affection[263] and give us a glimpse of your charity.[264] Your took on the attachment[265] of our weakness but only when you wished it, and were also able not to weep. O how sweet are your tears and how gentle. What savor and consolation they give to my troubled mind. *Look at how he loved him,* they said.[266] And look at how my own Simon was loved by everyone, embraced by everyone, cherished by everyone! But perhaps some stalwart persons at this moment are passing judgement on my tears, considering my love too human. Let them interpret [my tears] as they please. But you, Lord, look at them, observe them! Others see what happens outside but do not heed what I suffer within. That is where your eyes see, O Lord. Certainly in my eyes your servant had nothing to hinder his passing over into your embrace.

113. *No one knows what goes on in another human being, except the human spirit which is within him.*[267] But your eye, O Lord, *cuts through the dividing line of soul and spirit, of joints also and marrow, and discerns the thoughts and intentions of the heart.*[268] As an excellent servant said: *What a pity for man's life, praiseworthy though it may be, if you judge it without mercy.*[269] Look at the source of my fear, O Lord, look at the source of my tears.[34*] Heed them, O most tender-loving,

---

263 *affectio*
264 *charitas*
265 *affectus*
266 Jn 11:36
267 1 Co 2:11
268 Heb 4:12
269 St. Augustine, *Conf.* 9.13.34.

dearest and most merciful Lord. Receive them, O my only
hope, my one and only refuge, the object of my intentions, my
God, my mercy! Receive them, O Lord, as the sacrifice I offer
you for my most beloved friend and, if any flaws remained in
him, either pardon them or impute them to me. Let me, let me
be struck, let me be scourged, I shall pay for everything. I ask
only that you do not hide your blessed face from him, withdraw your sweetness, or delay your kindly consolation. Let
him experience the sweetness of your mercy, my Lord, which
he desired so ardently, anticipated with such great assurance,
commended with such great attachment and savored with
such delight that night when, after the others had retired to
rest and one brother was left at his bedside, in thanksgiving he
cried out aloud: 'Mercy! Mercy! Mercy!' He was trying, they
say, to recite in full the verse of the psalm: *mercy and justice
shall I sing to you, O Lord.*[270] Stopped, I think, by the sweetness of that first word, lingering with familiarity over its repetition and at last turning to the [brother] seated by his bed, he
repeated the same word over and over. Now noticing [his
attendant] overcome with a sort of drowsiness and as if indig-
nant at such lack of sensibility, because [the brother] was
obviously not plunged in similar sweetness or enjoying similar
savor, with his hand he began, as it were, to attempt to rouse
him from a deep sleep and repeated in a more expressive and
distinct voice: 'Mercy! Mercy!'

114. What is it I see in this, my Lord? Surely, as with my own
eyes, I seem to discern his mind refreshed by the draught of
this verse, freed by ineffable joy—while it discerns its sins
absorbed in the immense sea of divine mercy—to have left
nothing which burdens it, nothing which darkens its conscience in the least. What a joy to behold his soul, washed in
the fountain of divine mercy after laying down the weight of
sin. Striving upwards by the nimblest movements of its own
natural impulse and exulting to divest itself at any moment of
the remnants of the flesh, it meditates on the great mercy of

---

270 Ps 100 (101):1

God on whom it relies absolutely. Ah, *return now to your rest, O soul, because the Lord has treated you kindly.*[271] *Pass to the place of the wonderful tabernacle, even to the house of God, with the voice of joy and confession and the hymns of banqueters.*[272] I shall follow you with my tears, my tears whatever their worth. I shall follow you with my attachment. I shall follow you with the unique sacrifice of our Mediator. And you, Father Abraham, again and again extend your hands to receive this poor man of Jesus, another Lazarus.[273] Open your arms, welcome into your bosom, lovingly receive, cherish and console someone returning from the miseries of this life. To me, also, a wretch albeit his beloved, grant a place of rest some day with him in your bosom. Amen.

HERE ENDS BOOK ONE

---

271 Ps 114 (116):7
272 Ps 41:5 (42:4)
273 Lk 16:23

NOTES

1. *sicut pellem*: like a scroll. Cf. Augustine, *Conf.* XIII.15; *Enarr. in Ps.*
103, 1.8; and Aelred, *Spec car* I.32.90; Squire, *Aelred*, p.43.
2. Augustine, *Conf.* VII.18; *Enarr. in Ps.* 33, s. 1,4 & 6, see 30, s.1,9; Ps 8:5;
In Ioh. tract. 98.6. See G. Madec, 'Panis Angelorum (selon les Pères de
l'Eglise, surtout St Augustin)', *Forma Futuri*, Studi in onore M. Pellegrino
(Turin, 1975) 824: 'The bread of angels, for Augustine, is essentially the
Word of God and the Word was made flesh so that man might eat of the
bread of angels'. See *De libero arbitrio* III.10.29–30. Augustine therefore
interpreted the verse of the psalm as a summary of the christian doctrine of
salvation, as a soteriological formula which he liked to recall to the faithful.
3. Although *mens* has been consistently translated as 'mind', readers
should be aware that in the teaching of the Fathers *mens* carried a far deeper
and broader meaning than it does today, and meant far more than the
cognitive/perceptive consciousness. Robert Javelet, in his *Image et
ressemblance au douzième siècle, de saint Anselme à Alain de Lille*, 2
volumes (Paris: Letouzey et Ané, 1967), gives many references to *mens* (for
example, I:176–181, and accompanying notes in II:147–150). Among others
he cites Martin of Léon, *Sermo IV in nativitate Domini*, 2 (PL 208:109D–
110A) and *Sermo 34 in festo sanctae Trinitatis* (1276CD): 'The *mens* is the
image of God insofar as it is capable of him and can participate in his being';
Augustine, *De Trinitate* XV.7.11: 'Not the soul [*anima*] but what excels in
the soul, is called *mens*'; and William of Saint Thierry, *De natura et dignitate
amoris* 7.20 (PL 184:392C): '*Mens caput animae et principale ipsius mentis,
sedes amoris Dei.*' Javelet is of the opinion that *mens* deserves to be
translated 'heart', and that the rational character of *mens* does not exclude
the possibility of its being conceived in a broad sense embracing reason,
will, and memory (178–179).
4. Cf. Bernard of Clairvaux, SC 27.10 (CF 7:83–4); Augustine, *Conf.* I.2.2.
5. Cf. Aelred, *Spec car* II.10.25, and *Assumpt* PL 195:308D.
6. Cf. Augustine, *Conf. 1.1.1.*
7. *Natura, species, usus.* See *In Pent., Sermones inediti*, p. 109. Among
the numerous images of the Trinity elaborated by Augustine, two are found
joined together in this formula: 1) *aeternitas, species, usus* (*De Trinitate*
VI.10.11), which Augustine in turn had borrowed from Hilary of Poitiers (*De
Trinitate* II; PL 19:51);2) *natura, doctrina, usus* (*City of God*, XI.25). Note
that at the end of chapter 24, Augustine defined the action of the three
Persons as *est, videt, amat* (exists, sees, loves). In Hilary's *Trinity, usus* or
utilitas corresponds to the Holy Spirit, whereas Augustine considered *usus*
equivalent to *fructus*; he says so explicity in *De Trin.* VI.10.11. Aelred keeps
Hilary's word *usus*, and sees there the communication of goodness to the
person who is thus useful to others.
8. Cf. *Jesu*, 23–28. CCCM I;270–275; (CF 2:30–36).
9. *Beatitudo beatorum*: cf. Augustine, *Soliloquium*, I.1.3.
10. The trinitarian image of God in the soul: see Augustine, *De Trin.*
XIV.8.11; X.11.17; XI.1.1.
11. Cf. Augustine, *Enchiridion* 9.xxx: *nam libero arbitrio male utens et se
perdidit et ipsum* with Aelred, *et Deum.*

12. Cf. Bernard, *SC* 80:3–4 (CF 40:147–150); *Div* 12.2.
13. Augustine, *Conf.* VII.10.16.
14. Cf. Aelred, *Oner* 28 (29); PL 195:484D.
15. Cf. Augustine, *De libero arbitrio* III.24.72–3; *City of God* V.9.1.
16. Cf. *Spec car* I.8.24, first line: *non pedum passu, sed mentis affectu*; Augustine, *Ennar in Ps* 94; *In Ioh. tract.* 26.3. See also Gregory the Great, *Moralia in Job* 22.19.45: *cordis passibus*.
17. Augustine, *Soliloquia* I.14.24; Aelred, *Inst incl* 33 CCCM 1:677f; (CF 2:97f.).
18. Cf. I.8.24, near the end of the paragraph. On *compendium-circuitus*, see St Bernard, *Dil* VII.21 (CF 13:113) = *Spec car* I.16.49. Cf. Bernard, *Div* 93.2; Ep 64.1.
19. Cf. Bernard, *Dil* X.27 (CF 13:119–120).
20. Augustine, *Serm* 138.2; PL 38:764.
21. Aelred seems to follow Augustine (*De Gen. ad lit.* IV.2; PL 34:296–7) in his analysis of the number six.
22. *Spir amic* II.22–23; CCCM 1:307.
23. Augustine, *Conf.* XIII.9.2.
24. On the thirst for happiness (*beatitudo*), see also above I.3 and *Oner* 18; PL 195:431B. Cf. Bernard, *SC* 31 (CF 7:124f.), 48.8 (CF 31:19–20), 84.1 (CF 40:188–189).
25. Cf. *Oner* 1.5 PL 184:820BC: *onus Babylonis, mundus, cupiditas*.
26. *amare – amari*. Cf. *Spir amic* Prol. I.8 CCCM 1:287, and Augustine, *Conf.* II.2.1.
27. The classic mythological allegory of Scylla and Charybdis was used in a famous letter (14.6) from St Jerome to the monk Heliodorus, who had left the desert and whom Jerome wanted to bring back: 'Think of the meaning of the name of monk, since it is yours. What are you doing in the crowd, you who are alone? It is not as a pilot who does not know the waves and who has never known disaster that I warn you, but as someone who has recently been shipwrecked. It is from the shore and with a timid voice that I put you on guard against those who are in the sea. The boiling of sensuality, like that of Charybdis, engulfs one who gets lost in it (*in illo aestu Charybdis luxuriae salutem vorat*) whereas on the other hand Scylla, with the seductive face of a passionate virgin draws your modesty on to shipwreck.' (PL 22:350–51)
28. See Robert Thomas, 'Le Joug agréable, le fardeau léger du Christ d'après les auteurs cisterciens', *Collectanea* 37 (1975) 250–268. A reference to Augustine is added; from him comes the image of the wings which give the bird lightness; see *Sermons* 30, 69, 70, and 164 (PL 38), and Bernard *QH* 15.1: *Dulce onus, sed ei qui sentit, ei qui experitur. Alioquin...si non invenies, si non advertas, grave omnimo et periculosum....*(English translation CF 25:239–240).
29. Vocabulary from Augustine's *Conf.* X.27–28 is evident here. For example: When I shall be attached to you, there will be no more grief and labor for me' (X.27); *Clamasti, Domine, clamasti, vocasti, terruisti, rupisti surditatem meam* = *Vocasti et clamasti et rupisti surditatem meam* (X,27); *Audivi, sed heu, sero clamantem* = *Sero te amavi* (X.27). As Aelred Squire remarks in *Aelred of Rievaulx: A Study*, p. 159, n. 34: 'Most allusions of this

kind have been collected by P. Courcelle in *Les Confessions de St Augustin dans la tradition littéraire (Paris, 1963), pp. 291–305.'*

30. Cf. Bernard, *Pre* XIII.31, on observing an abbot's commands. (CF 1:128–129).

31. Bernard, *Pre* X.23 (CF 1:123).

32. Cf. Augustine, *Conf.* XIII.23.

33. See also III.106: *Cubitus unus,* the comparison is found in Origen's *Homily on the Book of Numbers* XXI.2: 'the summit is joined in one sole measure because everything converges in unity'(Sch 29:418). See also *Homily on Genesis* II.5: '...but the summit of the whole construction converges in the number one' (Sch 7bis:). See Augustine, *Contra Faustum* XII.16 PL 42:263, and Walter Daniel's *Life of Ailred,* ch. 40; Powicke, p. 48.

34. Cf. Aelred, *Nat Dom* PL 195:226.

HERE BEGINS BOOKS TWO

Chapter 1. What he proposed for consideration in Book One; it is clear that the vice-ridden should be excluded from these considerations.

I n the preceding part of this small work, when discoursing on the perfection of charity, we pointed out, as well as we could, that in charity consists the culmination of all the virtues. Nothing should be called virtue which that root has not produced; and no activity which does not end in charity should be thought perfect. In charity are recognized to be both fulfillment of the Law and evangelical perfection, since in it are spiritual circumcision of both the interior and exterior person and true sabbath of the mind,[1] true sacrifice, and complete fullness of the precepts. We have briefly mentioned circumcision above, and we have shown that the mind's sabbath does not, and cannot, exist apart from charity.

2. Charity is that easy yoke and light burden to which the Saviour's clemency invites us. *And you shall find rest for your souls,*[2] he said.

Yet because many of us who seem to have bowed our necks under this yoke demonstrably toil many ways, we have tried to show that the yoke of self-centeredness induces this labor. For this reason we proposed for consideration those three things in which the evangelist John seems to have summed up self-centeredness of all kinds: the concupiscence of the flesh, the concupiscence of the eyes, and pride of life.[3]

---

1 *mens*
2 Mt 11:29
3 1 Jn 2:16

But when the death of our dearly beloved friend inter-vened, this work was interrupted. Yielding to tears and mourning for a while, we set these considerations aside for another time.

3. To take Paul's words as our starting point, we say that the root of all evils is self-centeredness,[4] just as, on the other hand, the root of all virtues is charity. As long as this poisonous root remains in the depths of the soul, even though some of the twigs on the surface may be pruned back, others will inevitably continue to sprout from the re-invigorated base [of the plant] until the very root from which these pernicious shoots spring up has been utterly torn out and nothing more remains.

Yet there are some who are enmeshed in more evident and, I might say, ranker vices. One glance advertises the mark of their confusion. These, I think, should be excluded from these present considerations; that their minds are devoid of all restfulness has already amply been demonstrated. But we who seem to have bowed the shoulders of our minds beneath the Gospel yoke, which the Saviour's declaration shows to be very easy, and beneath the Lord's burden, which the selfsame authority likewise recommends as very light, we are still undeniably proved to toil. Let us, I say, who profess the cross of Christ, having taken up the key of God's Word, unlock the gates of our breast and, penetrating as far as the division of soul and spirit, of joints and marrow, let us discern the thoughts and intentions of our heart.[5] Without any wheedling flattery, let us scrutinize what lies deeply hidden in the inner recesses of our souls, and try harder to tear out the diseased roots themselves.

---

4 1 Tm 6:10
5 Heb 4:12

Chapter 2. Outward toil is determined by the quality of one's inward [toil], and outward toil is sometimes lessened by one's inward [toil].

4. Of course, this is a toil, not of the flesh, but of the heart, just as it is also evident that the rest about which we speak is one of the heart and not of the flesh, although outward toil is determined by the quality of a person's inward [toil] and it should not be said that there is outward toil if there is not already some within. For example: look at hunters and fowlers, or whoever else follows such vain pursuits. If you look closely at their outward, physical movements, what is more laborious? If at the state of their mind, what is more delightful? The same thing is very easily discovered in praiseworthy pursuits as well. How much outward toil the apostles endured when they were cast into prison, when they were bound with chains, when they were brutally scourged. And yet *they left the presence of the council rejoicing that they were counted worthy to suffer dishonor for the name of Jesus.*[6] How many sacrilegious people suffered similar torments in those times, but because their conscience was different, they were miserable in both respects. They toiled both inwardly and outwardly, whereas [the apostles] rejoiced in inward peace amid outward torments. We should not be astonished [at this], since outward toil is often lessened by inward, and the most oppressive ardors of the body are attenuated by the ardors of the spirit. What toil do adulterers have? What torment is there for thieves? For the former, to be received into wrongly-desired embraces; for the latter, to enjoy in the spoils of others. But the former, inwardly burning the torch of lust, are unaware of what they suffer outwardly, and the quiet covert flame of greed makes the latter insensitive to the obvious sufferings of the body. About such persons the prophet said: *They have toiled to commit iniquity.*[7]

---

6 Ac 5:41
7 Jr 9:5

5. Now that we have attentively examined these matters, it is perfectly clear that the outward sufferings of the body do not produce inward toil, but that the root remaining deep within[8] makes everything exterior conform to its nature.

Why is it that, when two people are sitting at the same table and have the same food placed before them, one is glad and the other complains? Why is it that when two people suffer the same wounds one is downcast with the lassitude of sorrow and the other is immersed in a marvelous joy? And when two people are stricken at the same time by the misfortune of bereavement or poverty, why is it that one blasphemes and the other gives thanks? The same object of beauty is set before the eyes of both; one is shamefully agitated, the other continues to enjoy his accustomed peace. When an opportunity for promotion to some kind of honor presents itself, one person is so inflamed with a craving to dominate that in his hope of reaching the summit of power he does not dread committing any kind of crime at all, whereas another remains so free from this worst of passions that he does not accept the marks of distinction offered to him or does so only reluctantly.

Chapter 3. By its tranquillity, charity tempers everything that happens; by its perversity, self-centeredness corrupts everything.

6. Is it not evident that the same thing happens with the body, so that according to one's healthy or unhealthy condition everything that happens outwardly is experienced either as vexing or pleasing? Food which aggravates the illness of one person benefits the health of another. And the sun which blinds the inflamed eye happily lightens the healthy.

Just as things that happen to the body outwardly are found to be either healthful or harmful according to the limits[9] of a

---

8 *in viscera*
9 *modus*

person's inward nature, so also one can easily perceive by what has been indicated above that one man's rest and another's toil depend on the inward quality of their minds. The mind which the Lord's very easy and tranquil yoke—I mean charity—holds in sway will transfer everything that happens to it into its state of tranquillity, not permitting itself to be upset by any disturbing events, but forcing the very changes of events to contribute to the benefit of its progress. But if a mind is habituated to the very heavy yoke of self-centeredness, its lax restfulness disguises itself as the sweetness of the Lord's yoke as long as there is no occasion for agitation. But as soon as some cause for indignation arises, the savage beast soon bursts from the recesses of the heart, as if from a deeply-hidden cavern. By the dreadful gnawing of the passions it tears and bloodies the poor soul, allowing it no time for peace or rest. So let this yoke rot in the presence of oil;[10] that is to say, the yoke of self-centeredness in the presence of charity. Then, all of a sudden, someone will experience how light, how easy, how joyful Christ's burden is;[11] how, as someone has said, it catches one up to heaven and snatches one away from the earth.[1*]

Wherefore, if we want to experience the sweetness of this rest, let us carefully seek out the causes and roots of our toil, not only by pruning what is outward with lukewarm attachments, as with a blunt knife, but by penetrating with quite vehement desire to the very sources of our ills.

Chapter 4. All inward toil arises from a threefold concupiscence.

7. I think, however, that if we investigate this question more keenly, we will very clearly realize that any toil which arises in us is derived from either concupiscence of the flesh,

---

10 Is 10:27
11 Cf. Mt 11:29

concupiscence of the eyes, or pride of life,[12] as though from some poisoned springs. If rather coarse food disheartens me, concupiscence of the flesh inflicts this toil on me. I toil, not because I have taken the yoke of Christ upon myself, but because I have not fully cast off the yoke of self-centeredness. Why is it that when I am burning with eagerness for more sumptuous food, I get upset if more commonplace fare is set before me? Or if there is less than usual, or something is not on time or rather carelessly prepared, why am I consumed with the plague of grumbling? What produces this anxiety in me? The passion of self-centeredness or the gentleness of charity? What if a monk demands from his superior the number of portions corresponding to the number of lessons at the Night Office, and wants to have tasty meals and exotic seasonings on each and every solemn feast? What if, when on some occasion any of these is lacking, he explodes in arguments and disputes and, unable to endure the raging of this worst kind of passion, disturbs the peace of his brothers with his uncivil complaints and secret murmuring? Has worldly concupiscence not put the yoke of this slavery on him and the affliction of the vilest toil? Rightly rebuking such persons, James said: *What causes arguments and disputes among you? Do they not come from your concupiscences, which are at war in your members?*[13]

Chapter 5. About an opinion of certain persons who say that outward toil is opposed to charity and to inward gentleness.

8. But, you say, it is clear that to waste the body away by unremitting vigils, to afflict the flesh by daily toil, and to weaken the strength of one's members by eating very poor food are not only [causes of] not inconsiderable toil, but are

---

12 1 Jn 2:16
13 Jm 4:1

opposed to the charity you are trying hard to recommend so that, emptying the mind of all pleasantness, they leave it drained of all spiritual gentleness.

This is the ludicrous opinion of those who put spiritual sweetness in a certain pleasantness of the flesh, asserting that affliction of the body is contrary to the spirit and that the sufferings of the outer man lessen the holiness of the inner. Since, then, they say, flesh and spirit cleave to one another by an attachment natural to them, each necessarily communicates its passions to the other. And if the joy of the one cannot remain undisturbed when the other is oppressed, so also a spirit downcast over some anxiety or sorrow certainly cannot catch the breath of spiritual joy. These things are seen to be closely investigated and proved.

O how shameful it is to seek spiritual grace by the rules of Hippocrates! Those who rely on physical arguments rather than on the apostles' teachings are so wrong, so very wrong!

9. This is clearly not the wisdom coming down from above, which is first of all modest and then pacifying, but one which is frankly earthly, animal, and diabolic.[14] This is the wisdom of words; while teaching pleasantness of the flesh, it strives to abolish the cross of Christ.[15] In the cross, of course, there is nothing pleasant, nothing soft, nothing tender, nothing at all delicate as far as the flesh is concerned. But it is not abolished. Rather, it upsets this self-indulgent doctrine which the nails driven into those sacred members have conquered, which the very lance thrust into that gentle breast has vanquished by its saving point.

I feel utterly opposed [to this doctrine], and declare boldly that affliction of the flesh is not contrary to the spirit, if it is inspired by a healthy intention and if discretion is observed. This should be taken, not from our own personal conjecture, but from the example of our forebears, so that laxness and slackness may not be camouflaged beneath the colors of

---

14 Jm 3:15
15 1 Co 1:17

discretion.[16] So I say, affliction of the flesh is not contrary, but necessary, to the spirit. It does not lessen divine consolation either, but rather, I think, elicits it. So much so that I would estimate that as long as we are in this life these two things, that is, outward tribulation and inward consolation, always balance one another.

10. What then, you say? Should I believe your opinion more than my own experience? And what if someone else were to declare that he has experienced something very different? Which of you should I believe in preference to the other? You assert that spiritual grace has lessened for you now that you have taken up a stricter way of life; he asserts that the more he is afflicted, the more he experiences the grace of divine comfort. Whose opinion should be trusted? Shall we think that divine grace is subservient to physical reasons? Far from it! Far from it! Clearly, he shows mercy to whom he wills.[17] He may therefore impart the sweetness of his consolation to someone affluent in riches and luxuries, yet withhold it by a harsh judgement from one of his poor little ones who for his sake dies to himself every day.[18] Far be it from me to think such a thing about our ever gentle, tender, loving, and compassionate [Lord]. Yet if I say it, you can doubt it; if Christ says it, not to believe it is heretical.

Chapter 6. The preceding opinion is refuted by apostolic and prophetic authority.

11. Let that most valiant athlete step forward, that most faithful witness, that remarkable debater in whom Christ speaks, who dies each day for Christ, who suffers all tribulations,[19] who is familiar with quarrels without and fear

---

16 Cf. III.35.95.
17 Cf. Rm 9:18
18 Cf. 1 Co 15:31
19 Cf 1 Co 15:31

within,[20] who chastises his body and subdues it,[21] who eats no bread without paying for it,[22] but works day and night, wearing himself out, whose hands provide what he and his companions need; who, finally, in labors and hardships, through many a sleepless night, in hunger and thirst, in cold and exposure,[23] toils beneath Jesus' standard like the keenest soldier. Let him settle this question, I say, and show whether such great tribulation and astonishing fatigue detracted from his spiritual consolation. Perhaps all the natural fluids in his head were so dried up by so many frequent vigils and so many labors that he could no longer bring out any tears. Perhaps his heart, withered by all the pressure on it, did not drink in any spiritual sweetness at all.

12. Yet I see him writing to certain men with great distress and anguish of heart, amid many tears.[24] I see him deploring people who had previously sinned and had not repented.[25] I see him rejoicing with those who rejoice and weeping with those who weep.[26] I hear him groaning because he wanted, not to be stripped of his present life, but to be clothed with new life.[27] What shall I say about his spiritual sweetness? Compared with its most pleasant taste, even the things that seemed gain to him he counted as rubbish.[28] Urged on by this wondrous sweetness, did he not long for the loving embraces of Christ, saying: *My desire is to depart and be with Christ, for that is far better?*[29] Aflame with wondrous love for Christ, did he not completely renounce all glory, *except*, as he said, *to glory in the cross of my Lord Jesus Christ?*[30] Stirred by the

---

20 2 Co 7:5
21 1 Co 9:27
22 2 Th 3:8
23 2 Co 11:27
24 2 Co 2:4
25 2 Co 12:21
26 Rom 12:15
27 2 Co 5:4
28 Ph 3:8
29 Ph 1:23
30 Gal 6:14

fervor derived from exceedingly great charity, did he not pronounce an anathema against those who do not love the Lord Jesus? *If anyone does not love our Lord Jesus,* he declared, *let him be anathema. Maranatha.*[31]

13. Let the apostle himself declare whether he was forsaken in his tribulations without consolation, and let him make known to us what we should hope for when we are in tribulation. With his apostle's sword, let him transfix the head of the serpent which hissingly released its deadly venom into human senses. For these opinions come from the one who crawls on his belly, eats dirt, and sleeps in swampy places in the shade.[32] Underneath the colors of holiness, he is preoccupied with the interests of the belly and lust. He thinks that simple people will be more easily frightened away from poverty as lived by the apostles and from evangelical purity, if they think they will have a greater grace of divine sweetness in a laxer sort of life. Perhaps they believe it is holier to display tear-smudged faces in the midst of sumptuous food and fine wines, amid portions fit for a king and carefully prepared feasts, amid idle chit-chat and all-night carousing, than it is to appear pale-faced and dry-eyed in the midst of toil and hardship, in numerous vigils, in hunger and thirst, in cold and exposure, in the fatigue of each day,[33] in the mortifications of one's own will, in scorning the world and disregarding the flesh.

14. Let Paul, therefore, declare whether the tender loving Comforter forsakes his own without any consolations during the tribulations of the present time, and let him by his authority settle beforehand Jovinian's heresy, which is sprouting up once again. This present heresy seems even more dangerous than Jovinian's, for his put feasting on a par with fasting, whereas this one gives it precedence.

---

31 1 Co 16:22
32 Jb 40:16 (21)
33 2 Co 11:27

Let those who have decided that a greater consolation of divine sweetness exists in pleasure of the flesh than in tribulation hear what Paul says: *Blessed be the God and Father of Our Lord Jesus Christ, the Father of mercies and the God of all consolation, who comforts us in all our tribulations.*[34] If we are emaciated from fasting or affected by the vigils or crushed by toil, therefore, blessed be God who consoles us in all our tribulations. If we are stoned, if we are bound with chains, if we are savagely scourged with rods, if we endure the confinement of prison, blessed be God who consoles us in all our tribulations. Let the world roar, let the world rage with fury, let it inveigh against us with hatred, assault us with curses, snatch away our belongings, and stain our reputation, blessed be God who consoles us in all our tribulations. *So that we may be able*, he says, *to console those who are in all kinds of trouble.*[35]

He promises his consolation not to those who live in wealth and luxury, but to those who are in all kinds of trouble. And leaving no question about it, he adds: *For as the sufferings of Christ abound in us, so also through Christ does our consolation abound.*[36] What could be clearer? What we said a little earlier is evident: that these two things are proportionate, outward sufferings and inward consolations.

15. Who, then, relying on physical reasons, would be so doltish and so presumptuous as to affirm with impudent absurdity (and contrary to the most manifest truth and apostolic authority) that sharing in the sufferings of Christ is opposed to the spirit and diminishes the grace of spiritual sweetness?[2]* To share in the sufferings of Christ means to submit to regular discipline, to mortify the flesh by abstinence, vigils, and toil, to submit one's will to another's judgement, to prefer nothing to obedience, and—to sum up many things in a few words—to follow to the limit our profession which we

---

34 2 Co 1:3–4
35 2 Co 1:4
36 2 Co 1:5

have made according to the Rule of Saint Benedict. This is to share in the sufferings of Christ,[37] as our Lawgiver bore witness when he said: *And so, persevering in the monastery until the end, let us share in the sufferings of Christ by patience, that we may deserve to share in his kingdom.*[38] And the apostle said the same thing: *knowing that as you share in our sufferings, so too you will share in our consolation.*[39]

16. How necessary affliction of the outward man is, the same apostle very clearly taught us when he declared: *Though our outward man may be wasting away, yet the person within is being renewed day by day. For our present slight affliction, which is momentary, prepares for us an eternal weight of glory which is beyond comparison.*[40] Finally, Solomon, with mystical words, identified those to whom divine consolation would be communicated by saying: *Give strong drink to those who grieve and wine to the sad-spirited. Let them drink and forget their need, and remember their sorrow no more.*[41]

By these words he clearly declares that it is not to those dissipated in idleness nor to those wasting their days in raucous laughing and story-telling, but to the sad-spirited that he promises the wine that rejoices the heart of man.[42] And he states that the cider made from new apples and old, which the bride reserved for the groom's delight, must not be given to those who feast and drink, but to those who grieve because of the difficulties of this life and to those who toil in want and sorrow. *Let them drink,* he said, *and forget their need*— plainly affirming by this that the magnitude of the toil is lessened by divine consolation. The psalmist very clearly harmonized with this opinion: *In proportion to the multitude of*

---

37 Cf. 1 P 4:13
38 RB, Prologue
39 2 Co 1:7
40 2 Co 4:16–17
41 Pr 31:6–7
42 Ps 103(104):15

the sorrows in my heart your consolations have given joy to my soul.[43]

Let no one therefore be terrified of the steep, rough road that leads to life.[44] Let no one turn back because of a timid moroseness to seek the laxer way he once abandoned. Rather, as our Lawgiver said, *Persevering, let him not grow faint, let him not fall away.*[45] Let him know that in proportion to the great number of toils he puts up with for Christ, Christ's consolations will gladden his soul.

Chapter 7. The question of why some persons are pricked by greater gentleness [of compunction] in a somewhat lax, rather than in a stricter, life.

17. Why is it, you ask, that when I lived in a rather more lax way, when I enjoyed richer food, relaxed a bit with good drink, indulged in a little more sleep and did not weaken my body by hard work or irritate it with such rough garments, and when I was not restricted to so much silence, I felt so much compunction, I was so affected, and so open to a certain sweetness of mind? Yet now, in this strictness, I go along so dry and parched that I cannot, even by force, wring any tears from my eyes?

18. And I ask you, what kind of judgement do you think should be made about someone who, once engulfed in a monstrous whirlpool of vice, gave himself up completely to filth and uncleanness and had no horror of any flagrant acts, yet in the midst of such a life was quite often touched with compunction and quite often shed tears, not only from fear of punishment and at remembering his sins—this would perhaps astonish no one—but, even open by a wonderful attachment

---

to the sweetness of Jesus' love,[46] seemed to embrace him with a mental kiss? What about that?

Should this person's life be envied? Should such habits be imitated? Should the flesh be delivered up to such enticements and the members given over to concupiscence so that we may enjoy a like sweetness? Would anyone be so out of his mind as to say this? I talk about these things, not as if they were doubtful, but as true and certain, as Jesus himself knew they are.

19. I, too, knew a brother who, after idling away the whole day gossiping and drinking in the company of worldlings, both men and women, came back to the monastery late and burst into such tears and sighs that he offended the ears of many brothers with his troublesome groanings. Yet he did not on this account refrain even in the slightest from pursuing this sort of enticements. In the hope of this compunction, should regular discipline then be abandoned? Should a like lewdness be sought after? Who would not be horrified at hearing such a thing?

Chapter 8. The cause for spiritual visitation is threefold.

20. We know, therefore, that a visitation of this sort is not always an indication of holiness, for often it urges a person onward to holiness, and often is a safeguard for holiness. As far as appears at present, the cause for this visitation is threefold. It is occasionally given to wake people up, sometimes to console them, and frequently to reward them. To wake up those who are sleeping, to console those who are toiling, and to reward those who are sighing for heavenly things. The first, then, awakens the sluggish, the second refreshes those toiling, and the third supports those making progress upward. The first compunction urges [a person] on to holiness, the second

---

46 *amor*

safeguards holiness, and the third confers reward. The first terrorizes the scornful or coaxes on the fearful; the second encourages someone making an effort and helps him along; the third embraces the person who arrives. The first is like a goad correcting someone swerving out of line; the second is like a staff supporting someone weak; the third is like a couch holding up someone at rest.

21. Just as divine Clemency urges those living tepidly or profligately on to salvation frequently by word, frequently by example, occasionally by reproach, and sometimes even by the whip, so too, by a secret compunction either awakened by fear or begotten by attachment, it invites others to a better state of life. The cause for this visitation is therefore twofold: it is accorded to the elect for advancement, and to the reprobate for judgement.

Chapter 9. The first kind of compunction, like certain other graces, occurs for the reprobate for judgement, but for the elect for advancement.

22. That this grace is frequently common to both the reprobate and the elect should not astound us, since we know that the more excellent charisms, that is to say, the words of knowledge, prophecy, kinds of tongues, and the grace of miracles, are bestowed even on the reprobate. For Saul also was among the prophets and Judas among the apostles. *On that day,* said the Lord, *many will say to me: 'Did we not cast out demons in your name and accomplish many miracles in your name?' And I will inform them, 'I never knew you!'*[47]

That we may likewise see this with regard to the grace of compunction, a contrite Balaam said, *Let my soul die the death of the just, and my last hour be like theirs.*[48] Deploring his own perversity, he also said: *Balaam, the son of Be'or, has*

---

47 Mt 7:22–23
48 Nb 23:10

spoken. He who hears the words of God has spoken, who in falling has had his eyes opened.[49] Nevertheless, he did not profit from this compunction at all. He taught Balak how to place a stumbling block in the way of the sons of Israel, to commit fornication, to drink, and to eat idolatrous sacrifices.

How often did the sons of Israel, rebuked by Moses, weep before the Lord in the desert? That compunction did them no good; they gave free rein all over again to their original concupiscence. But once they had been led into the promised land, when an angel spoke to them in the place of their weeping, they lifted up their voices and wept.[50] And still, after all this, they continued to do evil before the Lord.

23. And what about Judas? Was he not stricken with compunction when he said, *I have sinned in betraying innocent blood?*[51] The wise man who said, *If a man who washes himself after touching a corpse touches it again, what good does his washing do?*[52] gives witness that compunction of this type does no good for those who go back to their perversity. Someone washing himself after touching a corpse [is someone] who, when touched by compunction, weeps bitterly over a life devoid of all warmth of fervor, or indeed over a life fetid with vice and buried in it. But this washing will be of no avail if amendment does not follow. Yet the elect, *for whom all things work together for good,*[53] are awakened by compunction of this type, not to judgement but to advancement. Aroused by this heavenly visitation, they by no means languish securely apathetic in a rather remiss way of life, but the greater the sweetness of divine love[54] they enjoy, the more ardently do they gird themselves for a more courageous practice of virtues.

---

49 Nb 24:4
50 Jdg 2:4
51 Mt 27:4
52 Sir 34:30(25)
53 Rm 8:28
54 *dilectio*

Chapter 10. The twofold reason for the second visitation, and that this leads to the third, which is more excellent than the others.

24. Those who have abruptly shaken off their torpor to undertake sweat and struggles for Christ are singled out by Him for that more excellent kind of compunction which heals the infirm, strengthens the weak, and encourages the hopeless. It is consolation for those who moan, pause for those who toil, protection for those who are tempted, and food for those who are on their way. What consolation they deprive themselves of, who recoil abruptly at the first drop of sweat, and either slide back into their former torpor or seek out paltry consolations in frequent chatting, visiting with friends or, of course, in freedom of self-will. The holy prophet, scorning these dregs of consolations, said: *My soul refused to be consoled.*[55] What then? Were you forsaken without any consolation? Far from it! *I remembered God and was filled with delight.*[56]

25. The reason for this second visitation is likewise twofold. It sometimes occurs in persons who are tempted, that they may not fall, and sometimes in persons about to be tempted, that they may bear it more easily. People are refreshed by the first and armed by the second. Let no one measure his holiness by the first kind of visitation, therefore, because it is very clear that it sometimes happens to the wicked as well, or by the second kind, because even though it is more excellent , it still only prepares for, and does not indicate, holiness. One is born, we might say, in the first and nurtured in the second. When one has become used to experiencing compunction of this second kind frequently, and when one is nourished by frequent little draughts of divine sweetness, one is borne upward to that more sublime kind, on a more excellent level,

---

55 Ps 76:3(77:2)
56 Ps 76:4(77:3)

which no longer strengthens and sustains the weak man but rewards the quasi-perfect victor with more abundant grace.

Chapter 11., What God brings about in each of these visitations.

26. In the first state therefore the soul is awakened, in the second it is purified, and in the third it enjoys the tranquillity of the sabbath. In the first state mercy is at work, in the second loving-kindness,[57] and in the third justice. For mercy seeks what is lost, loving-kindness reforms what is found, and justice rewards what is already perfect. Mercy raises up one who is prostrate, loving-kindness aids one who combats, and justice crowns the victor.

What could be a greater indication of divine mercifulness than for that pleasantness, that joyfulness, that wonderful serenity in which no defilement intrudes, to impart the grace of its visitation to a soul that has, till then, been defiled? Not only does it shake the soul with terror but, by its force of penetration cutting through all the doors of the mind that have been locked with the bolts of vice, it imprints some kiss of its sweetness on lips still unclean and by its ineffable pleasantness coaxes the straying back, draws the hesitant close, and gives new life to the hopeless.

27. O sweet Lord! *What return can I make* to you *for everything you have given me?*[58] O how pleasant your Spirit is in all things! Truly, Lord, your mercy toward me is great.[59] You have stretched your hand down from above, snatching and delivering me from deep waters and from the hands of the sons of strangers.[60] You have snatched my soul out of the

---

57 *pietas*
58 Ps 115(116):12
59 Ps 85(86):13
60 Ps 143(144):7

depths of hell,[61] where I felt a drop of your sweetness on my tongue and heard your voice as if from far off.

What are you doing, worthless, squalid wretch? Why are you wallowing in squalor? Why are you delighting in shameful deeds? Look at what sweetness there is with me, what pleasantness, what joyfulness! Do you despair because of the enormity of your sins? But shall I, who pursue you when you flee from me, reject you when you come to me? Shall I, who embrace and draw you to myself when you turn your face from me, push you away when you hide under the wings of my mercy?

28. Your voice, O Lord, your inspiration. Where does such hope for the despairing soul come from, if not from your giving, O Lord, you who heal our infirmities in wonderful ways and restore form to our deformity?

But now, what should be said about the second state, in which divine loving-kindness works so wonderfully in man that he profits from temptation and gains greater strength from infirmity? And although every soul naturally flees from toils, temptations, and sorrows, he is quickened by so many consolations in the midst of temptations that not only can he endure them when they besiege him, but to some extent he can even summon them forth and ask for them when they are slow to appear. To this state that holy man had progressed who said, *Try me, O Lord, and test me.*[62] And further on: *Try me, O Lord, and know my heart.*[63]

In this state the mind accustomed to the countless incentives of heavenly attachments is moved along little by little to that most sublime kind of visitation experienced by very few. There it begins to have some foretaste of the first-fruits of its future reward. Passing on to the place of the wonderful tabernacle, right up to the house of God,[64] with his soul melting

---

61 Ps 85(86):13
62 Ps 25(26):2
63 Ps 138(139):23
64 Cf. Ps 41:5(42:4)

within himself, one is inebriated with the nectar of heavenly secrets. Contemplating with the purest regard the place of his future rest, he exclaims with the prophet: *This is my place of rest forever and ever. Here will I dwell, for I have chosen it.* [65]

Therefore, just as mercy alone is at work in the first state where no merits had preceded, so in this state where [God] crowns his gifts—which he has nevertheless willed to be our own merits—justice works along with mercy.

Chapter 12. In the first visitation, fear especially exists; in the second, consolation; and in the third, love.

29. I think it should be noted that although in this first visitation the sweetness of pleasantness is sometimes mixed with fear, and in the second the goad of fear is often brought to bear along with pleasantness, still the first has more particularly to do with fear and the second with the sweetness of consolation. But in the third, perfect charity casts out fear. [66] The beginning of wisdom is the fear of the Lord, [67] but the culmination of wisdom is love of God. Its beginning is in fear, its perfection in love. Here is toil, there reward. The first leads up to the second, yet no one attains it except through itself. Upon the mind often afflicted with fear, beset with grief, cast down by despair, absorbed in sadness, and gnawed by listlessness, falls a drop of this marvelous pleasantness trickling down from the balsam trees of that rich and densely-forested mountain, [68] as if it were overflowing in very peaceful downward course. At the splendor of its radiant divine light the whole dark cloud of irrational sensations is dispersed. At its very pleasant taste all bitterness is routed, the heart is

---

65 Ps 131(132):14
66 1 Jn 4:18
67 Sir 1:16(14)
68 Ps 67(68):16

expanded, the mind enriched, and its capacity for rising upward is primed in a marvelous way. Lukewarmness is banished by fear, and fear is tempered by the taste of divine sweetness. Lest the mind remain sluggish at the lowest levels, fear awakens it. Lest it faint away at toil, attachment nourishes it.

30. Educated by the alternation of these two until, entirely absorbed by ineffable charity, the mind no longer grows rich with love, but burning for the eagerly-desired embraces of him who is the fairest of all the sons of men,[69] begins to want to depart and to be with Christ,[70] saying each day with the prophet: *Alas for me that my sojourn is prolonged.*[71] And so the Lawgiver shall give a blessing,[72] dispensing the wine of compunction along with fear of himself to those who are beginning, and milk from the breasts of his consolation to those who are progressing. And when they are weaned from this milk, they shall feast as soon as they enter his glory.

The first visitation, then, casts reproach on wickedness. The second supports our infirmity, and the third manifests holiness. Let no one boast about the first therefore, in which the wicked or tepid person is accused, nor about the second in which the weak are tested. And in the third, let anyone who boasts boast in the Lord.[73]

Chapter 13. The fruit in each, and why certain persons are deprived of the consolation of the second visitation.

31. The fruit of the first visitation is true conversion to God. The fruit of the second, mortification of self-will and all the

---

69 Ps 44:3(45:2)
70 Ph 1:23
71 Ps 119(120):5–6
72 Ps 83:8(84:6)
73 2 Co 10:17

passions. The fruit of the third is perfect happiness.[74] So once
the fruit of the first compunction has been received in the
excellence of a perfect conversion, when that first kind has
ceased, as I have said, having finished its task, immediately
there follows the testing period of temptation and toil, so that
the [third], which is sweet devotion to God, may deservedly
come after. Surely, the attachment of this sweetness is not
readily given unless preceded, accompanied, or indeed
immediately followed by toil and temptation. By no means is
it granted for merit of life, but for the support of weakness and
the alleviation of temptation. Consequently, those who soon
recoil at the first temptations and toil are like some of the
Lord's disciples who, scandalized, shrank from sharing in the
body and blood of the Lord, that is to say, from imitating his
passion. They said: *This is a hard saying; who could accept
it?*[75] And so, less suited to the kingdom of God, they look
back, or indeed permit themselves the basest sorts of earthly
and human consolation. These people, I tell you, exclude
themselves from the sweetness of this consolation. They are
miserable everywhere and do not rise to that sublime kind of
visitation. Without consolation of this kind they find the practice of virtue loathesome, but because their conscience resists,
they do not have the presumption to return to their old ways.
Perhaps they could rightly complain about being deserted by
divine consolation if, perfectly renouncing their old ways and
fully mortifying their self-will, they did not in any way prefer
the vile and base consolations of the world to God's consolation.

32. Now once they have set out along the way of a more
demanding vocation, they will immediately begin to dream of
I know not what badges of honor, and to usurp liberties for
themselves with the vainest sort of presumption. These
wretches do not wait to be told, *Friend, move up higher,*[76] but

---

74 *beatitudo*
75 Jn 6:60
76 Lk 14:10

push themselves impudently toward the higher places the best they can. If I may use the Gospel's words, they crave the seats of honor in synagogues, the places of honor at banquets, the greetings of honor in the market place, and to be called Rabbi by other men.[77] These men who have never spent one day learning to be disciples pretend to be teachers. Since they are conscious of such absurdities in themselves, I am therefore astounded at the shame and irreverence with which they think divine sweetness should be bestowed on them, or that their souls, defiled by earthly affections, should be caressed in Jesus' purest embrace.

Certainly, if a drop of heavenly sweetness were to trickle down on them, it would surely happen not on account of merit for holiness or relief for toil, but to wake up those who are at the lowest level, as it were. Yet grace of this kind is hardly ever, or never, lavished on those who sin wilfully or who remain apathetically indolent after they have received some notion of truth and taken to the way of perfect purity.

We should say however that it is one thing simply to be tempted by these earthly attachments, another thing very rarely to fall into one of them hardly at all, yet another to yield and consent or to give oneself over to them completely. And [it is] still another thing to accept preoccupations of this sort against one's will if they are imposed.

Chapter 14. Some divine witnesses are proposed, by which each person may judge his own state.

33. If, then, you wish to have a clearer idea of the causes and reasons for your visitation, first investigate with keen scrutiny the state to which you have progressed. Then examine the quality of your life and habits, not according to your own fancy but according to the rules given in Scripture, the outlines of the heavenly precepts and the norm of your own

---

77 Mt 23:6

profession. [Do this] giving close attention, with your conscience as witness. Did the Lord not say, *Watch out that your hearts are not weighed down with dissipation and drunkenness and the cares of this life?*[78] And likewise: *Everyone who is angry with his brother shall be liable to judgement. Whoever insults his brother shall be liable to the council. And whoever says 'You fool', shall be liable to hellfire.*[79] Elsewhere: *Whoever among you wants to be greater should be the servant of everyone.*[80] Also: *Anything you want men to do to you, you do to them.*[81] And: *On the day of judgement men will answer for every careless word they have uttered.*[82]

The apostle Paul also said: *Not in reveling and drunkenness, not in debauchery and licentiousness, not in quarreling and jealously, but put on the Lord Jesus Christ and forget about the flesh with all its desires.*[83] And he said: *No soldier in God's service gets involved in civilian pursuits.*[84] To the Galatians: *If you snap at and devour one another, see that you are not destroyed by one another.*[85] He said to the Thessalonians: *We beseech you, brothers,…to make more progress,*[86]*…and to endeavor to live quietly, to mind your own affairs and to work with your own hands…so that you may have the respect of outsiders and may be dependent on no one for anything.*[87] In the second letter to the same he also wrote: *If anyone does not want to work, let him not eat.*[88]

James, too, said: *My brothers, show no partiality to persons as you hold the faith of Our Lord Jesus Christ.*[89] Likewise: *If*

---

78 Lk 21:34
79 Mt 5:22
80 Mt 20:27
81 Mt 7:12
82 Mt 12:36
83 Rm 13:13–14
84 2 Tm 2:4
85 Gal 5:15
86 1 Th 4:1
87 1 Th 4:11–12
88 2 Th 3:10
89 Jm 2:1

you have bitter jealousy and disputes in your hearts, do not boast.... Wherever jealousy and dispute exist are fickleness and every kind of evil practice.[90] And a bit further on: *Whoever wants to be this world's friend becomes God's enemy.*[91] The same apostle says further on: *Do not speak slanderously about one another, my brothers.*[92]

Let us come to the Prince of the Apostles: *I beseech you,* he says, *as strangers and pilgrims, to abstain from the desires of the flesh.*[93] And in the same letter: *Putting aside all malice, all guile, and insincerity and all slander....*[94] Further on: *If anyone speaks, let him speak words that seem to come from God.*[95] A few verses later on he says to pastors: *Feed the flock of God entrusted to you, not for shameful gain nor as domineering over clerics.*[96] *Likewise, you young people, be subject to the elders. Deal humbly, all of you, with one another.*[97] In a similar way, in his second letter, he says: *Escaping the corruption of the concupiscence that is in the world....*[98] And again: *Be sober and vigilant.*[99]

34. Now we must turn to that disciple whom Jesus loved:[100] *Anyone who says he knows God and does not keep his commandments is a liar.*[101] And, *Do not love the world or anything that is in the world.*[102] A little further on: *Anyone who hates his brother is a murderer.*[103]

Jude the apostle also said: *Woe to those who walk in the way of Cain and with the same error of Balaam abandon*

90 Jm 3:14–16
91 Jm 4:4
92 Jm 4:11
93 1 P 2:11
94 1 P 2:1
95 1 P 4:11
96 1 P 5:2–3
97 1 P 5:5
98 2 P 1:4
99 1 P 5:8
100 Cf. Jn 21:7
101 1 Jn 2:4
102 1 Jn 2:15
103 1 Jn 3:15

themselves for gain,[104]*and perish in rebellion like Korah.*[105]
These carousers are blemishes on their feasts.[106] A few verses
further on he says: *These are grumblers, complainers, following their own desires.*[107] And later: *Hating even that contami-
nated garment which is the flesh.*[108]

35. Putting before yourselves these attestations of evangelical and apostolic teaching, and others like them, like a spiritual mirror, contemplate your soul's countenance quite
carefully. If you find that you have been floating from banquet
to banquet, or glowing rather often on wine, or mixed up in
worldly affairs, distracted by the cares of this world and intent
on the desires of the flesh, that you spend the day in quarrels
and gossiping, that you tear your brothers' flesh to bits with
vile back-biting, that you are careless with an apathetic inactivity and agitated by anything that pricks your curiosity; if you
find that you flit hither and yon excitably and that you procure
delicacies for your belly not by your own toil but by the blood
and sweat of the poor, finally, if you are quite often stained
with bad-temper, impatience, envy and disobedience, and
more solicitously concerned with your stomach than with
your mind, if you endlessly transgress the limits of your profession, if you strut around sleek and fat in the midst of all this,
do not, I beg you, boast much about your paltry tears. They
do—so that we may say something in keeping with what
physicians say—slip out more easily when the blood vessels
are puffed up from wine or the fluids in the head increased by
the varied scents of foods and flavors. If you are touched with
compunction, by fear of God, or by attachment in this state,
do not rashly abuse so great a grace of God by wallowing
even more securely in your squalor. By your lukewarmness
you would compel God (who seems by this sign not yet to
have rejected you completely from the warmth of his heart) to

---

104 Cf. Nb 22:23
105 Cf. Nb 16:32
106 Jd 1:11–12
107 Jd 1:16
108 Jd 1:23

spew you out. Your latest misfortunes would be worse than your former. We are well taught by many daily experiences that this does happen.

Chapter 15. The ways by which one passes to spiritual consolations.

36. If, on the other hand, when aroused by such stings of the attachments, you have cast away the filthy flesh-pots of the Egyptians and have preferred the poverty of Jesus to all the world's wealth; if you have traded regal platters for the fare of coarser bread and the cheapest vegetables; if you have balanced subjection and abjection against honors; if you have stripped yourself of the cares and affairs of this world and have chosen to seek your daily bread not by abusing peasants[3*] but by your own toil and by work shared with your brothers; if you have put on silence in place of loquacity and the attachment of brotherly love[109] in place of frequent quarreling; if you have already begun to fulfill the promises which your lips have pronounced;[110] if, I say, by these and like signs you perceive that you have left Egypt and like a true Israelite have crossed the waves of this great and spacious sea,[111] that is to say, the sea of this world, and if the manna of heavenly sweetness has not immediately begun to pour down on you, do not murmur against God. Do not tempt God and say; *Is God among us or not?*[112] For fulfillment of his precepts is the clearest sign of his presence, as he himself said: *If anyone loves me, he will keep my commandments and my Father will love him, and we will come to him and make our abode with him.*[113]

---

109 *dilectio*
110 Ps 65:13(66:13–14)
111 Cf. Ps 103(104):25
112 Ex 17:7
113 Jn 14:23

Do not murmur, I say, and do not fall into that blasphemy so that you say: *It is useless to serve God, and what advantage is there for us who have kept his precepts?*[114]

And that saying of the psalmist: *Then I have kept my heart pure to no purpose and washed my hands among the innocent. I have been plagued all day long and chastised each morning, while sinners and the wealthy have obtained riches in the world.*[115] And above all, spiritual riches. If more abundant grace is given in the midst of more abundant riches, why are we put to death all day long, and why should we consider ourselves as sheep for slaughter?[116] Is it not better to eat and drink and enjoy good things both in this life and in the next? Is someone not silly to seek in cruel bodily torment what can easily be acquired without toil?

37. But where is what Paul says: *It is through many tribulations that we must enter into the kingdom of God?*[117] And to the Thessalonians he said: *No one should be unsettled by these tribulations. You yourselves know these are bound to be our lot.*[118] Yet you marvel that heavenly sweetness does not overtake you immediately. Nevertheless the sons of Israel, who had quite often been spurred on by the glory of divine miracles in Egypt and had been fed with the holy flesh of that mystical lamb, did not deserve the consolation of angelic nourishment immediately after they had crossed the Red Sea. On the contrary. First they were led to the waters of Mara, and there were tempted.[119] Then, coming by way of the twelve watersprings to the hidden places of more remote desert, they were miraculously feasted with bread from heaven.[120]

38. And you—if, having left Egypt therefore, you have passed by dry tracks through the billowing waves of this

---

114 Ml 3:14
115 Ps 72(73):13–14, 12
116 Ps 43(44):22
117 Ac 14:22
118 1 Th 3:3
119 Cf. Ex 15:23
120 Cf. Ex 15:27

world— you must first be led to the waters of Mara, that is, to bitter[121] waters, to be tested by the bitterness of physical toil and to experience the gospel verse: *harsh is the road that leads to life.*[122] There you will be tempted by the Lord, if by chance you deserve to pass on to the fellowship of those to whom he said: *You are the ones who have stood by me in my temptations.*[123]

From there you will pass to the twelve fountains on a more excellent level, that is, to the flowing waters of apostolic teaching, so that when you have become used to assiduous meditation on the Scriptures, you will in some way be taken out of this world and, borrowing for yourself the silver wings of the dove[124] from the divine words which are truly like silver tried by fire, you will fly away like the purest turtle dove to the spiritual desert. There, if the Creator's loving-kindness pours out some spiritual dew on you, know that it is not for you to decide when to gather it up or how much to gather or how long to keep what you gather.

If you go out on the sabbath and try to gather in some of this heavenly food, you will not be able to find anything. On other days, the measure of divine justice will prescribe a fixed quantity for you, that is, an omer.[125] Furthermore, if you try to keep anything for the morrow to be able to enjoy this nourishment from heaven without your daily toil, your anticipation will beget only worms for you.

39. And in truth, once you have tasted this spiritual sweetness you will not immediately be freed for leisure. Soon there will loom up at your side a spiritual Amalek,[126] to be vanquished not by arms but by prayers. And so while some consolations follow one another because of divine loving-kindness, but you still experience much toil because of your

---

121 *amara*
122 Mt 7:14
123 Lk 22:28
124 Cf. Ps 67:14(68:13)
125 Ex 16:18
126 Cf. Ex 17:8–16

own concupiscence, you will, after countless struggles, rise to that ineffable kind of visitation to receive your reward. Aflame with the unsullied ardor of charity as soon as you enter the glory of God, you will be happily satisfied as if by the fruit of the promised land. Once the fire of divine love[127] completely destroys the yoke of concupiscence, you will rest in the mellow glow of gold, in the splendor of wisdom, and in the pleasantness of divine contemplation. You will experience fully that the yoke of the Lord is easy and his burden light.

Chapter 16. A person should not forsake his intention of living more strictly, even though he may experience no gentle attachment.

40. But suppose that none of this sweetness flows over you, no pleasant tear soothes you. You must not return to your old ways. Rather, the fruits of each of these ways of life should be considered and weighed in the balance of your conscience by fair examination, so that lesser things may not outweigh greater in your estimation, meaner things be compared with better, dubious things be prejudicial to things indubitable or a few considerations outrank more numerous ones. If you cannot do otherwise, it is certainly more advantageous for you to continue on your way with one member disabled or, if necessary, amputated, but with the others strong and healthy, than to rely dangerously on the health of one member alone after all the rest have withered up.

Chapter 17. The questions of a certain novice, and the answers, are inserted.

41. Not long ago, when a certain brother renounced the world and entered our monastery, our most reverend abbot

---

127 *amor*

entrusted him to me, meager fellow that I am, for his formation in regular discipline. One day, astonished, he began to ask what seemed to me the reason why formerly, when he was still in secular condition and way of life, he was so often moved by compunction, open to an attachment of divine love[128] and enjoyed such great pleasantness of spirit, whereas now, he said, I will say not only that I cannot retain it for a longer time, but that I cannot even rarely taste it.

Then I said: I ask you, do you think your previous way of life was holier and more acceptable to God?

I would not say that at all, he replied, especially since if I had done then even one of the many things I do now, everyone would have thought I was not only holy but, I might say, worthy of adoration.[4*]

42. I ask you, I went on, on how many occasions have you experienced the apostolic insight that *through many tribulations we must enter the kingdom of God*,[129] or what blessed Job said: *If I am just, I shall not lift up my head, full of affliction and misery as I am?*[130]

I remember feeling none of these things, he said. But often, deep within me, I felt that I loved Christ more expressly and more sweetly.

I continued: Were you suffering for Christ as much then as you are now?

Not for one hour did I put up with what I put up with here all the time, he replied. For, not to mention other things, I would by no means have allowed myself to be restricted by so much silence for one single day, and for no reason would I have restrained myself from idle and empty talk. Instead, after the tears I mentioned earlier, I returned immediately to loud laughter and story-telling, and I flitted hither and yon at whim. Having freedom of my will, I enjoyed the company of my relatives and amused myself in conversations with my friends.

---

128 *amor*
129 Ac 14:22
130 Jb 10:15

I attended sumptuous dinner parties and did not shrink from drinking. I caught up on my sleep in the morning as I liked, and stuffed myself with food and drink far beyond the limits of necessity. I say nothing of the stabs of anger which sometimes spurred me on, of the quarrels and disputes, or my cravings for worldly things, on which I was as intent as could be.

43. And now, I said, what is your conduct? What is your life? What are your actions?

Smiling, he replied: That's easy to answer, because these things do not allow themselves to go unnoticed. My food is scantier, my clothing rougher, my drink comes from the well, and I often get my sleep over a book. Finally, a mat with very little softness to it is spread out for my exhausted limbs. When it would be nicer to sleep, we have to get up to a clanging bell. I say nothing about the fact that we eat our bread by the sweat of our brow, that we speak with only three people—and then extremely rarely and seldom even about necessities. That apostolic dictum: *Mortify your members which are on earth*,[131] is very clearly realized in us, is it not? And the psalmist's saying: *I have become like a beast of burden before you*.[132] We surely have become like beasts of burden, going wherever we are led without objection, bearing whatever is put on us without resistance. There is no place for self-will, no time for idleness or dissipation. I think I should not leave out certain other things which please me no less than these weary me. Nowhere are there quarrels, nowhere conflicts, nowhere the wailing complaint of peasants about dreadful oppression, nowhere the pitiful outcry of poor people wronged; no legal trials, no secular courts. Everywhere is peace, everywhere tranquillity, and wonderful freedom from the hustle and bustle of worldly affairs. There is among the brothers such great unity, such great harmony, that what each has is considered as belonging to everyone, and what everyone has to each one.[5*] What pleases me in a marvelous way is that there is no

---

131 Col 3:5
132 Ps 72:23(73:22)

partiality and no favoritism because of birth [rank].[6*] Necessity alone gives rise to diversity, and infirmity alone to disparity. What the common work of all produces is distributed to each, not as physical attachment or personal likings dictate, but according to the needs of each person. Also, how wonderful it is that for three hundred men—as I calculate—the will of one man alone is law, so that whatever [words] issue from his mouth just once are observed very carefully by everyone, as if they had all sworn together to do that very thing or had heard the words from the mouth of God himself.

To summarize many things in a few words, I hear nothing about perfection in the precepts of either the Gospel or the apostles, I find nothing in the writings of the holy Fathers, I understand nothing in the sayings of the ancient monks which is not in harmony with this order and this profession.

44. Then I said: You are a novice, so I would attribute these [reflections] not to boasting, but rather to fervor. Still, I want you to be careful not to suppose that there is any profession in this life that does not include impostors, and not to be troubled if, contrary to your expectations, you perhaps see someone transgressing the rule either by word or deed, as I know does happen. Nevertheless, do you suppose that all these things you so fervently enumerate should be set in comparison with those tears of yours?

Far from it, he said, for shedding tears never gave me back a secure conscience. It never rid me of the fear of death. But now I worry very little about death. On the contrary, I hope very much that my Maker will take me before long. Although this may perhaps be because of faintheartedness—for which you are always scolding me, that is, because I prefer to be released from my labors—there is no way without sure hope in God's mercy that I could do this. And so I wonder why I loved God with greater love when I enjoyed less security.

45. I ask you, I continued: if you had two servants, one of whom not only complied with your orders very obediently but would even put up with considerable work on your behalf, whereas the other disobeyed your precepts every day

and would not consent to bear any adversity for you; and if both were to say 'I love my Lord', which would you choose to believe?

Who cannot see, he replied, that the former should be rewarded very generously and the latter rebuked, not only for his disobedience but also for his extreme impertinence?

So you must judge between these two states of yours, I said.

But, he retorted, so that I may not trust my own experience, what reasonable argument might convince me?

If someone, I said, were to ask you: who is better, someone who loves God more or someone who loves him less, wouldn't you declare without hesitation that the one you know loves God more is better?

Only a simpleton would even hesitate about this.

46. Now I ask you, I went on, if any worldly pleasantness still entices you now that you are a novice, and if any pleasure you have experienced makes sport of you, break with it! Pay attention, not to what the flesh suggests, but to what reason indicates, and answer me in keeping with the rules of truth and the witness of your conscience, whether you would now prefer to be in that state rather than in the one in which you now are.

Certainly, he replied, if I am unwilling to deceive myself or to behave in a way that would make my own words like a sinner's oil for anointing my head,[133] I must necessarily confess that if I had chosen that former state, it would certainly not have been for Christ but for the world, and not in a desire for greater perfection but in loathing for the present toil or, of course, in a craving for greater pleasure.

47. Now, I told him, as if conscious of your fervor, I do not hesitate to affirm that you do not now wish to be in that other state of life.

You are not mistaken, he said.

But in that state, I remarked, you loved God more and were certainly better. If you were better then, why are you more

---

133 Ps 140(141):5

secure now? Do you choose to be safer than better? If someone were to say that a man who applies himself more to fulfilling the Lord's precepts is better than someone who does so less, I think that you would not deny this.

I am cornered on all sides, he replied, and I am tossed about as if from reef to reef by the force of reason. I find no way out. That I then loved God more and was more often refreshed with sweet tears at his love,[134] as something I experienced, I should not doubt. But that someone who is more fervent in God's love is the better person I dare not deny. In fact, the entire authority of Holy Scripture is incompatible with preferring that life to this way of living.[135] Reason opposes it, and our conscience itself cries out against it. Hence, I judge it very insane to doubt that the person whose conduct[136] is more in harmony with the authority of the Scriptures is the better man. But since these things are more than a little repugnant [to me], I must reflect whether it is less perilous to doubt the truth of Scripture, extremely manifest reason, or the conjecture of my experience.

But no Catholic is against Scripture, I told him, and no peace-lover is against manifest reason. Really, in his estimation of himself, does error not easily creep up on a person? Experience is misleading and, as Scripture says, *Not every spirit is to be trusted,*[137] and *Sometimes Satan transforms himself into an angel of light.*[138]

48. It is possible, he replied, that I loved God more then, yet because I am now more submissive to his will and more intent on fulfilling his precepts and now afflict myself more for his name, my mind is in greater security, my conscience happier, and my spirit,[139] aware of so much toil, is readier to suffer even death itself in the hope of rewards.

---

134 *amor*
135 *conversatio*, used to designate the monastic way of life.
136 *mores*
137 1 Jn 4:1
138 2 Co 11:14
139 *animus*

49. You affirm two very contradictory things, I told him. That is, that you loved God more and were less submissive to his will. The Saviour's own words cancel out this opinion of yours. He said this: *If anyone loves me, he will keep my commandments.*[140] And again: *Someone who has my commandments and keeps them is the one who loves me.*[141] And again: *Someone who does not love me does not keep my commandments.*[142] Hence the disciple whom Jesus loved,[143] and for whose head that holy breast became a resting place,[144] said: *In this is the charity of God, that we keep his commandments.*[145]

In the same vein, some saint said: 'Those who transgress the commandments of God in word or deed, or even in shameless thoughts, believe in vain that they love God.'[146] Hence blessed Gregory also said: 'The love[147] of God is never idle. Either it does great things, if it is love, or if it scorns action, it is not love.[148] The test of love,[149] therefore, is the demonstration of its activity.'[150]

50. What then?, he asked. Must we believe that wonderfully sweet attachment was worthless, and shall we decide those tears were deceptive?

Not at all, I replied. On the contrary, they have been highly fruitful, provided you understand. First of all, you know that love of God must by no means be weighed according to some momentary, or I might say, hourly attachment. This is plainly to be seen by contrasting examples.

Sometimes in tragedies[7*] or epic poetry a character whose

---

140 Jn 14:23
141 Jn 14:21
142 Jn 14:24
143 *diligere*
144 Cf. Jn 13:23
145 1 Jn 5:3
146 Unidentified.
147 *amor*
148 *amor*
149 *dilectio*
150 Gregory the Great, Homily 30.

attractive handsomeness, admirable courage, and agreeable attachment are extolled, is portrayed as persecuted or oppressed. If someone hearing these things being sung or listening to them being recited is moved by some sort of attachment even to the point of weeping, would it not be terribly absurd on this basis of worthless devotion to make some inference about the quality of his love? Could it be claimed that such a person loves one of the characters in the play, for whose rescue he would not be willing to spend even a tiny part of what he possesses, even if all these things really were taking place before his eyes? Likewise, if by God's inscrutable design, someone who is tepid and debauched is touched with compunction because of some inward attachment, then goes back again to his empty, ludicrous and base former ways after those sterile tears and momentary attachments, it is certainly foolish, and even much more than that, it is insane, to come to this judgment about his love: that he is believed, because of these attachments, to love God more than someone who devotes himself so totally to God's service that he detests and has a deep horror of anything he knows to be contrary to God's will, and embraces with fervor any toil imposed on him in the Lord's name.

51. At these words he blushed and, with his head bowed and his eyes fixed on the ground, he said: True, very true. For when reading fables that are being made up in common speech about some Arthur—I don't know exactly who—I remember being moved sometimes even to the point of weeping. So I am not just a little ashamed of my vanity if [when I hear] those things which are read with piety about the Lord or chanted or, of course, said publicly in sermons, I can succeed in squeezing a tear out of myself, and immediately congratulate myself on my holiness, as if some great and extraordinary miracle had happened to me. It is, in fact, the mark of a very vain mind to become puffed up with vainglory because of the attachments (even if they perhaps come about in proportion to piety) which used to move it in reading fables and falsehoods. But since you said a little while ago that there

is no small fruit in these attachments, continue, I beg, with what you began to say.

52. Very gladly, I replied. Recognition of truth, for the sake of which you believe you must not spare yourself, should not be refused you. Most people, if they happen to hear some argument against their apathy, fabricate some sophistic, petty rationalizations by which they resist the truth, even when their conscience screams at them. Turning their hearts to words of malice, they love excuses for their sins.[151] It is certainly better to praise the Lord and say *Have mercy on me, for I am weak,*[152] than to say *I am rich and wealthy, and I lack nothing, while you are wretched, miserable, blind, poor, and naked.*[153]

But let us return to our subject.

Chapter 18. In what we should believe the love of God consists.

53. Therefore, as we have said, no spiritual person fails to realize that the love of God should be appraised, not according to these momentary attachments which are not at all dependent on our will, but rather according to the abiding quality of the will itself. To join one's will to the will of God, so that the human will consents to whatever the divine will prescribes, and so that there is no other reason why it wills this thing or another except that it realizes God wills it: this surely is to love God.

The will itself is nothing other than love, and good or bad will should not be called anything but good or bad love. The will of God is itself his love, which is nothing other than his Holy Spirit by whom charity is poured out into our hearts.[154] It

---

151 Ps 140(141):4
152 Ps 6:3
153 Rev 3:17
154 Rm 5:5

is an outpouring of divine charity and a coordination of the human will with, or certainly a subordination of the human will to, the divine will. This happens when the Holy Spirit who is the will and love of God, and who is God, penetrates and pours himself into the human will. Lifting it up from lower to higher things, he transforms it totally into his own mode and quality, so that cleaving to the Spirit by the indissoluble glue of unity, it is made one spirit with him. The apostle clearly intimated this same thing: *Someone who cleaves to the Lord,* he said, *becomes one spirit with him.*[155]

54. This will should surely be judged by two [criteria], namely: suffering and activity. That is to say, according to whether it bears patiently those sufferings which God sends or allows to befall it, and whether it fervently accomplishes those things which he commands. Moreover, as blessed Gregory said: *Without good works, let no one believe what his mind tells him about his love of God.*[156] For this is the affirmation of him who does not lie: *Someone who has my commandments and keeps them is the one who loves me.*[157]

55. Therefore, in whatever way the judgements of God, which are an unfathomable abyss, may dispense these extraordinary attachments and interior visitations, and for whatever reasons they are, as I have already said, sometimes suddenly communicated to those who neither seek nor plead for them, and are withdrawn from others who toil with all their might to obtain them, the person whose will is in harmony with God's will, that is, who patiently bears whatever God sends and accomplishes with fervor whatever he has commanded, must, without any hesitation, be said to love God. Otherwise, if our love[158] had to be measured by those attachments, so that we would be said to love God or even another human being only when we experience attachments

---

155 1 Co 6:17
156 Cf. Gregory the Great, Homily 30.
157 Jn 14:21
158 *amor*

of this sort, we should by no means be said to love constantly but only during certain very rare intervals. We must say, however, that if by chance a just person at some time or other wills something that God does not will—the salvation of some person, for example—,his will is still not at odds with God's will insofar as God's will is undoubtedly at work that he may will this thing. He wills that all persons be saved,[159] for he causes his disciples to hope for it.

56. Furthermore, this love has its foundation, its development, and its perfection. This is not the time to treat of all these things more explicitly, and perhaps this is not within our capacity. To feel those attachments is not so much to love God, as you claim, as at this gentle touch to perceive in advance a drop of that sweetness offered to—or rather infused into—the mind, present there, as it were, to the inward palate. It is one thing for someone desirous of this honeyed sweetness to toil with all his might to obtain it, and another thing for someone not to be able to escape the taste of this sweetness when it is poured on his lips, even if he neither seeks nor likes it. The one does not taste it, yet loves it. The other does not love it, yet tastes it.

To say this in simpler words so you may understand more easily, anyone who keeps trying to the best of his ability to reach God—that is, by obeying his commandments and living soberly, justly, and godly,[160] according to the teachings of the Gospel and the apostles—even though he does not taste any of this sweetness, should be said to love God, on the testimony of him who said *The person who keeps my commandments is the one who loves me.*[161]

But anyone who experiences this attachment daily, and still puts his own desires before God's will, must be believed not to love God, but to be unable not to feel the spiritual sweetness passing by divine dispensation into his mind.

---

159 1 Tm 2:4
160 Tit 2:12
161 Cf. Jn 14:23

Chapter 19. [In reply] to the novice's questions, the fruit of the various types of compunction is explained.

57. The experience of this sweetness is a great stimulus to good works for the negligent, a much-needed consolation for those who toil laboriously at good works, and a pleasant, sure refreshment for those who arrive at the summit of perfection. He who is wonderfully merciful works out our salvation by these wonderful and ineffable means. He himself is enlightening wisdom, terrifying justice, and the enticing sweetness of pleasantness. It is as if you would want to arouse an appetite for honey in someone who does not know what it is. Observing that he takes delight in other, albeit less tasty, kinds [of food] and that neither talking about nor praising it kindles any desire for it in him, you would take a little dab of the liquid and drop it in his mouth. Once he had tasted it he would burn with such an appetite for it that, to acquire it, he would not dread undertaking even immense labor. As often as you saw him exhausted by the enormity of the toil and becoming tepid again after his initial fervor, you would soothe him with a similar drop of sweetness. So, by a like taste of inward sweetness, the clemency of our most tender-loving Saviour draws toward salvation those who are sunk in the enticements of the flesh whom neither the light of reason nor the fear of judgement to come succeeds in holding back from ill-charming pleasantness. Little by little, as they are attracted by their own pleasure—as that saying goes: *Each one drawn by what gives him pleasure*[162]—he puts upon them the yoke of his service.

58. But because anyone who enters God's service hears Scripture say: *Be steadfast and prepare your soul for temptation,*[163] it is necessary as the toils of temptation press in on him every day that some spiritual savor flow into him while he is still faltering and near despair. Refreshed by its drops, he

---

162 Virgil, *Eclogues* 2.65
163 Sir 2:1

takes up the struggle against his faults with more intense
mental ardor, endures it more generously, overcomes it more
easily, or escapes it. Examine yourself more carefully. After
that experience of utterly sweet attachment, when you
returned to those silly vain occupations, once you regained
your composure again did you not feel disconcerted and, as I
said, did you not simmer with a sort of salutary hatred for
yourself? Then you thought about adopting a stricter life and
imposing such great obligations on yourself so that, even if
your will consented to such things, there would be no opportunity of returning to them.

That is entirely so, he said.

59. Do you see then, I asked, that your fervent conversion
and your very strict way of life are, as it were, the fruit of those
tears? This is why they were given to you. They brought this
about little by little, or rather, through them God brought it
about. Is it any wonder then that, as I already said, they have
stopped now that their work is completed? Now you must
endure sufferings for Christ, you must exercise the virtue of
patience, chastise the insolence of your flesh by frequent
vigils and fasting, undergo temptations. Your must turn your
spirit away from all earthly preoccupations. But most particularly, you must mortify self-will by the virtue of obedience.

Yet in all this, whenever your spirit is excessively weary,
hasten to the maternal breasts of Jesus in earnest, devoted
prayer.[8]* Drawing from their abundance the milk of wonderful consolation for yourself, you will, with the apostle, say:
Blessed be God who consoles us in all our tribulations.[164] And:
*As the sufferings of Christ abound in us, so also through Christ
does consolation abound.*[165] That devout attachment, which
first awakened you when you were in torpor so you would
not perish, will console you in toil so you do not faint away.
Finally, after countless victories, when you have become like
an old soldier and when those temptations which now wear

---

164 2 Co 1:3–4
165 2 Co 1:5

you out as a novice will be thoroughly deadened, you will repose in the pleasantness of the virtues. Admitted by the grace of the divine loving-kindness to that most sublime kind of consolation which is, as it were, the reward of the just, you will say with the prophet: *How great is the abundance of your sweetness, O Lord, which you have hidden for those who fear you.*[166]

60. Then, with tears brimming over, he said: I like what you say and like it very much, because not only can I conclude by what reason teaches me that it is so, but by this light I really perceive it within myself more clearly. For I have certainly experienced that first kind of visitation, as you affirm. But by what you are teaching me, I sense that second kind beginning to be active in me, and I am confident that someday I will reach the kind that is sublime and ineffable.

Chapter 20. The novice is convinced that when he supposed he loved God more, he loved him less. Those who profit from shedding tears is also shown.

61. See then, I said, how contrary to your opinion this matter has turned out.

How? he asked.

Perhaps you are not convinced, I told him, that when you believed you loved God more, you loved him less.

For some time now, this reasoning has begun to dawn on me. All the same, I would like to understand it more fully by having you explain it.

Is it not true, I asked him, that the more negligent someone is, and the more fickle-minded, the more imperfect he will be proved to be in love of God?

That cannot be denied, he replied.

And as you say that you yourself see more clearly now, I continued, that first attachment reproached you when you

---

166 Ps 30:20(31:19)

were erring and the second sustained you when you were weak.

Quite right, he said.

Then these facts convince you that you loved somewhat imperfectly.

62. With a sigh, he said: O how miserably mistaken are those persons, and what traitors they are to their own salvation, who, if they experience even a tiny bit of this attachment we are speaking about while they are entangled in countless and damnable vices, not only assure themselves that they are pardoned for their past [sins], but even return to the same things and, in a certain way, with greater security. They derive no profit at all from this spiritual incentive. Supposing themselves holier because of it, they wallow yet more impudently in their squalor and negligence. Perhaps it is about such people that the apostle said: *God has given them a spirit of compunction: eyes, that they may not see, and ears that they may not hear.*[167] Does this kind of compunction not blind their eyes and stop up their ears to the point that they think the frightful squalor of their vices can be washed away by a few tears, without the fruits of repentance?

63. Shedding tears, I continued, is certainly very pleasing and acceptable to God, and a holocaust compensating for all offenses, but [only] for those who are repentant and confess their sins, those who do not repeat the things they have repented of, those who flee to Jesus' compassion with a spirit of humility and with a contrite spirit,[168] those who to their utmost ability persevere in fruits befitting repentance.[169]

For this reason, you and everyone concerned about his salvation must take pains to the point that this mortification of the flesh, this concern for vigils and toil, this cheapness of clothing, this coarseness of food, this sobriety of silence, these things, I say, like the most pleasing spiritual holocaust of all

---

167 Rm 11:8, Cf Ps 113(115):5–6
168 Cf. Ps 50:19(51:17)
169 Cf. Mt 3:8

the members of the inward and outward person may grow rich with the fatness of tears, as I said, and with the sweetness of very devout attachment, so that once the fire of charity is lighted on the altar of your heart, it may give off a sweet scent. And so, as the prophet said, *May your holocaust become rich.*[170]

Otherwise, if you cannot have both, it is better to live in apostolic poverty and evangelical purity without tears than to transgress God's commandments daily with daily tears. Even if those who have been workers of iniquity raise the dead, cast out demons, and give sight to the blind, they will nevertheless hear from the Lord: *Depart from me.*[171]

Chapter 21. From those things which have been inserted here, we can ascertain what charity, and what self-centeredness, do in someone making progress.

64. It has perhaps not been useless that we have inserted these remarks. If all these things are examined attentively, diligently, and finally, humbly, it will—if I am not mistaken—be easy to see that by a new inpouring of charity a person converted [to the Lord] is raised up to higher things by his zealous effort and by some very nimble movements of his mind. But since self-centeredness presses him downward and everything he clings to continually pushes him by its natural heaviness toward the lowest things, he toils somewhat in the midst of his very efforts.

The more deeply in the recesses of his soul a deadly plant has fixed its roots, the more difficult it will be to tear them out and the less easy the ascent. Just as a lazy, slothful person, unskilled in farming, clears and cleans up his field more slowly, though only a small part of it is overgrown with

---

170 Ps 19:4(20:3)
171 Mt 7:22–23

thistles and thorns, on the contrary an energetic, hardworking man, industrious in this occupation tears clumps of brambles out by their roots more quickly, even if they cover the whole surface of the field, and makes it rich and productive where it was sterile and unfruitful. In just the same way, surely, someone who forsakes the world will progress more slowly toward serenity of conscience and the freedom of charity if he remains sluggish and lukewarm, and if he takes less care to correct himself, even if he had been less defiled while in the world. But if he is fervent of spirit, diligent, and attentive, if he is firmly anchored in the virtue of discretion, then on taking up the instruments of spiritual exercises, he will vigorously tear the shoots of vices out of the field of his heart and will more quickly breathe the fresh air of a purer conscience.[9*] Having thrown off the yoke of self-centeredness and set down the burden of the passions, he will discover that the yoke of the Lord is easy and his burden light.[172]

Chapter 22. What great joy exists in contempt for, and conquest of, yearnings.

65. And so, having experienced it, he will provide proof that being steeped in the sweetness of chastity is not only not laborious, but supreme joy, although it may be burdensome to hold in check by the bridle of temperance the natural impulses and unclean desires which arise from concupiscence of the flesh. Likewise, when concupiscence of the palate has been conquered, it is not only joyous but even glorious to see oneself not as the slave of one's belly but as its master, and to be carried away with wondrous exultation: *I have learned in whatever state I may be to manage. I know how to be abased and I know how to abound. And in any and all circumstances I have learned how to bear hunger and accept plenty, to enjoy abundance and suffer deprivation.*[173]

---

172 Mt 11:30
173 Ph 4:11–12

66. If love of the flesh has been thoroughly lulled to sleep or really absorbed by the fire of divine love,[174] there will be no toil over outward things, because the mind will not be able to be vexed by any affliction which cannot be melted by love.[175] Even if some people shamefully misuse enticing scents, I refrain from saying any more about them since those of whom we are now speaking toil little or not at all out of appetite for them or deprivation of them.

On the other hand, yearning of the eyes and ears brings down considerable toil on many persons. It is not at all right to attribute this to the Saviour's yoke, for all of it is instead engendered by bad habits. Because they feel it is too burdensome to break [these habits], they prefer to plead as an excuse the harshness of the Lord's yoke, the lightness of which they have not experienced. Since this [lightness] comes with contempt for yearning, the freedom it confers on those who do have contempt for them surely is not less than the damnable sweetness the empty and ridiculous yearnings engender.

Chapter 23. The vain pleasure of the ears.

67. Because we have thought that overtly evil persons should clearly be excluded from these considerations, let us now discuss those who disguise their preoccupation with yearning under the appearance of religious observances, those who wrongfully usurp for the use of their vanity the things which the Fathers of old[176] practised in a wholesome way, as types of things to come. Where, I ask, with these types and figures now passing away, where do all these organs in the church come from, all these chimes? To what purpose, I ask you, is the terrible snorting of bellows, more like a clap of

---

174 *amor*
175 *dilectio*
176 The Fathers of the Old Testament, who used musical instruments in worship

thunder than the sweetness of a voice? Why that swelling and swooping of the voice? One person sings bass, another sings alto, yet another sings soprano.[177] Still another ornaments and trills up and down on the melody. At one moment the voice strains, the next it wanes. First it speeds up, then it slows down with all manner of sounds. Sometimes—it is shameful to say—it is expelled like the neighing of horses, sometimes, manly strength set aside, it is constricted into the shrillness of a woman's voice.[178] Sometimes it is turned and twisted in some sort of artful trill. Sometimes you see a man with his mouth open as if he were breathing out his last breath, not singing but threatening silence, as it were, by ridiculous interruption of the melody into snatches.[179] Now he imitates the agonies of the dying or the swooning of persons in pain. In the mean-time, his whole body is violently agitated by histrionic ges-ticulations—contorted lips, rolling eyes, hunching shoul-ders—and drumming fingers keep time with every single note. And this ridiculous dissipation is called religious obser-vance! And it is loudly claimed that where this sort of agitation is more frequent, God is more honorably served.

---

177 *Hic succinit, ille discinit, alter supercinit.... Succinit* from *sub-canere* means to sing below the melody, *discinit*, as in descant, to sing a higher counter melody, and *supercinit/super-canere*, a yet higher line. Aelred presumes in this that the reader knows that the melody would be sung by the tenor, whom he therefore does not mention. (The editors appreciate the insights of Chrysogonus Waddell ocso in unravelling Aelred's meaning.)

178 Aelred is echoing a general Cistercian caution against exaggerated musical embellishment. See Joseph M. Canivez, *Statuta Capitulorum Gener-alium Ordinis Cisterciensis ab anno 1116 ad annum 1786*, 1:30, Statute LXXIII; *De falsis vocibus.* 'Viros decet virili voce cantare, et non more femineo tinnulis, vel et vulgo dicitur falsis vocibus veluti histrionicam imitari lasciviam. Et ideo constituimus mediocritatem servari in cantu, ut et grav-itatem redoleat, et devotio conservetur.'

179 A reference to a musical style known as the hocket, or ochete or *hoquetus*, etymologically a blending of words meaning rhythm and hic-cough. It was an early medieval contrapuntal style which interspersed notes of a melody with rests, creating a staccato effect. See Paul Henry Lang, *Music in Western Civilization*, 140, and Gustav Reese, *Music in the Middle Ages*, 321ff (both published by W.W. Norton, New York).

Meanwhile, ordinary folk stand there awestruck, stupefied, marvelling at the din of bellows, the humming of chimes, and the harmony of pipes. But they regard the saucy gestures of the singers and the alluring variation and dropping of the voices with considerable jeering and snickering, until you would think they had come, not to an oratory, but to a theatre, not to pray, but to gawk.

68. They do not fear the awesome majesty in whose presence they stand, nor do they honor that mystical crib before which they render cult, where Christ is mystically wrapped in swaddling clothes, where his most sacred blood is poured out in the chalice, where the heavens are opened and angels attend, where earthly things are joined to heavenly, and where human beings keep company with angels. What the holy Fathers instituted to awaken the weak to an attachment of devotion is usurped for illicit pleasure. Sound should not be given precedence over meaning, but sound with meaning should generally be allowed to stimulate greater attachment.

69. Therefore, the sound should be so moderate, so marked by gravity, that it does not captivate the whole spirit to amusement in itself, but leaves the greater part to the meaning. Blessed Augustine, of course, said: 'The soul is moved to a sentiment of piety on hearing sacred chant. But if a longing to listen desires the sound more than the meaning, it should be censured.'[180] And elsewhere he says: 'When the singing delights me more than the words, I acknowledge that I have sinned through my fault, and I would prefer not to listen to the singer.'[10*]

Therefore, after someone has scorned that ridiculous, ruinous vanity and has applied himself to the ancient moderation of the Fathers, if the noble gravity causes his itching ears frightful aversion when he remembers such theatrical nonsense, and if in consequence he despises and condemns as rustic crudeness all the Fathers' gravity in their way of singing (which the Holy Spirit instituted by these holy Fathers, that is,

---

180 *Confessions* 10.35.

by Augustine, Ambrose, and especially Gregory, as though by
his own instrument) and prefers what they call Iberian lulla-
bies[11*] or I know not what kind of tom-foolery of certain
schoolmen; if then because of these a person is tormented,
grieved, or sighs anxiously for those things which he has
spewed out, what, I ask you, is the origin of this toil: the yoke
of charity or the burden of worldly concupiscence?

Chapter 24. Concupiscence of the eyes is found in outward and inward curiosity and afflicts those who have been converted to a more perfect way [of life].

70. A few words should now be said about concupiscence
of the eyes, which the holy Fathers realized should be called
curiosity.[12*] They thought that it concerns not only the outward but also the inward person.

Outward curiosity concerns all the superfluous beauty
which the eyes like in various forms, in bright and pleasing
colors, different kinds of workmanship, clothing, shoes, vases,
pictures, statues, or various creations exceeding necessary
and moderate utility—all those things which people who love
the world seek out to attract the eyes. Outwardly pursuing
what they make, inwardly they forsake him by whom they
were made, and they destroy what they have been made to
be.[13*] So it is that even in cloisters of monks you find cranes
and hares, does and stags, magpies and ravens—which are
certainly not means [used by] Antony and Macarius, but effeminate amusements. None of these things are at all expedient
for the poverty of monks, but feed the eyes of the curious. If,
preferring the poverty of Jesus to these things which attract
the eyes, someone has restricted himself to the limits of what
is necessary and has sought the cells of some poor brothers
instead of buildings of extravagant size and unnecessary
height; if perhaps, on entering an oratory built of unpolished
stone he finds no paintings, no sculpture, nothing of great
value, no marble strewn with carpets, no walls covered with

purple hangings decorated with folk sagas or battles of kings, or at least a series of scriptural scenes; if there is no awe-inspiring glow of candles, no splendor of gleaming metal of the various vessels; if, when none of these meets his gaze, everything he does see begins to seem sordid to him; if he complains that he has been banished from paradise and plunged into some kind of squalid prison, what is the source of this mental anguish, of all this toil?

71. I ask you, if he had learned from the Lord Jesus to be meek and humble of heart, and to contemplate, as the apostle advised, *not those things which are seen, but those which are not seen, for the things which are seen are for a time, but those which are not seen are eternal,*[181] I ask you, if he had tasted even a little of that inner glory of which it has been written: *All the splendor of the king's daughter is within,*[182] and that saying of the apostle: *Let each person examine his own work* and *in this way he will have reason to boast in himself alone and not in his neighbor*[183]....If this is not to be found in any other man, how much less shall it be found in mute and lifeless metal? If, I say, he had interiorly bowed his neck under the yoke of divine love[184] and there, there within, that sweet Jesus had become savory to him, would he, I ask you, have become so attached to these petty exterior vanities?

72. Now we should speak a bit about that inward curiosity which is found especially in three things: an appetite for harmful or valueless knowledge; prying into the life of another person, not to imitate him but to envy him if his life is good or to scoff at him if it is bad, or simply by curiosity alone to know whether it is good or bad; and lastly, a sort of inquisitive restlessness to know about events and things in the world. No little toil arises for minds captivated by all these things when they either indulge in them intemperately or,

---

181 2 Co 4:18
182 Ps 44(45):14
183 Gal 6:4
184 *dilectio*

liking to indulge in them, are forbidden to do so. Hence it is
that numerous persons who have devoted their minds[185] to
worthless philosophy and whose habit it is to meditate on the
Bucolics along with the Gospel, or with eagerness to read
Horace along with the prophets, and Cicero with Paul,[14*] or
then again, to play with metrics and weave love poems into
bits of song or provoke one another with invective, when they
have entered a place where all these things are condemned by
the strictness of the Rule as seedbeds of vanity or sources of
quarreling or incitements to desire, they begin to get sad and
to get angry. And since they have no means of casting out the
seeds of a vanity once conceived, they seem (in these words
of Elihu) to burst out: *Look, my belly is like unvented new wine
which bursts a new wineskin.*[186] Where this toil comes from,
he is slow to discern.

Hence it is also that, when by looking at inane shows or
intently listening to gossip, we have in some way gone out of
ourselves, and we do return to ourselves again, we usher in
with us the images of these vanities[15*] and, bringing a heart
full of pictures even to our place of rest, we pass sleepless
nights because of this utterly absurd nonsense. In the most
idiotic kind of daydreaming, we depict battles of kings and
victories of dukes as though they were before our eyes, and
we straighten out all the affairs of the kingdom with our idle
ramblings, even as we sing psalms or pray.

73. There is still another, the worst, kind of curiosity, which,
however, assails only those who are conscious of their great
virtues: testing their holiness by working miracles. This is
tempting God. This kind of curiosity is forbidden by the Law
of Moses in these terms: *You shall not tempt the Lord your
God.*[187] The apostle also said: *And let us not tempt Christ, as
some of them tempted him and were destroyed by serpents.*[188]

185 *animus*
186 Jb 32:19
187 Dt 6:16
188 1 Co 10:9

If anyone consents to this worst vice, when he does not obtain his wish he may fall into the snares of despair or the sacrilege of blasphemy because of excessive anguish of mind.

Chapter 25. Pride of life.

74. Of this harmful root there remains the third branch, which the holy apostle called pride of life.[189] Although there are many kinds of it, for our present discussion it is pertinent to speak only of two of them.

The first is the kind which infuses love of empty praise; the second implants a desire to dominate. Who can tell how much affliction and how much mental anguish arise from these two? As often as I am disturbed at being corrected or contradicted, of course, or as often as I am upset by any detraction or slander, or (still more disastrous) as often as I am consumed by the plague of sadness, if I want to hunt out the causes of this affliction more exactly, I find the root of vanity lying deeply hidden in the recesses of my soul.[190] Because of it, my spirit[191] presumes great things about itself, and in its delusion paints its own portrait accordingly: not only should it not be corrected or blamed, but—still more—it should be praised and honored by everybody. Or when infected with the poison of this abhorrent plague the mind may have fancied itself to be holy and deserving of admiration in other peoples' esteem, as soon as it notices that others disagree with its vanity, it feels frustrated in its joy and glory. That is to say, because by its false opinion [of itself, the soul] has based these on the estimation of others, it is inevitably gnawed by the stabbing pains of sadness. Also, because of this very dreadful malady the soul shamefully craves the best seats, the highest marks of respect, the first turn at speaking in assemblies,[192] and the first seat at

---

189 Cf 1 Jn 2:16
190 *anima*
191 *animus*
192 Cf. Mt 23:6–7

meetings. To the same degree that all these things delight us when offered or acquired, so they vex us when refused or taken away.

Chapter 26. The desire to dominate.

75. If desire to dominate has corrupted a mind, the suffering it imposes can only be known by someone who, after experiencing the tyranny of this worst passion, has at last been freed from its power by God's help. As soon as the unhealthy mind has contracted this noxious virus it is subjected by ignoble baseness to anyone whom it hunts out to obtain fulfillment of its desire. And before such a person gains precedence over others, he becomes the most abject slave to those who he realizes can either stand in his way or be useful to him. Hence, out of fear of them, truth is quelled; in currying their favor flattery becomes disgraceful. He loses all freedom of speech, so that he is forced to praise what his conscience sees should be reproached, and to reproach what it shows him should be commended. Finally, if he notices that someone is getting rather familiar with the person he depends on, his fettered mind is soon stabbed by darts of suspicion. He is afflicted with the sickness of fearing that the other person might be raised more quickly than he to those honors he ambitions. He is so torn up by the iron rods of envy that food does him no good and sleep procures no rest for him.

76. Then he turns to detraction and whispering, and discloses and noises abroad anything reproachable he notices in his rival. Anything he cannot reproach him for publicly, he discolors with a perverse interpretation. Indeed, if the other is given advancement and all his hopes are frustrated, what tortures and torments of soul does he then not suffer? He is confounded, exhausted, upset, torn to pieces, and unable to tolerate the [rage] burning within himself. He is either driven out of the community, violently harassed by the pricks of so many passions, or, if he is overcome with human respect and remains in the community, he becomes inexorably opposed

to everything. Unable to bear the flame of his ambition once kindled, he gasps, seethes, and is so tortured that his bitterness is apparent in his silence and his indignation in his speech. In the heat of [this] hidden furnace, with agitation of the outer man, like an earthen vessel he creaks unhappily, snaps when speaking, glances around truculently, and answers all criticisms with puffed-up arrogance. Those whom he previously flattered shamelessly, he now resists barefacedly, contradicts and slanders, gnawing at them secretly with staining detraction and finding fault with them publicly without any respect or honesty. Intent, with an evil sort of curiosity, on every word of his seniors, he tries to trap them at each syllable, and he scrutinizes anything they do. Keeping close watch with shameless eyes on all their activities and on their comings and goings, he keeps track of everything, judges everyone, and interprets everything according to the spitefulness of his own malice. If by chance, as happens with human frailty, a senior is caught in some fault, this fellow then seizes the occasion to avenge what he considers an injury to himself. He raises his eyebrows, wrinkles his forehead, and opens wide his lips in uncivil uproar.

77. But to hoodwink those watching him into thinking he is acting out of zeal for God, from time to time he wrings some droplets of tears from his eyes, heaves deceitful sighs, complains in a querulous voice that charity has been forsaken, and groans that purity is being transgressed and justice trodden underfoot. You would say—if you did not know—that he is acting by that spirit which blazed long ago within the prophet Jeremiah: *The words of the Lord,* he said, *became like a fire burning in my bones, and I fainted away, unable to bear it.*[193]

And so, proclaiming that his inner being is consumed by the fire of zeal for God, he lies that he is standing up for justice, battling for order, and has endured even hatred for the sake of charity.

---

193 Jr 20:9

What more? In the end he is found to be so rebellious and obstinate that extreme necessity makes it urgent that he be sent away, or at least pacified by some liberty for his self-will. Hence an astonishing sort of abuse has arisen.

Formerly, when religious life was led with so high a degree of purity as to be considered a rule of truth, those who were humbler, more placidly obedient, readier for reproach, more fervent in all good works, did not seek honors above all else. Such monks as these were, I shall not say promoted but compelled to govern others or to assume certain administrative duties. Now, on the contrary, while the insolence of certain monks is feared or their rebellion warded off, or their dishonesty dreaded because they are quarrelsome, irritable, frivolous, or ill-tempered, incapable of keeping their feet in the house—now in, now out—or, precisely, because they are feared, they are given advancement. What should be a cause for abjection and humiliation for them becomes tinder for their pompous pride.

78. But let this be enough about this three-fold self-centeredness. If, in all these things, anyone looks attentively on the countenance of his soul as if in a mirror, he will find, unless I am mistaken, not only whatever deformity there is in him, but in the light of truth he will also recognize the hidden causes for this deformity. And so he will blame it not on the harshness of the Lord's yoke, which is not harsh at all, but on his own perversity.

Once these roots of the passions, the causes of all our toil, we might say, have been completely torn out, and once the shoulders of our mind have submitted to the yoke of charity, we will learn from the Lord Jesus that he is gentle and humble of heart, and we shall find rest for our souls,[194] by keeping not a sabbath according to the flesh with the Jews, but an eternal and spiritual sabbath in the sweetness of charity.

HERE ENDS BOOK TWO

---

194 Cf. Mt 11:29

NOTES

1 Augustine, *Enarr in Ps* 59.8. CC 39:760, 45–47.

2 Cf. *Oner* I.4; PL 184:919.

3 *rusticorum maledictione.* Cf. II.**17**.43: *rusticorum ob diram oppressionem querulus planctus.*

4 Cf. Bernard, *QH* 4.3 (CF 25:137–138).

5 Cf. Charles Dumont, 'Personalism in Community according to Aelred of Rievaulx', *Cistercian Studies* 12 (1977) 250–271, especially 254–259. See also, Augustine, *In Ioh Tract* XXXII.8.2– 15 (community); and Leo the Great, *De jejunio septimo mensis, Sermo 3,* and *Sermo* 75.4–5.

6 Aelred, *Nat Dom;* PL 195:222AB.

7 Cf. Augustine, *Conf.*III.2.

8 *ad materna ubera Jesu.* Cf. *Inst incl* 26. CCCM p.658 (CF 2:73).

9 *in auras conscientiae purioris…*an augustinian expression. See the note to I.**8**.25.

10 Cf.Augustine, *Conf* 10.33.

11 *iberas naenias.* This expression is found in Saint Jerome's *Praefatio in Pentateuchum* (PL 28: 147A–152B), which formed the first lesson of the Septuagesima Night Office in the twelfth century and was therefore familiar to Aelred. Jerome considered the *Iberi* prone to follow heretical novelties. See also his *Commentary on Ezechiel,* XI.38: *Alii…multo peiores fingunt nenias…de quibus scribit Irenaeus qui per Marcum Aegyptium, Galliarum primum circa Rhodanum, deinde Hispaniarum nobiles feminas deceperunt* (CC 75:526), and *Ad Hedibiam, Ep* 119, q. 10, (PL 22:998), on Rm 9:14–29: … *Melius est simpliciter imperitiam confiteri, et inter caetera quae nescimus…quam dum volumus Dei probare justitiam, Basilidis et Manichaei haeresim defendere, et Iberas naenias, Aegyptiaque portenta sectari;* and *Contra Vigilantium* (PL 23:360C): …*ut facilius per has naenias vulgus indoctum provoces ad bibendum.…* For Aelred, the word *naenias* had nothing to do with *Iberi,* properly speaking, but is simply a cliché referring to the twelfth-century counterpart of the innovators in the time of Irenaeus, that is, pseudo-intellectuals or new cantors who preferred the degenerate modern musical practices and theatricalism in the execution of sacred music to the authentic tradition canonized by Augustine, Ambrose, and Gregory.

12 Cf. Augustine, *Conf.* X.35.54; Bernard, *Apo* XII.28 (CF 1:63).

13 Cf. Augustine, *Conf.* X.34.51 and 53.

14 Cf.Jerome, *Ad Eustochium, ep. 22,29.* PL 22:394–425. Also Gilbert of Hoyland, *Tractatus* 7, part 2, 10. PL 184:287C (CF 34: 78).

15 Cf. *Inst incl* 2.35–37 CCCM 1:638 (CF 2:46).

Chapter 1. The law about distinguishing sabbaths is presented.¹*

*W*e read in the Old Testament about certain distinctions of sabbaths. We are going to devote the beginning of this book to a consideration of these. As a matter of fact, in the Law you have three times consecrated to the sabbath rest: the seventh day, the seventh year and, after seven times seven, the fiftieth year.¹ The first, then, is a sabbath of days, the second of years, and the third is not inappropriately called the sabbath of sabbaths. It consists of seven sabbaths of years plus one, so that the number seven, which proceeds from unity and is perfected in unity, may be concluded in unity. Likewise, every good work is founded on faith in the one sole God and progresses by the seven-fold gift of the Holy Spirit to reach him who is truly one, where all that we are is made one with him. And because there is no division in unity, let there be no outpouring of the mind in various directions, but let it be one in the One, with the One, through the One, around the One, sensing the One, savoring the One—and because always one, always resting, and therefore observing a perpetual sabbath.

2. Meanwhile, you have the sabbath of days, the sabbath of years and, by a kind of foretaste, the sabbath of sabbaths. Has anyone been so enlightened by the Spirit of God that he has no need to borrow these distinctions of sabbaths from the words of others by the mediation of his memory, but, sensing within himself that it does happen, may speak not only from memory but also from insight?

---

1 Lv 23:3; 25:3–4,8,10

Good Jesus, be present! Be present to this little pauper of yours who is not begging for the crumbs of a rich man clad in purple but,like a puppy, for those crumbs which fall from the table of my masters, your sons.[2] That great man was your son, and because he was your son, my Lord—I mean holy Moses— who has surely been admitted to your table and has feasted on your bread in the bower of Solomon. I know, my gentle Lord, that you said, *It is not fair to take the children's bread and to throw it to the dogs*.[3] But since the puppies eat the crumbs which fall from their masters' table, break some of that bread up for your puppy, so that someone who cannot manage to eat the crust may gather up the crumbs.

Chapter 2. The distinction between these sabbaths is to be sought in three-fold love. Also, the bond which exists among these three distinct loves.[2*]

3. Let us listen to him as he breaks [this bread]: *You shall love the Lord your God,* he said, *with all your heart, with all your soul, and with all your mind,* and you shall love your neighbor as yourself. On these two commandments depend all the Law and the prophets.[4] If, therefore, we believe—or better, *because* we believe—the truth, we must look for the distinctions between these sabbaths in these two commandments, for they come from the Law. Yet if you diligently examine these two commandments, you discover that three things must be loved: yourself, your neighbor, and God. When it says, *You shall love your neighbor as yourself,*[5] it is clear that you ought also to love yourself. This is not a commandment because it is inherent in our nature. *No man has ever hated his own flesh,* the apostle testifies.[6] If one does not

---

2 Cf. Mt 15:27
3 Mt 15:26
4 Mt 22:37–40
5 Mt 22:39
6 Eph 5:29

hate his flesh, much less does he hate his mind. Everyone, even if unwittingly, loves his mind more than his flesh. There is no one who would not choose physical infirmity over mental unsoundness.

Let love of self, then, be man's first sabbath, love of neighbor the second, and love of God the sabbath of sabbaths. As we said above, the spiritual sabbath is rest for the spirit,[7] peace of heart, and tranquillity of mind. This sabbath is sometimes experienced in love of oneself, it is sometimes derived from the sweetness of brotherly love and, beyond all doubt, it is brought to perfection in the love of God. Surely a person should be careful to love himself in a suitable way, but to love his neighbor as himself and to love God more than himself; and not to love either himself or his neighbor except for God's sake.

God willing, we will explain later how this love should be shown toward oneself and toward one's neighbor. But at present we must consider that although there is an evident distinction in this triple love, a marvelous bond nevertheless does exist among the three, so that each is found in all, and all in each. None of them can be possessed without all. And when one wavers they all diminish. Someone who does not love his neighbor or God does not love himself, and someone who does not love his neighbor as himself does not love himself. Furthermore, someone who does not love his neighbor is proven not to love God. *For how can a man who does not love the brother he sees love God whom he does not see?*[8]

4. Somehow, then, love of neighbor precedes love of God. Likewise, love[9] of self precedes love of neighbor. It precedes it, I say, in sequence, not in excellence. It precedes that perfect love about which was said: *You shall love the Lord your God with all your heart, with all your soul, and with all your mind.*[10] Of course, a certain part of this love, even if not

---

7 *animus*
8 1 Jn 4:20
9 *dilectio*
10 Mt 22:37

its fullness, necessarily precedes both love of self and of neighbor. Without it both of these are dead and, consequently, non-existent. It seems to me that love of God is, so to speak, the soul of the other loves. It lives of itself with perfect fullness, its presence communicates to the others their vital being, its absence brings about their death.

That a person may love himself, the love of God is formed in him; that one may love one's neighbor, the capacity of one's heart is enlarged. Then as this divine fire grows warmer little by little it wondrously absorbs the other loves into its fullness, like so many sparks. And so it leads all the soul's love[11] with it to that supreme and ineffable good where neither self nor neighbor is loved for self or for neighbor, but only insofar as each fades away from self and is borne totally into God.

5. Meanwhile, these three loves are engendered by one another, nourished by one another, and fanned into flame by one another. Then they are all brought to perfection together.

What is more, it happens in a wondrous and ineffable way that although all three of these loves are possessed at the same time—for it cannot be otherwise—still all three are not always sensed equally. At one moment that rest and joy are sensed in the purity of one's own conscience. At another time, they are derived from the sweetness of brotherly love. At another they are more fully attained in the contemplation of God. Just as some king who possesses various perfume cellars[3]* enters now this one, now that, and is steeped in the fragrant scent now of this kind of perfume, now of that, so the mind preserves within the enclosure of her consciousness several cellars filled with spiritual treasures. As she enters now this one, now that, she balances the measure of her joy with the variety of her treasures.

---

11 *dilectio animi*

Chapter 3. How the spiritual sabbath is experienced in love of self.

6. When a person withdraws from exterior commotion into the secret retreat of his mind and, once the gate is closed on the throng of noisy trifles around him, surveys his inward treasures he finds nothing disturbed, nothing disordered, nothing to torment or worry him, but rather, everything pleasant, everything harmonious, everything peaceful, everything tranquil. The entire throng of his thoughts, words, and deeds, like a very well-ordered and very peaceful family, will beam on his spirit like a father's household. This gives rise to marvelous security, and from security to marvelous joy[4*] and from joy to a kind of jubilation which bursts out yet more devoutly in God's praise the more clearly [the soul] recognizes whatever good there is in her is his gift. This is the joyful solemnity of the seventh day. Six days must precede it, that is, the perfection of deeds. First we sweat at good works and then, at last, we pause in tranquillity of conscience. For purity of conscience, by which love of self is judged, is born of good works. Just as someone who accomplishes or loves iniquity does not love his own soul, but hates it, so also someone who loves and accomplishes works of justice does not hate, but loves, his soul.

This is the joyful solemnity of that first sabbath. On it no servile works of the world are performed in even the slightest way; on it the shameful fire of concupiscence is not lighted and the burdens of the passions are not carried.

Chapter 4. The kind of sabbath attained by brotherly love,[12] and how the six years which precede the seventh are connected with charity.

7. Yet if, from the quite secret chamber in which a person celebrates this first sabbath, he directs himself to that inn of his

---

12 *dilectio*

breast where he usually rejoices with those who rejoice, weeps with those who weep,[13] is weak with those who are weak, burns with those who are scandalized;[14] and if he senses there that his soul is united with the souls of all his brothers by the cement of charity, and that it is not vexed by any pricks of envy, set afire by any heat of indignation, wounded by darts of suspicion, or consumed by the gnawing of rapacious sadness, then he clasps all of them to the utterly tranquil bosom of his mind. There he embraces and cherishes them all with tender attachment and makes them one heart and one soul with himself. At the very pleasing taste of this sweetness the whole tumult of self-centered desires soon falls silent and the din of evil habits quiets down. Within, there is absolute holiday from everything harmful, and in the sweetness of brotherly love an agreeable and joyful interlude.

8. The apostle Paul, who kept continual sabbath, is a witness that in the quiet of this sabbath fraternal charity permits no evil habits to dwell. For he said this: *You shall not commit adultery, you shall not steal, you shall not bear false witness, and if there are any other commandments, they are summed up in this sentence: you shall love your neighbor as yourself.*[15]

Steeped in the rest and pleasantness of this sabbath, the prophet David burst into a song of festive thanksgiving: *Behold, how good and pleasant it is when brothers dwell together in unity.*[16] Truly good, truly pleasing. Good surely, because nothing is more useful; pleasing because nothing is more savory. Just as only one day is set aside for the first sabbath—it is evident that it is one because it consists of tranquillity of one's own conscience—so it is not without reason that an entire year is devoted to this sabbath. Just as a year is made up of many days, so also in the fire of charity one heart and one soul are molten from many souls.

---

13 Rm 12:15
14 2 Co 11:29
15 Rm 13:9
16 Ps 132 (133):1

If you wish to carve some mystical significance out of those six years which precede this spiritual sabbath, know that there are six kinds of persons on whom the spirit's love must be exercised. Just as a year is made up of many days, so also in each of these kinds there are many people united to us by the bond of love.[17]

9. Our love turns first of all in the order of nature to our blood relatives. Since to have this love is inherent in our very nature, not to have it is extremely inhuman. Hence the apostle said: *Anyone who does not provide for his relatives, and especially if they live with him, has disowned the faith and is worse than an unbeliever.*[18] No one should consider this apostolic statement contrary to the Lord's words when he said: *Whoever comes to me without hating his father and mother cannot be my disciple.*[19]

But we shall look into these things in what follows. Since, therefore, there are some people who are more monstrous than beasts and do not look after their relatives, anyone who loves[20] his own as he ought already approaches this spiritual sabbath a little. This love, since it proceeds from nature itself, moreover, is sanctioned in first place among the precepts having to do with love of neighbor. As God declared: *Honor your father and your mother.*[21]

Hence our love goes out to those who are linked to us by a bond of special friendship or bound to us by an exchange of services, and it widens out from a heart somehow grown larger. Still, this love does not go beyond the justice of the Pharisees, to whom was said, *You shall love your friend and hate your enemy.*[22]

Surely this love, practised in either of these [forms], earns slight reward, inasmuch as natural law impels us to it and the

---

17 *dilectio*
18 1 Tm 5:8
19 Lk 14:26
20 *diligere*
21 Ex 20:12
22 Mt 5:43

grace communicated to us urges us to it. To neglect it, however, brings down the worst kind of damnation. The Lord
spoke of these things in the Gospel: *If you love those who love
you, what credit shall you have? Do not even the heathens do
this? And if you greet only your brothers, what more are you
doing than the others?*23

That our love may be extended to something larger, therefore, let it also embrace those who are subject to the same
yoke of profession as we are. This love will certainly not be
cheated of its reward, because the reason it is proffered is
God. In this state the mind clings to Jesus' garments and licks
some of that ointment which, running down from the head of
the true Aaron, flowed into his beard and reached even the
hem of his garment.5* Anointed by its richness, the mind
expands for a while. Into its widened heart it first receives to
be loved all those whom that ointment, by its touch, makes
partakers of the name of Jesus. Anointed by the Anointed, that
is to say, by Christ, they are called Christians.6* 24

10. There still remain two other kinds of person. If they are
bound to our breast by the links of love,25 surely nothing will
prevent us from enjoying the rest of that true sabbath. We
must grieve over the ignorance of those who are outside—I
mean pagans and Jews, heretics and schismatics. We must
have compassion for their weakness, deplore their ill-will, and
with a devoted attachment share with them the solace of our
prayer, so that they, too, may be found with us in our Lord
Jesus Christ.

From there we should pass on to that love which constitutes
the summit of fraternal charity. In it, a person is made a son of
God; in it the likeness of divine goodness is more fully
restored. As our Saviour said in the Gospel: *Love your enemies
and do good to those who hate you. Pray for those who*

---

23 Mt 5:46–47
24 Cf. Ac 11:26
25 *amor*

persecute and slander you, that you may be sons of your Father who is in heaven.[26]

11. After that, what will remain but the seventh year, during which we are not allowed to ask our debtors for payment, during which the slave is granted freedom? Someone who knows how to look even his enemies straight in the eye is someone who can really say, *Forgive us as we forgive.*[27] *Everyone who commits sin*, he said, *is a slave of sin.*[28] A person is delivered up to this deplorable servitude until, himself loving and forgiving, he is forgiven and loved. From being a slave, he becomes not only a freeman but even a friend.

This is truly a time of peace, a time of quiet, a time of tranquillity, a time of glory and exultation. What trouble, what disturbance, what grief, what anxiety can tarnish the joy of someone who, from that first sabbath (on which he feeds upon the fruits of his labors), progresses by a fuller grace to the state of this divine likeness? There, embracing the whole human race in the one love of his mind, he is not troubled by any injury from anyone. Rather, just as a very fond father has a tender affection for a dearly-beloved son suffering delirium, so likewise will he not think unkindly of his enemies, so that the more injured he is by them, the deeper will be the attachment of charity by which he has compassion on those inflicting trouble on him.

12. A person possessing this virtue should be said to celebrate this sabbath especially when he enters into his heart and applies his spirit to the sweetness of brotherly love. Completely surrended to this very agreeable attachment to those dearest to him, he tastes how good and pleasant it is for brothers to dwell together in unity.[29]

---

26 Mt 5:44–45
27 Mt 6:12
28 Jn 8:34
29 Ps 132(133):1

Chapter 5. How each of these loves is preserved by the love of God.

13. As we said earlier, it is true that each of these loves—the one by which we are concerned about our own salvation and the one by which we are united to our neighbor by pure attachment—has to be animated by some portion of divine love.[30] We must realize that the love[31] of God inclines us toward and fosters this twin love, because *the Word was made flesh and dwelt among us.*[32] Indeed, in this twin love innocence is acquired, and this [innocence], it is clear, consists of two things. A person is innocent, in fact, who harms neither himself nor another person. But someone who corrupts himself by the stain of some vice or foulness harms himself. Toward this corruption pleasure and delight of the flesh strongly impel us, yet anyone can repel or avoid it easily if, having put on tender attachment to the flesh of our Saviour, he rejoices to look with spiritual eyes on the Lord of majesty bowed down even to the narrow dimensions of the manger, nursing at the virginal breast, clasped in his mother's embrace, or being kissed by the happy lips of a trembling old man—I mean Simeon. He considers it sweet to imagine with the eyes of his mind how meek in appearance the Lord was, how gentle in his way of speaking, how compassionate with sinners, and how sympathetic with the infirm and wretched; [to imagine that], with wonderful kindness, he did not shrink from the prostitute's touch or the publican's table; [to imagine] that he took the defense of one adulteress so she would not be stoned and conversed with another that she might somehow, after being an adulteress, become an evangelist. Is there anyone who would not find the delights of fetid flesh despicable at this dear sight?

---

30 *amor*
31 *dilectio*
32 Jn 1:14

And so there easily well up in our eyes gentle tears to quench all the heat of concupiscence, cool the flesh, temper ravenous gluttony, and sedate all titillation for trifles.

14. Nothing animates us so much to love of enemies—which is the perfection of fraternal charity—as grateful consideration of the Lord's admirable patience. By it, the fairest of all the sons of men[33] offered his comely face to the ungodly to be spit on. By it, he subjected to the veil of the iniquitous the eyes whose glance governs all creation. By it, he bared his back to scourges. By it, he bowed beneath the sharpness of thorns the head before which principalities and powers tremble. By it he delivered himself up to insults and outrage. By it, finally, he patiently endured the cross, the nails, the lance, the gall, the vinegar, all the while remaining mild, meek, and calm.

As a sheep he was led to slaughter, and as a lamb before the shearer he was silent and did not open his mouth.[34] O human pride, O proud impatience, consider what he bore, who bore it, why he bore it, how he bore it! Let these things be pondered, I say, not written about!

15. Who is there whose wrath would not instantly be cooled at this marvelous sight? Who, hearing that marvelous voice full of sweetness, full of charity, full of invariable tranquillity, say, *Father, forgive them,*[35] would not instantly embrace his enemies with his entire attachment? *Father,* he said, *forgive them.* What mildness, what charity could be added to this prayer? And yet he did add (more). To pray for them was not enough; he also wanted to excuse them. *Father,* he said, *forgive them for they know not what they are doing.* They are indeed great sinners, but puny judges of value, and so, *Father, forgive them.* They crucify, but do not know who it is they crucify. Had they known, they would never have crucified the Lord of glory.[36] Therefore, *Father, forgive them.* They think he

---

33 Ps 44:3(45:2)
34 Is 53:7
35 Lk 23:34
36 1 Co 2:8

is transgressing the Law, someone pretending to be God, someone leading the people astray. I hid my face from them; they did not recognize my majesty. And so, *Father, forgive them, for they know not what they are doing.*

16. Therefore, that a person may love himself, let him not corrupt himself by any delight of the flesh. That he may not succumb to the concupiscence of the flesh, let him extend his full attachment to the attractiveness of the Lord's flesh. Moreover, that he may rest more perfectly and pleasantly in the delight of fraternal charity, let him embrace even his enemies with arms of true love. But lest this divine fire die in the gales of injustice, let him gaze with the eyes of his mind on the tranquil patience of his beloved Lord and Saviour.

Chapter 6. How the perfect sabbath is found in God's love, and how the fiftieth year may be compared to this love.

17. The greater its devotion, the more securely does the soul purified by this twin love pass to the blissful embraces of the Lord's divinity, so that, inflamed with utmost desire, it goes beyond the veil of the flesh and, entering into that sanctuary where Christ Jesus is spirit before its face[37], it is thoroughly absorbed by that ineffable light and unaccustomed sweetness. All that is bodily, all that is sensible, and all that is mutable are reduced to silence. The soul fixes its clear-sighted gaze on what is and is so always and is in itself: on the One. Being at leisure[38] it sees that the Lord himself is God, and in the tender embrace of charity itself it keeps a sabbath, doubtlessly the Sabbath of sabbaths.

18. This is the jubilee year in which man returns to his possession,[39] that is, to his very Creator, so that he may truly

---

37 Cf Lam 4:20
38 *vacare*
39 Lev 25:10

be possessed by him and possess him, be held by him and hold him, be taken by him and take him. This is the possession that was sold for the price of cheap sin when man's love slipped away from the One who made him and clung to the thing that had been made. Not without reason is the number fifty applied to this sabbath on which servile fear is cast out, concupiscence of the flesh is not only silenced but the memory of it is lulled to sleep, and the fullness of the spirit is received.[7*] *As yet,* it says,—that is to say, before Pentecost— *the Spirit had not been given because Jesus had not yet been glorified.*[40] This means, of course, not that the Spirit had not been given at all, but that he had not yet been given with such great fullness or such great perfection. He is indeed given on the first sabbath, and on the second too, but on the Sabbath of sabbaths his fullness is poured out. On that twin sabbath Jesus is seen as being little not great, humble not exalted, wronged not glorified. For that reason, then, the Spirit had not yet been given, because Jesus had not yet been glorified.

19. It is true that charity is not poured into our hearts otherwise than by the Holy Spirit who has been given to us.[41] The number seven is kept in each case, but it is in the multiplication of seven that the development of this charity is recognized. For the seventh day is, as it were, the foundation of charity, the seventh year its increase, and the fiftieth year— which comes after seven times seven—its fullness. On each of these there is rest, on each of these there is leisure, on each of these there is a spiritual sabbath. First there is rest in purity of conscience, then in the very pleasant joining together of many minds, and finally in the contemplation of God himself.

On the first sabbath the soul keeps free from fault, on the second from self-centeredness, and on the third from absolutely everything that dissipates it. On the first sabbath the mind tastes how sweet Jesus is in his humanity; on the second it sees how perfect he is in charity, and on the third how

40 Jn 7:39
41 Rm 5:5

sublime in his godhead. On the first the soul is recollected within itself; on the second it is extended outside itself; on the third it is caught up above itself.

Chapter 7. What love[42], charity, and self-centeredness are.

20. The place and the time require that we pursue in more detail what we have discussed above, that is to say, how this charity should be shown. To make this more evident, I see we must demonstrate more articulately what charity is.

It is evident enough that charity is love, although it is not less evident that not all love is charity.[8*] Wherefore closer examination is necessary so that what love is may first of all become apparent to us as we reflect and that, once its *genus* is recognized, its species may not remain hidden from us as we search.

Observed habits of speaking indicate that love is said to be two-fold. We call 'love' that certain power or nature of the rational soul whereby it has the capacity within itself of loving something or not loving it. We likewise call 'love' an act of the rational soul exercising this power, when the soul uses it with regard to those things it should or those it should not [love]. Such an act is usually called 'love' with some qualification. For example, love of wisdom, love of money. This love is necessarily either good or evil. That power or nature of the soul by which this love (either good or bad) is exercised is a good of the soul and, in both good and evil [applications], can never not be a good. It belongs to the nature of its very substance, which comes from the infinite Good that made all good things, all of which are very, very good.[43]

21. Yet man, being endowed with free choice, uses this just as he uses all the other goods of his nature: either well (aided

---

42 *amor*
43 Gen 1:31

by grace) or badly (when justly forsaken). Because, as someone has said, *nothing makes a man's behavior good or bad
except good or bad loves,*[44] good use of any given good makes
a person good because it makes his love good, but abuse
makes his love bad and so makes the person bad. Why then
do we hesitate to say that charity is the right use of love itself,
and that its abuse is self-centeredness?

Chapter 8. How the right or perverse use of love depends on the choice, the development and the fruit.[9*] [45]

22. Let us now make a finer distinction between right and
wrong use of love. It seems to me that its use consists of three
things: the choice, the development, and the fruit. The choice
proceeds from reason, the development is in desire and act,
and the fruit is in the object. Created with a capacity for
happiness, the rational creature is always eager for this happiness. But he is quite incapable of this happiness by himself.
Consequently, since he is taught by his own unhappiness that
he is incapable of happiness, he sees that he should look for
enjoyment in something other than himself if he is to obtain
the desired happiness. And so each person, according either
to the degree of his faith and understanding, or to illusions
arising from error or to his sensory experience, puts his happiness in the fruit of one thing or another. Then, without any
hesitation, he chooses for his enjoyment what he supposes
capable by its fruit of making him happy. Love[46] makes this
choice, for the rational soul does this by that force or nature
which we earlier called love. To be sure, love always has
reason as a companion; not that the soul always loves in a

---

44 Augustine, *Ep* 155.4
45 *electio, motus, fructus*
46 *amor*

reasonable way by means of it, but that by it, with alert circumspection, it distinguishes what it chooses from what it rejects. Lastly, it is for reason to distinguish between Creator and creature, between what is temporal and what is eternal, between what is bitter and what is sweet, and between what is harsh and what is delightful. It is, however, for love to choose what it wants for its enjoyment.

23. This choice, in turn, is called love and is an act of the soul. Although the love by which it makes its choice is itself always a good thing, still this choice (which is likewise called love) is necessarily either good or bad. Because of this, the love is either good or bad. If the mind, enticed by the experience of some delight or deceived by some error, chooses for its enjoyment objects it should never enjoy, it certainly loves injudiciously. By *enjoy* we mean possessing something with delight and joy. A secret development of this love immediately follows the choice, or even accompanies it, awaking the spirit in some way and moving it to desire that object which it has decided should be chosen. Similarly, this development is an act of the spirit. It comes from love and is called love. If it is directed toward what it should be and as it should be, it is good love. But if it is directed toward what it should not be or otherwise than as it should be, it is bad love.

24. If, by actions proportionate to its wish, it attains the object it has chosen for its enjoyment, and once chosen has desired, it soon is at rest in using it with joy and delight. This use, to express it in one word, we call the fruit.

Therefore, charity or self-centeredness seems to consist of these three things: a choice in the spirit, a development, and the fruit. The choice is the beginning of love, either good or bad; the development of love is its course; and the fruit of love is its object. And so, if the mind selects for its enjoyment what it should, if it moves toward its object as it ought, and enjoys this object as is suitable, this salutary choice, this appropriate development, and this advantageous fruit rightfully deserve to be reckoned by the name charity. Charity is founded on this choice, it is extended by the development, and it attains perfection in the fruit. But if the soul chooses foolishly, or is moved improperly, or misuses [love] shamefully, it is easy to see that by these steps, as it were, self-centeredness reaches its consummation.

These are two fountains, two sources of good and evil things, since the root of all evils[47] is self-centeredness and the root of all good things is charity.

Chapter 9. What we should choose for enjoyment.

25. Now that we have drawn a distinction between good love and bad, it remains for us to show—as he in whose hands we are may deem to inspire both ourself and our words—what the spirit ought to choose for its enjoyment. In that way we will recognize what we should love and how we should love it.

We should mention that we should not say we love everything we choose for our use, but only what we choose for our enjoyment. The mind which is sunk in the dungheap of the flesh and does not strive to aspire to anything fine that goes beyond the grossness of the senses, chooses delusive riches or futile honors or bodily indulgences or worldly favors—either some or all of these things together—to reach its goal. By a mistaken opinion it depicts happiness as the attainment of such things. Yet not all persons strive for the fruit of these things by the same route. One man chooses to engage in business, another in military affairs, another to practise some craft, still another inclines toward thievery and robbery to reach his goal. Of all of these, one should be said to love only those things toward which his entire intention hastens for enjoyment. The others he uses as so many props by which he may more easily achieve the attainment of the desired object.

---

47 1 Tm 6:10

26. As long as a perverse mind does not attain its hopes, it paints a picture of happiness for itself in their fruit. Once able to gratify its wish, however, it feels that it struggles in its usual insatiableness or it shrinks in disgust from the things it has abused and its appetite for some other object builds up. Yet it will not be satiated. On the contrary, the same absurd vanity will delude it shamefully all over again.

This is the circle of the ungodly,[10*] whose miserable insatiableness has been sufficiently discussed above in the first part of this work. But someone with a healthier soul, a purer eye, a serener life, will look into matters with loftier senses. Since it is evident that no one can supply his own happiness, he understands perfectly well that something inferior to, and lower than, his own nature can drag man down by his love for it, not raise him higher, and that it involves him in misery far more than it bestows the solace of true happiness. Hence, beginning to reckon himself at his proper value and to estimate the privilege of his own nature, he perceives how worthily , how magnificently, and finally how justly, the divine law prescribed: *You shall adore the Lord your God and him alone shall you serve.*[48] That certainly would not have been said if there were some higher nature to whom human nature owed that unique homage, or from which it might expect the reward of blessedness. He should be chosen by us, therefore, in preference to all else, so that we may enjoy him. This is the foundation[49] of love. He should be desired above all else; that is, as it were, the course and progress of love. In attainment of him there will also be perfect blessedness, because there will be perfect love of the perfect good.

27. Rightly did the divine law connect the first and greatest commandment with love of God, when it stated: *You shall love the Lord your God.*[50] Yes, because when we attain this beatifying good, each of us will enjoy it according to his own

---

48 Dt 6:13, Mt 4:10
49 *inchoatio*
50 Dt 6:5

capacity. All together, we will be capable of enjoying it to a greater extent than each one could singly, so a person's blessedness will surely be more abundant if, having less capacity for it in himself, he begins to possess in another what he cannot have in himself. The good of another will not be his, however, unless he loves that good in the other person. And so divine authority very fittingly decreed the second precept: *You shall love your neighbor.*[51]

28. Yet, since God will be our highest good, we are commanded to love him always, above all else, in himself, in us, in others. Therefore, *You shall love the Lord your God with your whole heart, all your soul, and all your strength.*[52] But because our neighbor's good will confer as much joy on us as does our own, we are rightly told: *You shall love your neighbor as yourself.*[53] It is clear, therefore, that we should choose for our joy these two: God and neighbor, although not in the same way. We should choose God that we may enjoy him in himself and because of himself, and our neighbor that we may enjoy him in God and God in him. For although this word *enjoy* is usually taken in a stricter sense—that it may be said that we should take our joy in no other thing but God alone—still, when speaking to a fellow man, Paul said, *So brother, may I take my joy in you in the Lord.*[54]

When reason perceives, as we said, that these two should be chosen, and when by contemplation of them everything else has been scorned and the soul makes a choice by consenting, then there really is a foundation for pure love[55] of God and neighbor, because there is conversion of the very love[56] itself toward what it should love.

---

51 Mt 5:43
52 Mt 22:37
53 Mt 22:39
54 Phm 20
55 *dilectio*
56 *amor*

Chapter 10. Our love is moved to action and desire, and it is moved to each of them sometimes by attachment, and sometimes by reason.

29. As far as choice is concerned, we have said enough to allow us to proceed to what should be said about the development of love. This development occurs toward two things: either inwardly toward desire, or outwardly toward action. The spirit is moved toward desire when, by an inward development and appetite, it tends toward what it has deemed [worthy] of its enjoyment. It is moved toward action when some hidden force of love[57] itself impels the mind to accomplish some outward act. Accordingly, I think we should investigate what the things are which, like goads, arouse love and move it in these two directions, and which also in some way fix its course and guide it. Then we should examine more precisely which of these things it should follow and how far it should follow, which it should reject, which it should allow, and which it ought to diminish and which increase, so that the development itself may suit its end.

30. There are, it seems to me, two things which move and provoke the spirit in the two directions we have mentioned: they are attachment[58] and reason. Sometimes it is only by attachment and sometimes only by reason that our love is fanned to overt action or to hidden desire. Hence we will endeavor to treat each of these insofar as it seems necessary. It should, of course, be noted that since reason has taught us in the foregoing which two—God and our neighbor—ought to be chosen for our enjoyment, we should put other things aside and treat next how our love ought to be moved toward these two. Therefore, from among all those developments from which our love derives its many-sided diversity, let us see which one we should especially follow. First, however, let

---

57 *amor*
58 *affectus*

us continue with what we began to say about the two-fold origin of the development itself.

Chapter 11. What attachment is, and how many types of attachment there are. That spiritual attachment may be understood in two ways is also shown.

31. Attachment is a kind of spontaneous, pleasant inclination of the spirit toward someone. Moreover, attachment is either spiritual, rational, irrational, dutiful[59], natural, or, of course, physical.

Spiritual attachment can be understood in two ways. The soul is stirred by spiritual attachment when, touched by a hidden and—we might say—unforeseen visitation of the Holy Spirit, it is opened either to the sweetness of divine love or to the pleasantness of fraternal charity. I recall that I have demonstrated above as clearly as I could the modality and causes of this visitation.[60]

This is the opposite of that attachment which is brought about by the devil's meddling. By this sort those of whom the prophet said, *A prostituting spirit has led them astray,*[61] were enticed to commit shameful deeds.

32. This highly unclean enemy attacks the modesty of the holy by two torments: first, he enkindles the flesh by intolerable flames, and then he weakens the mind by the attachment of dangerous sweetness. Unless I am mistaken, David's son Amnon, unhinged by an attachment to culpable pleasure, at the instigation of that extremely crafty enemy, burned with desire for the forbidden embraces of his own sister. He stained the house of his noble father with incest and brought his brother's sword on himself.[62] He also sowed opportunities and causes for the attempted patricide which the unfortunate

---

59 *officialis*
60 II.**8**.20–**14**.35.
61 Hos 4:12
62 2 S 13

Absalom, coveting the kingdom, plotted against his own
father.[63] Let no one be horrified because we call this attachment spiritual, because it is born of spiritual wickedness. And
let us not quibble about its name, when the matter itself is
evident.

Chapter 12. Rational and irrational attachments.

33. A rational attachment is one that arises from reflection
on the virtue of another person, that is, when we have observed someone's virtue or holiness with our own eyes or
have learned of it either by his growing reputation or, of
course, by reading about him. It floods our mind with a kind
of charming pleasantness. This is the attachment which pricks
us with very pleasant devotion when we hear about the
triumphant suffering of the martyrs or depicts for us in delightful meditation the memorable deeds of those who have gone
before us, as if we were eyewitnesses. Hence, that voice with
which the admirable athlete of Jesus—I mean Paul—often
related his brave deeds drew tears to the eyes of his listeners
in token of their admiration, and soon moved their hearts with
sudden tenderness to want to embrace him. Who, hearing
about the dangers of the deep, the dangers from robbers, the
dangers from his own people, the dangers from pagans,[64] and
above all, hearing that voice of virtue say, *In any and all
circumstances I have learned the secret of facing plenty and
hunger, abundance and want; I can do all things in him who
strengthens me,*[65]—who, I ask, hearing or reading about these
things would not be moved to wonderful attachment to such a
man? This attachment consecrated the first-fruits of the sacred
love between David and Jonathan, and through a pact of the
most grace-filled charity forged a bond of social grace[66] which

---

63 2 S 15
64 2 Co 11:26
65 Ph 4:12–13
66 *vinculum gratiae socialis*

not even paternal authority could break. When [Jonathan] saw the unswerving constancy of heart with which the unarmed youth laid the armored giant low,[67] what would have been a seedbed of envy for another person became a cause of increase of virtue for this best of young men. The friend of virtue was stirred by attachment for the virtuous lad. As Scripture says: *Jonathan's soul was knit with David's soul,* because *David loved Jonathan like his own soul.*[68]

Jesus himself, who was wonderfully merciful, mercifully transformed this attachment within himself when he looked at the young man who declared his virtues to him. As the evangelist says, *he loved him.*[69]

34. The opposite of this attachment is the irrational, by which a person aware of someone's defects is moved toward him by an inclination of mind. Many people incline the souls of others to themselves either by the most inane philosophy or by the stupidest audacity in military affairs. What is still more doleful, many lure and bend the affection of others to themselves because they are spendthrifts or libertines, or betrayers and persecutors of modesty, or supporters and followers of disreputable men, or very foolish, but very intent, spectators at the silliest kind of spectacles.

Chapter 13. Dutiful attachment.

35. Next, we call 'dutiful' that attachment which arises from services or marks of deference. When the holy Moses fled from Pharaoh's ambush he won the affection of the priest of Midian by a dutifulness worthy of being remembered. Since he had very tenaciously protected the priest's two maiden daughters against the wickedness of certain shepherds, even though he was a stranger, the priest admired the youth's

---

67 Cf. 1 S 17:50
68 1 S 18:1
69 Mk 10:21

kindness and asked him not only to be his friend but also to become his son-in-law.[70] Barzillai the Gileadite also inspired King David's grateful attachment because of his services (he had taken David in with extremely dutiful devotion when he was fleeing from Absalom[71]). The king remained so unswervingly attached to the spirit of this faithful man that, when he was about to die, by the terms of his will he directed his son Solomon to reward such great generosity.

Chapter 14. Natural attachment.

36. In addition to these, there is the natural attachment everyone has for his own flesh, a mother has for her son, and a man has for his blood relatives. *For no man has ever hated his own flesh.*[72] *A woman cannot forget her little child to the point of not pitying the son of her womb,*[73] and *Anyone who does not provide for his relatives, and especially if they live with him, has disowned the faith and is worse than an unbeliever.*[74]

The first of these did not exempt even the holiest men. Because of that attachment by which no one has ever hated his own flesh, they were concerned about their burial, and it is said that they bound their sons by oath not to inter them in a foreign land when they died, but in the tombs of their fathers.[75] As to the second, when the prostitutes disputed in the presence of the ever-wise Solomon over the surviving child (for the mother had smothered the other child), he thought the matter should be investigated.[76] In the end, when a sword had been brought and his royal majesty had reached

---

70 Ex 2:16ff
71 1 K 2:7
72 Eph 5:29
73 Is 49:15
74 1 Tm 5:8
75 Cf. Gn 47:29–30
76 1 K 3:16ff

the decision that the child should be divided, natural attachment revealed the mother, and she who had yielded to treachery disclaimed all attachment; and she who had taken great pains that the true mother not be deprived of her offspring, began to take pains that he be given over to the other woman. *I beg you,* she said, *give this baby to her while he is still alive, and do not let him be killed.*[77] [The other woman], on the contrary, devoid of loving tenderness, hardened her heart to the other and said, *No, let him be neither mine nor yours, but divide him.*[78]

37. In the breast of the ever-holy Joseph, the third type of attachment outweighed even a fratricidal offense. After branding his fratricidal brothers with the crime of spying, with the severity befitting someone in charge of affairs, and seeing that they were more than a little harassed and adequately tormented by their belated regret over betraying their brother, he yielded to his attachment. As Scripture says: *He left them for a little while and wept.*[79] Nor did the cruelty of David's patricidal son efface this attachment from the patriarch's loving heart. When his son was seeking to put him to death, he sent men who would resist his madness. He was oblivious to the injury and mindful of nature, so he might know himself to be a father while pretending not to recognize his persecutor. *Save the boy Absalom for me.*[80]

With wonderful compassion, the Saviour himself was steeped in this attachment when he looked at the city which was his home according to the flesh and from which his ancestors according to the flesh had come. Moved by natural pity he wept profusely over its future destruction.[81] His imitator, Paul,[82] touched by natural attachment, I think, once

---

77 1 K 3:26
78 Ibid.
79 Gen 42:24
80 2 S 18:5
81 Lk 19:41
82 Cf. 1 Co 11:1

wished to be cut off from Christ for the sake of his kinsmen according to the flesh.[83]

Chapter 15. Two different ways of understanding physical attachment.[84]

38. Next, the origin of physical attachment appears to be twofold. Very frequently it is not someone's virtue or vice, but a certain bearing of the outward person which attracts the spirit of someone looking at him. An elegant appearance, a pleasant way of speaking, a mature bearing, and a comely countenance easily invite and ensure attachment, even if one does not know what kind of a person this is. This charm glowed in Moses when he was still a little boy so that, contrary to Pharaoh's tyrannical order condemning the Hebrews' male children to death, he was kept by his parents for three months. As the apostle said: *because they saw that the child was so fine.*[85] When he was exposed to danger, his fine appearance drew the loving kindness even of Pharaoh's daughter to him. She adopted him as her son and he became great among all Pharaoh's servants.

On the other hand, no one of sound mind will have any doubt that a man prodded by evil and seductive pleasure toward some object of beauty is moved by physical attachment, by the memory of harmful pleasure. At the sight of Bathsheba's beauty this attachment overcame David, caught off guard as he walked on the roof of his house.[86] It led him astray once he was overcome and brought ruin on him once he strayed. The man it unnerved in the unlawful embraces of another man's wife, it steeled, on the other hand, for the cruel killing of one of his own soldiers.[87] This attachment blotted

---

83 Rm 9:3
84 *affectus carnalis*
85 Heb 11:23, Ex 2:2
86 2 S 11:2
87 2 S 11:17

out Solomon's wisdom and, once he had been led astray by carnal lust, it hurled him into a chasm of spiritual fornication by his infamous worship of idols.[88]

Chapter 16. What our view of these attachments should be.

39. These are the attachments which occur to my mind for the time being. They are, as I have said, the fountainheads or roots of love, as it were, not love itself. We do not consider being aroused or stirred by these attachments especially praiseworthy if they are good, or ruinous if bad. To their own detriment, many persons abuse the first we stated, even though it is the best, as we have explained in the preceding booklet.[89] And by the latter, which is adjudged more formidable than others, the best of men are sometimes titillated to their merit by this trial.

For this reason, what we consider either useful or harmful is not being moved by these attachments, but rather being moved according to these attachments. When these attachments move the spirit there is either a visitation or a temptation. When it is moved according to these attachments there is full consent of the will itself. This consent is either hidden or manifest. It is hidden when one is inwardly aroused by consent to a desire; it is manifest when the desire itself erupts outwardly into activity. Whether our love ought to be moved according to these attachments and how far it ought to be moved, we shall endeavor to investigate. But first we will make a few remarks about reason, which we have called the other cause of this development.

---

88 Cf. 1 K 11
89 Book II.7 and 17.

Chapter 17. How the mind is moved by reason to love God and neighbor.

40. The spirit which no attachment moves to love of God and neighbor reason frequently does move. This is as much holier as it is more secure, as much more secure as it is more refined, as much more refined inasmuch as nothing can be more useful or purer than a rational love. In order to arouse a lukewarm spirit to desire its Creator, reason therefore relies on three arguments: its necessity for us or usefulness to us, and his worthiness. Reason persuades us that we should love God because this is necessary for us, because it is advantageous, and because it is worthy. Necessary for us to escape damnation; advantageous for us to arrive at glorification; and worthy because he loved us first and rightly demands requital of his love.

A person should desire God as his good. Without him, one will of necessity always be miserable; with him, one can never be anything but supremely happy. Not needing any good thing we have, he willed to become poor for us. If the mind consents to this reasoning, it will be aroused to desire God by the will, even if not by a [sense of] attachment. Reason immediately follows up its work by demonstrating that, if one wills to attain what it desires, one must resolutely struggle to fulfil his commandments.

Hence, as reason urges it on, a desire born deep within[90] us moves into action. Yet because the greatest of God's commandments is that a person have as much concern for his neighbor as he does for himself, reason insists that the spirit be moved to devote itself to doing good for its neighbor. Everyone is our neighbor, whether a friend, not a friend, or even an enemy. A friend because he either benefits us or has done so; a non-enemy because he neither harms us nor has done so; an enemy because he either injures us or has done so. A friend for reasons of blood or favor; a non-enemy by

---

90 *internis visceribus*

reason of innocence; an enemy by reason of injury. Consequently, reason proposes three [motives] why a person should exert himself for a friend, two for a non-enemy, and one for an enemy. Kindness is owed to a friend by reason of nature, obligation, and precept; by nature because he is a human being or even a member of the household, by duty because he is his friend, and by precept because he is his neighbor. Kindness if owed a non-enemy by reason of nature, because he is a human being, and precept, because he is a neighbor. To an enemy [it is owed] only by precept, because it is the Lord's precept that we love our enemy.[91]

If the spirit yields to these three arguments and resolves to exert itself in doing good not only to its friends but also to its enemies, then even though it may feel no attachment, it will nevertheless not lose the merit of charity.

Chapter 18. The distinction between the twin loves between which wavers the spirit of anyone making progress.

41. A distinction must be made then between these two loves: one [stems] from attachment, the other from reason. Between the two loves the spirit of someone making progress and desirous of having an ordered love wavers and is often fearful, imagining that it loves less someone whom it should love more, or loves too much someone whom it should love less. Ordered love is this: that a person not love what ought not to be loved, and that he love everything that ought to be loved but not more than it ought to be loved, and that he not love equally the things that should be loved differently, nor differently the things that should be loved equally.

42. Let us set before our eyes two persons: one of them is gentle, charming, peaceable, pleasant, and good at getting along with all good people. He attracts others to close

---

91 Mt 5:44

acquaintanceship with himself, is soft-spoken, and well-man-
nered. Yet he is less perfect in certain virtues. The second
person, although more advanced in the highest virtue, has a
sadder mien, a severer countenance, and a brow furrowed by
his austere habits. He may do good to everyone and give what
is demanded of him, but he is not pleasant company and he
does not attract everyone to him by his kindness. By a sort of
spontaneous attachment, the spirit is moved to love the first;
reason and the rule of ordered charity urge it to love the
second. And so, when a person feels his spirit taking to the
first with some pleasure and hardening toward the other
because of his lack of pleasantness, he is anxious and grieved.
He fears that he is transgressing the rule of charity and thinks
he loves the first more than he should and the second less
than he should.

**Chapter 19. By twin comparisons is explained why a
kind and pleasant person, although less perfect, may
be loved with more agreeable attachment than
someone who is austere but more perfect. The love of
either of these persons is shown not to be dangerous.**

43. Now I want first of all to explore the hidden recesses of
my own conscience, so that this attachment may not trick me
[as would be the case] if I happened to be ignorant of its cause
and origin. When someone towards whom my spirit is moved
by a pleasant inclination, although less than perfect, is not
vice-ridden but indeed adorned with many virtues, why
should this attachment not be believed to have its source in
virtue, and therefore be something I should not fear but rather
embrace? But if I had said that its source or cause is virtue,
why does it not turn itself with a readier—or at least a similar—movement toward someone whom I recognize as more
virtuous? Must this attachment (which is engendered by some
attractiveness of the outward person) be considered merely
physical? If this is so, why is it that I do not cherish with the

pleasantness of this same fondness, another person equally attractive in his outward ways because I, however, consider him vice-ridden?

It has sometimes happened to me that someone's outward bearing has inclined my spirit to him very much as long as I either hoped to find virtue in him or ignored his vice. But when his vice was discovered it blotted out all that attachment and caused no end of repugnance in my mind.

What then? Virtue and vice must perhaps be considered food for the soul—nutritious or harmful. The austerity or affability of the outward person should be adjudged as a container, either crude or elegant. Nutritious food is very often taken in ugly-looking containers, but harmful food is not accepted even in exquisite ones.

44. It happens, however, and quite often, that somewhat cheaper food is more happily accepted on account of the attractiveness of the container, but that even the most exquisite food is taken unpleasantly on account of repugnance for the container. Also it sometimes turns out that a vice-ridden person displeases us even though very handsome, and that virtue is extremely pleasing even when accompanied by some harshness and austerity in a person's outward appearance. Still—and it is evident that this happens—one more readily notices lesser virtue in a person who is kind and joyful, while a greater virtue is less savory in a harsh austere person.

The comparison will be finer, I think, because also more expressive, if virtue is considered as truth and vice as falsehood: excessive severity of bearing as harsh, rough language; and agreeable pleasantness of the outward person as polished, eloquent language. Just as falsehood expressed in sweet talk should not be accepted, so also truth expressed in harsh, rough language should not be spurned. In the same way, outward faults should not be pleasing in a handsome person, nor virtue displeasing in however harsh and austere a person.

45. Then again, suppose two men begin pleading some cause: one of them does it insipidly, gracelessly, and coldly;

the other cleverly, splendidly, agreeably, and forcefully. As long as the listener does not know which of them is relying on the truth and which is overflowing with falsehood, it is no wonder if he enjoys more the language of the one who by his forcefulness in speaking knows how to convince his adversaries, stir up the inattentive, and by introductory remarks gain the good will, attention and docility of the listener. To those who do not know where his presentation is leading, he hints at what they should expect.

Even if both are known to present arguments that are equally true, equally worthwhile, it is with some bitterness that we accept what is wholesome in the words of the one and hearken with better grace and more eagerly to the pleasant wholesomeness and wholesome pleasantness of the other's words. The more the agreeable pleasantness of a true statement is craved, the more easily will its wholesomeness have an effect. Yet if each adduces arguments that are true, but the less eloquent (speaker) tries to affirm truths which are nobler and more profound, the arguments presented in the more pleasant manner will fall more agreeably on the listeners' ears, even though they may be of less value. We must exert more than a little effort so that when we hear these arguments of greater importance our soul does not get bored at the awkwardness of the words in which they are presented, with the result that we are not pleased to understand them and finish by becoming unwilling to believe them.

46. It is no different if two persons are put before us, one of whom is kind, affable, pleasing in appearance, and delightful in his manner of speaking. By a certain pleasantness in his outward person he overwhelms the hearts of those who see him. The other is harsh and austere. By his excessive seriousness he strikes fear, as it were, into those who see him. As long as the virtue or vice of each lies hidden, who would blame someone for letting his intimate feelings accept the former more easily and letting his attachment—though not his will and reason—reject the other? But if one recognizes that both are equal in other virtues, or if one even discovers that

the happier one is less perfect in certain virtues, it would be neither surprising nor unreasonable for one to relish more delightfully the inward virtue put before him in outward pleasingness, like truth presented in beautiful language. He will accept virtue amid an excessive austerity of bearing with a certain degree of mental anxiety or even reluctance, like truth in harsh, rough language.

But just as there is a certain eloquence which is becoming to youth, but another to older people, and that which in youth is considered fervor and vivaciousness in maturity becomes silliness, so, of course, if kindness in a young person is more joyous, prompter, more inclined to deference, more agile in activity, in an older person it is noble, serious, without any dissipation, joyous, free of silliness, and fully mature. The former should not be accused of frivolity or the latter of austerity.

47. However the attachments of a loving person may vary, therefore, he does not overstep the law of charity if he resists giving any influence over himself, or anything else which goes beyond reason to someone whom his spirit attachedly cherishes, yet does not withhold from another what reason demonstrates should be accorded him. Yet since these attachments are not located in our free choice—we are sometimes moved by some of them very much against our will and sometimes unable to experience others even though we want to do so—love never grows from attachment when attachment moves the mind, but it grows when the mind directs the development itself according to the attachment. The same thing should be thought to hold good for the development engendered by reason.

Chapter 20. The three loves: from attachment, from reason, and from both together.

48. Love arises from attachment when the spirit gives its consent to this attachment, and from reason when the will

joins itself to reason. A third love can also be brought about from these two when the three—reason, attachment, and will—are fused into one. The first is pleasant, but dangerous; the second is harsh, but fruitful; the third, having the advantages of the other two, is perfect. The sense of the sweetness we experienced draws us to the first; the evidence of reason impels us toward the second; and in the third, reason itself savors [the sweetness]. This last differs from the first because, although in the first we sometimes love what we ought to love, we love it more for the sake of the sweetness of attachment. In this last we love it not because it is pleasant, but because it deserves love and is consequently sweet.

Chapter 21. A review of what has been said; and how true love of God may be recognized.

49. From all that has been said, then, let us briefly summarize what makes up the whole force of love. First, if the mind chooses something for its enjoyment, then reaches out to it by a kind of inward desire, and finally does what will enable it to attain what it desires, this should without any doubt be called 'to love'. The more fervently and insistently someone carries this through, the more also does he love. If he does this out of attachment, he surely loves more sweetly and therefore acts with greater facility. If another person does out of reason alone everything that the first does solely by attachment, he loves[92] less sweetly yet will not less promptly obtain what he desires.

If the choice has been perverse, so that someone selects for his enjoyment something he should not, then what follows on this choice will be perverse and the love will be perverse and should be tallied under the word 'self-centeredness' and not 'charity'.

---

92 *diligit*

As we have taught above, anything that the seduced or deceived mind chooses for its enjoyment, other than God in himself or a neighbor in God, exceeds the boundaries of real love.[93] The choice may in itself be sound then, but one of the two developments perverse.

50. It may happen that the choice and the subsequent development in the desire are founded on reason, but that the other—which is in the act—corrupts the entire love. This will be made clearer by examples.

If someone chooses God for enjoyment, that choice is sound. But if he were to desire something sensual as the fruit, thinking—as some of the Jewish stories have it—that when he attains God he will be able to steep himself in banquets and repose in pleasures which flatter the senses, the integrity of his choice followed by such great perversity of desire will profit him nothing.

If he chooses God to be the fruit of his felicity and desires in God nothing but God, and yet aims to attain so great a good by acts other than he should—for example, by Jewish ceremonies or pagan sacrifices or any other kind of superstition—he will surely void the entire fruit of love.

51. Let the choice therefore be sound, the desire correspond to it, and the act be reasonable. In that way we will not overstep the bounds of charity. In this love it is very important how attached a person is, how discerning, and how strong.[11*] He should be attached, that he may love sweetly, discerning, that he may love prudently, and strong, that he may love perseveringly. Attached, that he may savor what he chooses by desire; discerning, that he may not overstep moderation in activity; strong, that temptation may not lead him astray. Attachment is useful against perverse pleasures, discretion against deception, fortitude against persecutions. If anyone is recognized as perfect in these three, he loves not only felicitously but also pleasantly. If he cannot feel attachment, let him nevertheless be discerning and strong, and it will be equally to

---

93 *dilectio*

his advantage, if not for immediately pleasantness, at least for his future felicity.

Chapter 22. What considerations should be entertained in love of neighbor.

52. Let us consider these same things in love[94] of neighbor. If we choose our neighbor for the fruit of his company, which is in God, then our choice is sound. But if base desire or inordinate activity follows upon this choice, the soundness of the choice is totally stained. In our love of God we are really concerned with ourselves and not with him. He is our God and does not need what we have.[95] In mutual love, however, since we have a mutual need, we must have concern for each other's interests. Hence desire should reach out to two objects, and activity should no less be undertaken in a two-fold way.

Desire should be directed toward this: that we enjoy one another mutually in God (as is fitting) and we enjoy God reciprocally in one another. Yet since man is composed of body and soul, our action should certainly keep both in view, insofar as our means make this possible. The more fervent and prudent a person is in these respects, the more perfect he is in charity, too. Besides, the greater the attachment, the more pleasant is charity itself. As we have said, just as attachment sometimes moves the soul [to charity] and sometimes reason does, so each of them vies to arrange the measure of the desire and the activity according to its own qualities. Therefore, careful consideration is required for us to see which of these attachments should be followed, and how far they should be followed.

---

94 *dilectio*
95 Ps 15(16):2

Chapter 23. Which attachments are unacceptable, and how far spiritual attachment, which is from God, should be pursued.

53. There is, then, a spiritual attachment which comes from the devil, an irrational attachment that fosters vice, and a physical attachment which leads to vice. Not only should these three attachments not be pursued, they must not even be allowed. Still more, they should be torn out of our hearts by the roots to the furthest extent this can be done. But the spiritual attachment which comes from God should be not only allowed, but stimulated and increased in every way. It is very salutary for our desire to pursue it, as the more agreeably its great excellence is revealed to us, the more fervently its desirable presence is desired. Our activity, of course, should also be stimulated by this attachment, but it should not be regulated according to it. It has to be stimulated so the will never becomes lukewarm about doing what is good, and even perfect. But the doing itself should not be regulated according to attachment, lest it overstep the limits of physical capability. For this body is a kind of instrument which has to be exercised. Since it has the quality of clay, it is subject to innumerable dangerous passions and cannot support the force of an ardent spirit. If its outward action is not tempered by a certain moderation, it will undoubtedly flag and succumb, leaving its undertaking unfinished.

54. Attachment has, moreover, this characteristic: very often it pays no attention to moderation, does not gauge human strength, uses up physical energies, rushes towards the object of its love with a blind impetuosity, ponders only what it craves, and despises everything else. Furthermore, in undertaking something burdensome, arduous, even impossible, as though it were slight and effortless, because of the delight of the inward attachment, it does not feel the very annoying afflictions to the outward person. That the will may glow with constant fervor for this yoke, that someone may patiently, even joyfully, endure sufferings inflicted on him from without,

the impetus of this attachment must be brought to bear on the development of the desire itself. And so that he may not overstep the limits of physical capabilities as he proceeds to voluntary activities, he must be restrained by the moderation coming from reason. Some people pay no attention to this measuring of life and, stubbornly following all the impulse of their attachment, they become weaker instead of holier. As their attachment becomes tepid because their action lacks moderation, their very will also becomes tepid, immoderately weighed down.

If the Spirit who inspires and regulates good attachments, but merely regulates evil ones, may wish to suggest something useful to us about the healthy moderateness of action which is necessarily undertaken according to reason, we will take note of this in its proper place. Now let us continue with what we began to say about distinctions among the attachments themselves.

Chapter 24. Rational attachment, and the extent to which it should be pursued.

55. It is certain, then, that the rational attachment arising from contemplation of someone else's virtues is more perfect than the other attachments by which we are kindled to love[96] of neighbor. Love[97] of virtue is no slight mark of virtue. To give our consent to this attachment is therefore extremely useful, as much for rousing us to emulate those virtues— something quite easily aroused by attachment—as for rousing dread of vices, which turn sordid when considered by some- one who loves virtues. But I think our desire is neither dangerous nor harmful if it is directed according to this attach- ment. It is not an obstacle—on the contrary, it is very useful— for us to desire the presence of someone by whose example

---

96 *dilectio*
97 *amor*

we may be corrected if we are wicked, helped along if we are good, and strengthened by mutual conversation if we are equally advanced in perfection.

56. This temporal presence of holy persons is indeed to be desired and still more that [presence] which with Christ will be eternal in heaven. Although we may be roused to desire both by a similar attachment, we do not attain both by similar activity. We tend toward the physical presence of holy people, if they happen not to be present, by travelling some distance on earth, but we tend toward the eternal presence by living in a holy, just, and godly manner.[98] If, by the same attachment, we are therefore roused to each of these actions, the latter may follow its force without any hesitation as far as inward practices are concerned, for excess poses no threat to inward holiness. The outward practice of virtue, however, about which it has been said, *Do not be over just*[99], must be tempered by the moderation of reason.

Although usefully desired, the physical presence of holy people is not always sought in a useful way. Hence in this act we must heed reason, not follow attachment. How pleasing the physical presence of Paul and Barnabas was to the brethren at Antioch. They were instructed by their knowledge, strengthened by their example, and protected by their arguments against those who expounded different opinions. Still, when they heard these words from the Holy Spirit: *Set apart Barnabas and Saul for me for the work to which I have called them,*[100] they sent them off, laying their hands on them and praying, even though attachment fought against this. Did not Paul have proof of Timothy's attachment in the copious tears he shed? If the man had only given him his consent, Timothy should surely have followed closely upon Paul's tracks, even unreasonably. *I thank my God,* he said, *when I remember you. I remember your tears...that I may be filled with joy.*[101]

---

98 Tt 2:12
99 Qo 7:17
100 Ac 13:2
101 2 Tm 1:3–4

Chapter 25. The extent to which we should be wary of, or allow, dutiful attachments.

57. Next follows dutiful attachment, something more dangerous than the others which are allowable. If indeed it is to be allowed, we should be extremely cautious about it. For what is so deserving, so consonant with reason, as to make requital to someone who loves you, to render service to someone who shows you deference, to give thanks to someone who offers you gifts? Yet what should you be more wary of than fostering vices or fawning on someone riddled with vices once you are flattered by deference and enticed by gifts? This is not a matter of people who love gifts and seek rewards, and who, holding justice cheap, fawn over not a man but his favors. It is a matter of those who, touched by deference or gifts, cherish a certain inward attachment not to the gifts but to the man.

58. We should allow this attachment, I say, but we should also be wary of it. We should allow it, lest we be ungrateful for a service; we should be wary of it lest we reward not so much the man as the vice. Furthermore, however much discretion should be observed in accepting gifts or tokens of deference, we must be careful about the attachment that moves us toward someone from whose kind deeds we derive benefit, or by whose deference we are aided. The worthiness of the person himself should be very carefully examined, so that, if he is perhaps deserving, dutiful attachment may be turned into rational, and someone we started to love because he pleased us may begin to be loved because he is endowed with virtues.

59. It happens sometimes, as we said before, that because of outward austerity even the best of men does not easily inspire attachment in the heart of someone regarding him. If, after some occasion presents itself, we have experienced his generosity toward us, the attachment which his austerity somehow held down and concealed is stirred, without our being aware of it, and awakened. Then the virtue which first

pleased us, but we did not savor, works its way in by its pleasantness and floods the attachment like the palate of the heart. Even though it may be attracted to something else, it takes delight in it and savors it in a marvelous way. If he should by chance be someone with no pleasing virtue, the attachment should be allowed to the degree that correction may be hoped for. The simple affection that embraces someone irrespective of any other grounds must in all circumstances be tempered, even though it has been set in motion by, and continues for, some determinable reasons.

Let requital for deference of gifts be made to each person according to reason and not according to attachment. So, too, let the desire by which the presence of each is desired, or the activity by which their presence is obtained, follow reason and not attachment.

Chapter 26. The measure to be kept in natural attachment; what it means to love 'in God' and 'for God's sake'.

60. Now let us examine quite carefully the measure to be observed in natural attachments. Just as it is clearly impossible not to allow this attachment, so not to follow it is the summit of virtue. No one has ever hated himself, and yet, *Anyone who comes to me,* said the Saviour, *and does not hate his own life cannot be my disciple.*[102] Likewise, *Anyone who comes to me and does not hate his father and mother cannot be my disciple.*[103]

The apostle, on the other hand, says: *Anyone who does not provide for his relatives, especially if they live with him, has disowned the faith and is worse than an unbeliever.*[104] What then? Should master and disciple, servant and Lord, very Truth

---

102 Lk 14:26
103 *Ibid.*
104 1 Tm 5:8

and Truth's friend, be thought to have had contrary points of view? Far from it!

61. Between these two loves[105] about which we have spoken above, a distinction must be made: the one [is] according to attachment; the other according to reason. It is natural for a person to have an attachment for himself and his own [relatives], but one ought not form his love according to attachment. It ought rather to be according to reason. This attachment was meant when the apostle said, *No one has ever hated his own flesh.*[106] Yet love according to attachment is forbidden on the authority of the Saviour himself, who said, *Anyone who comes to me and does not hate his father and mother, yes, and even his own life, cannot be my disciple.*[107] Love according to reason was indicated when the apostle said, *Anyone who does not provide for his relatives, especially if they live with him, has disowned the faith and is worse than an unbeliever.*[108]

Love according to attachment was denounced when Paul, foretelling ills to come, said among other things: *There will be persons who will love themselves.*[109] The following words teach us that here he understood this as love according to attachment: *For there will be persons who love themselves, who will be avaricious, proud....who will love pleasure rather than God.*[110] Attachment always suggests things that are pleasant[111] and soft. It willingly embraces what is delightful and tender, what is pleasurable and delicate. But anything arduous and harsh, anything that goes against self-will, it flees in utter dread and avoids. Hence, following this attachment through is perverse love; it strips a person of his humanness and vests him in animal form, destroying in a way and hiding every

---

105 *amores*
106 Eph 5:29
107 Lk 14:26
108 1 Tm 5:8
109 2 Tm 3:1–2
110 2 Tm 3:2–4
111 *suavis*

trace of reason, of integrity, and ultimately, of usefulness. This love is characteristic of beasts, and excusable in children, because reason has not been bestowed on the former and is dormant in the latter.

In only a few words, the Saviour himself amply distinguished between these two loves. *Anyone who loves his life will lose it,* he said, *and anyone who hates his life in this world will find it in life eternal.*[112]

Furthermore, as the saint said: *If you have loved badly, then you have hated; if you have hated well, then you have loved.*[113] Anyone who loves according to attachment we might say, hates, because *anyone who loves iniquity hates his soul.*[114] But anyone who hates according to attachment loves according to reason. To this he added *in this world,* because *everything that is in the world is concupiscence of the flesh* or *concupiscence of the eyes* or *pride of life.*[115]

So anyone who loves his soul according to attachment loves it in the world because he loves it in concupiscence of the flesh, in concupiscence of the eyes, and in pride of life. All these things are inspired by attachment.

62. By this distinction an explanation is also given to this question some people ask: What is the difference between the love which is 'in God' and that which is shown 'for God's sake'. Surely, attachment is not taken on for God's sake, but arises in the soul itself either naturally or accidentally. Hence, if all one's love is shown someone on whom his spirit lavishes itself by some spontaneous, pleasant inclination according to attachment, that person is loved neither in God nor for God's sake, but rather for his own sake. But if the one whom that attachment encircles is also taken into a person's love of God, that love savors of attachment, but its expression is subject to the moderating control of reason. At the outset love of this

---

112 Jn 12:25
113 Augustine, *In Ioh. tract.* 51.10
114 Ps 10:6 (11:5)
115 1 Jn 2:16

person is not taken on for God's sake, but it is exercised in God in a wholesome way. Moreover, if in regard for the divine precept we have shown this, as we ought, to someone whom our [personal] attachment rejects and avoids, and if we oblige him in everything reason dictates proportionate to his needs, that person is loved not for his own sake, but solely for God's.

63. And so, let the friend whom it is impossible for us not to love, be loved in God, and let the enemy whom it is impossible to love for his own sake be loved for God's sake; the first, in virtue of attachment and the second in virtue of reason. Let this moderation be observed in natural attachment, so that we may possess and feel it, but that it may be tempered toward everyone and in every circumstance by the moderating control of reason.

Finally, holy Joseph first declared his natural attachment for his brothers by his tears.[116] If this saintly man had put reason aside and followed his attachment, his brothers would never have been exculpated by salutary affliction of their crime of betrayal. The Saviour, too, inspired by tender-loving attachment to his people, wept with wonderful compassion over the city which was going to be destroyed.[117] Yet because of his strict justice, he chastised the same city's crime with a very great calamity.

64. If only those who govern the Church would chastise their own attachments according to this rule! Many of them surround their relatives with an all too human attachment. Not only do they fail to restrain them with any strictness from the vanity and pleasure of the world, but, still worse, with damnable presumption they even provide them with the wherewithal to satisfy their passions—from the very price of Christ's blood. What a sad thing! To enter the homes of some of our bishops—and still more shameful, of some of our monks—is like entering Sodom and Gomorrah.[12*] Effeminate, coiffeured young men, dressed up like courtesans, strut around with

---

116 Gen 42:24
117 Lk 19:41

their rumps half bare. Scripture says about them: *They have put the boys in brothels.*[118] Amidst the wantonness of such as these your blood is received, Lord Jesus, your cross is lifted up, your wounds are laid open, the price of your death is squandered. So they can go around with hunting dogs and hawking falcons and lathered horses, your sides are laid bare in the persons of poor people, your scourgings are mocked, your entrails are poured out.

You see these things, my Jesus. You see them and you remain silent. But surely you will not keep silent forever? *No,* you say, *I shall groan as a woman in labor.*[119] But let us return to our subject.

Chapter 27. Physical attachment; that it should be neither utterly rejected nor completely allowed.

65. Physical attachment, which comes from a certain charm in the outward man, should therefore neither be rejected utterly nor allowed just as it gushes out. This attachment is akin to the one that leads to vices; unless a person stays rather prudently on guard, it will slip in almost without being noticed by the person affected.

Provided it is allowed grudgingly and with some degree of moderation, this attachment is wholesomely allowed, therefore, to this end: that if virtue shines out in a person, it may be more easily embraced; but that if, on the other hand, vice [shows up], one may insist more strongly on its correction. We think everything we have said about dutiful attachment should be thought to apply equally to this type. This attachment should, however, be deliberately rejected by those who are still being assailed by vices of the flesh. For them to experience it without some titillation of vice is extremely rare.

---

118 Jl 3:3
119 Is 42:14

Chapter 28. An examination of the origin of the attachments and also their development and end, and examples of how one kind of attachment leads to another.

66. Not only must we examine the origin of these attachments, but we must also give discerning attention to their development and their end. Very subtly sometimes one of them springs up and finishes by becoming another or, at least, is changed. It suffices to show this by two or three examples. Someone's interest is aroused by hearing about a nun extolled for her holiness of body and spirit, her sincere faith, her outstanding discretion, her rock-solid virtue of humility even to complete disregard for herself, her remarkable abstinence, her excellent obedience. In admiration for such great virtues, one venerates her with the strongest attachment.[13]* Earlier, we termed this attachment 'rational'. If one should begin to develop a familiarity with her, to honor her with deference, to seek diversion in conversing with her, to have frequent contact with her by keepsakes or letters or little gifts, that rational attachment imperceptibly changes into dutiful attachment. She whom one began to love because her holiness deserved it begins to be frequented for mutual favors. Then as this attachment extends to flattering compliments, even that physical attachment which is more dangerous than the others creeps in at vice's temptation.

67. I have known it to happen to very chaste ascetic men who detested every trace of dissoluteness with the greatest horror that, when they noticed those of tender years arriving at the summit of virtue and unbelievably attaining, if I may say so, spiritual grey hair by their remarkable gravity of conduct and holiness of life, they cherished and embraced them with very devoted and very dear attachment. As they ceded to them more influence over themselves, and with increasing pleasure found repose at the sight of them (and I might say, their embrace), they have very often been quite insidiously tormented by a vice-prone attachment. Those who, I do not say,

would not countenance others equally guilty of that crime, but far more would cast them with the greatest horror from the bosom of their nauseated soul—these very modest, very sober men, these serene men with perhaps even maidenly decorum, whom no unchaste person could glance at without shame for his own hopeless condition—could scarcely keep company with them without some titillation of vice.[14*]

68. Why is this? Surely because one attachment changes into another more easily than either an unchaste person can esteem someone with a chaste breast or someone manifestly chaste can be attracted to someone unchaste. Hence when our attachment, however rational or even spiritual, extends itself to someone of suspect age or sex, it is extremely advisable that it be held back within the bosom of the mind and not permitted to spill over into inane compliments or soft tenderness, unless perhaps, because of this, the attachment may occasionally develop maturely and temperately until virtue loved and praised may be more fervently practised.

Chapter 29. Various attachments very often struggle in the same mind; which is to be given preference is made clear by examples.

69. It must now be said about attachments that several of them sometimes war in a single mind, and in some way strive to best one another. When this happens, great discernment is necessary that a person may recognize which [attachment] is to be preferred. Virtue is also needed that a higher [attachment] may not be driven out by an inferior. So it was that Abraham, ordered to immolate his own son, lacked no natural attachment and did by no means become hardened towards his own flesh and blood. But when the natural attachment by which he cherished his son and the spiritual attachment with which he cherished God warred with one another in this holy

man's breast,[120] he set the higher above the lower. Rather, he scorned the lower because of the higher.

Or again, it was not with the intention of doing injury to his father that Jonathan, that outstanding young man, betrayed the plot by which [Saul] had marked David out for death—[David] to whom he was linked by a sacred pact.[121] By legitimate right he put rational attachment before natural. No wonder that in his ever-holy breast favor[122] for his friend wiped out his attachment to his father. Because of it, he scorned with unswerving courage the harm to himself that people imputed to him. Finally, when this man of invincible charity hurried to the hiding place to meet David when he was fleeing Saul, as he was about to reveal his father's plot to him, they both burst into tears, embracing and kissing one another. With sincere weeping they declared their tender attachment. After they had renewed their pact, Jonathan spoke out: *You shall be king and I shall be second after you.*[123] O man worthy of being proclaimed with highest praise! Man free of envy, devoid of self-centeredness, who preferred a friend to a kingdom! Who wished that what seemed to be his should belong to another! *I*, he said, *shall be second after you.*

70. O breast of sublime humility! A man of royal seed who by right of succession could hope for inheritance, for whom rank of birth, courage, the favor of warriors, and the acclamation of the people had increased the expectation of arriving at the height of power—as also had the admirable renown of that triumph when, assisted by only one attendant, he infiltrated the armed troops of the enemy lines and gained an unhoped-for victory for his people! Lowering himself even beneath a servant, he said, *You shall be king, and I shall be second after you.* He, I repeat, in whose praise [people] even today sing: *The arrow of Jonathan never turned back and*

---

120 Gn 22
121 1 S 20
122 *gratia*
123 1 S 23:17

[Saul's] sword did not return empty,[124] said, *You shall be king
and I shall be second after you*—as though he were overlook-
ing himself to give recognition to his friend.

Who, I ask you, would have such thoughts even about his
own blood brother without frightful envy? Who, for the sake
of a friend, would reduce so great a hope to renunciation? The
sons of the patriarch Jacob, inordinately envying the favor
which their father lavished on one [of them] more fondly than
the others, brought slavery down on their brother and sadness
on their father.[125]

The high priest, led on by his prophetess sister to disparage
his meek brother out of envy, only barely escaped divine
vengeance, unless I am mistaken, and then only because of
Moses' prayer.[126] The ever-wise Solomon seized an opportunity to do away with his brother, a rival for his kingdom.[127]

Jonathan alone had less esteem for his father, his country,
and his kingdom than for his friend, and said, *You shall be
king and I shall be second after you.* If he had said, 'I shall be
king and you shall be second after me', he would have violated neither the law of friendship nor his friend's love. *They
both wept,* Scripture says, *but David wept more.*[128]

71. That separation, certainly more bitter than death, which
was to deprive those two hearts of the sight of one another
was close at hand. Because of it their enjoyable conversations
had to end, as did the consolation that sustained them in all
their dangers and that confiding of mutual secrets which is
preferable to life itself. And so they both wept. I ask you, look
at this man with such well-ordered love. Jonathan owed
attachment to his friend, but deference to his father. He owed
his friend favor, but his aged father protection. If he had
followed his attachment and clung to his friend he would have
betrayed the rights of a father's love. Yet if, when warned—or

---

124 2 S 1:22
125 Gn 37:28
126 Nb 12:1–13
127 1 Kg 2:25
128 1 S 20:41

still more, forced—by his father, he had withdrawn his favor from his friend, he would have violated the pact he had made with him and also the law of most sacred friendship. Being together was pleasing to both of them because of their attachment, but separation was agreeable to them because of reason. By weeping, they paid what they owed to attachment, but by separating, even though forced to do so, they yielded to reason. Both wept because each loved. Why then did David weep more? Jonathan had surely somehow foretold his own demise and his friend's increase, that he would be deprived of his kingdom and that David would come into possession of it. The law of friendship, therefore, required the one to weep with compassion over the wrong done to his friend, but the other, in order not to seem to grieve over his friend's success, held his tears back a little.

He put natural attachment before rational attachment, but he set his action in order according to reason. After David's loyal army had reported its victory over his parricidal son, he too yielded to natural attachment and mourned the death of his son.[129] Yet, when one of his soldiers rebuked him for this, he put dutiful attachment before natural, and set aside his grief to go out to meet and to celebrate with his victorious people.[130]

72. Even our Saviour, when—because of the natural attachment by which no one has ever hated his own flesh—he cried out: *Father, if it be possible, let this chalice pass from me,*[131] he subjected it by right of reason to the spiritual [attachment] by which he forever clung to his Father. *Still,* he said, *not as I will, but as you will.*[132] In these attachments, therefore, this rationale must be kept: that the one by whom our spirit is urged towards God is to be put before all others. Next, rational [attachment] is to be put before dutiful, dutiful before natural, and natural before physical.

---

129 Cf. 2 S 19:1
130 2 S 19:6–9
131 Mt 26:39
132 *Ibid.*

Chapter 30. What utility is to be sought in attachments.

73. Now that we have carefully examined these things which have been said about the distinctions among the attachments, it is clear, if I am not mistaken, that we should ask what utility is to be sought in them. Surely it is that we may be urged on by these attachments, as by goads of love, to desire those things which should be loved; that we may maintain this love more agreeably, and consequently more diligently, by the infused sweetness of the attachment; and that we may thus practise those acts by which we tend toward the object of desire with greater attachment to the extent there is greater pleasure, and with greater pleasure to the extent there is greater fervor.

Even if desire itself has been aroused by attachment, only very rarely should it follow this attachment, as we have shown above. Likewise it is of the greatest utility to be urged on by attachment to practise good works and to be sustained in these good works by attachment. Regulating these works according to attachment, however, is contrary to order.

It remains for us to say a few words commensurate with our modest capabilities about setting works in order according to reason. Desire itself is uniformly a matter of reason. It is felt only in the love which comes from attachment, whereas in the love coming from reason it is weighed by the will alone.

Chapter 31. By what acts we should tend toward God, and by which we should have concern for ourselves and our neighbor.

74. There are certain actions by which we strive toward that infinite good which we should love above all else and desire above all else. There are other [actions] in which we are concerned for either our own needs or the needs and salva-

tion of our neighbors. Yet we have no doubt whatever that this latter precaution is equally to be referred to the same end. The apostle seems to have suggested the whole condition of the life of perfection in a few words when he said: *Let us live soberly, justly, and godly in this world.*[133] Sobriety is a certain measure in human living, or temperance which prudently avoids extremes in both directions and leads us on our course along the royal road, between right and left. The sages of this world call this virtue 'frugality', and the most eloquent of them all explained its excellence lucidly enough: *Let everyone understand this as he wishes,* he said, *I think that frugality— that is, moderation and temperance—is the greatest virtue.*[15*]

Since the One toward whom we are tending above all is in a way infinite moderation,—to him nothing is lacking, nothing is an obstacle, in him there is nothing excessive and nothing lacking—when we reach him there will be nothing outside which we desire and nothing within which we shun. We really must maintain ourselves in a certain moderation or measure or we will either go to our ruin from having less than is necessary or, with disastrous presumption, will exalt ourselves from having more than we should.

75. The justice I think the apostle means here is that [justice] by which we have concern for the needs or salvation of our neighbor. Discerning which acts of kindness are fitting for each and which person is to be given precedence over another, we accord to each what is just. So that neither philosophers nor anyone else foreign to the faith of Christ may glory in these two virtues—sobriety, that is, and justice—he very judiciously added godliness, which consists in sincere faith and pure intention. Now this intention seems to consist of the choice made by love, which we have already talked about. Here, perhaps, the reader may ask us to explain in greater detail this moderation of life which it seems dangerous, even ruinous, to exceed. Can anyone not see how arduous and difficult it is to deal with this, when there are as many human

---

133 Tt 2:12

aptitudes as there are human beings, and it is very rare to find even two at a time for whom all things are equally suited. What is enough for one is too little for another. What is profitable for one is harmful to another. And what is necessary for one appears superfluous for another. Yet it seems something must be said that suits everyone, something each [person] can adapt for himself. And with reason as his guide, he can draw conclusions whether he is exceeding the necessary moderation in his life.

Chapter 32. Beginning to treat moderation of human life, [Aelred] shows what sobriety should be observed in the natural order.

76. Three orders of human life therefore come to mind.[16*] The first is natural, the second necessary, and the third voluntary. The first is conceded, the second imposed, and the third is offered [to humankind]. The first depends on enablement, the second on necessity, and third on will. To the first grace is due, to the second mercy, and to the third glory. But let us develop as lucidly as we can what it seems should be said about each of them.

77. There exists a natural order. That is, if a person who has not committed illicit actions so chooses, he may make use of everything licit, provided [he does so] licitly. For example, eating flesh meat and drinking wine are licit, as are also the use of marriage and the possession of riches. As the apostle said: *To the pure all things are pure,*[134] and *nothing which is accepted with thanksgiving should be rejected.*[135] Heretics who forbid marriage and order people to abstain from food which God created for his faithful to receive with thanksgiving[136] are condemned by the same apostle.

---

134 Tt 1:15
135 1 Tm 4:3–4
136 *Ibid.*

So that use of these things may be licit, moderation must be observed, and rather careful attention given to circumstances of time and place and the nature[137] of the thing. Moderation is to be sensibly observed by everyone and under no circumstances should anyone exceed it. The Saviour himself commanded, *Watch yourselves, that your hearts be not weighed down with dissipation and drunkenness and the cares of this life.*[138] And on the use of marriage, Paul said, *Let each one of you know how to possess his vessel in holiness and honor, not in the passion of desire.*[139] And on the use of clothing, Peter wrote: *Not in expensive clothes.*[140]

In using licit things, therefore, this moderation should be respected, so that in taking food or drink a person refrains from overeating and intoxication, in possessing wealth he puts aside anxious preoccupation, in using marriage he avoids ignominious passions, and in choosing clothing he looks not to the price but to the need.

The time suitable for making use of each of these must also be taken into account. For example, during those seasons when Church tradition orders the faithful to abstain from food, fasting should not be broken without reasonable need; at the times when one should be free for necessary prayer one should not exercise marriage rights; on those days which the authority of christian tradition has consecrated to salutary leisure for listening to the Word of God one should not be intent on worldly concerns, and on those days which our holy religion has set aside for expressing sadness and penance by a change of vestments one should not inappropriately wear festive garments.

Place should also be taken into consideration every time something necessary is used. Who would not consider it sacrilegious to pass one's time idly at a banquet in church, or exercise marriage rights there, or carry on business? Writing to

---

137 *genus*
138 Lk 21:34
139 1 Th 4:4–5
140 1 P 3:3, cf. 1 Tm 2:9

the Corinthians, the apostle upbraided them for not having kept to the legitimate times in taking food and drink: *When you meet together,* he said, *it is not to eat the Lord's supper. Each person presumes to eat his own meal.*[141]

Those who dared to take ordinary food before receiving the Eucharist, contrary to apostolic decree, did not keep to the appropriate time. Reproaching the same people also for exceeding moderation, he added: *One goes hungry while another is drunk.*[142]

Then, reprimanding them for contempt for the place they were, he said, *Surely you have houses where you can eat and drink? Or do you have contempt for the church of God?*[143]

78. Finally, we must make finer distinctions about the kind of things it is licit to use. Not that anyone may consider any of God's creatures impure without impious sacrilege, but because using things that are known to have been offered in sacrifice to demons, or something we are sure has been taken from others by theft or plunder, would give the wicked or the weak the impression that we consent to wrong-doing, holy authority obliges us to abstain from them. Hence the apostle says: *If someone tells you, 'This has been offered to idols', do not eat it.*[144] When the holy Tobias—whose eyes were impaired, it is true, but who was perfectly sound of mind— recognized the bleating of the kid which his wife had brought home as pay for her work, and feared that by eating it illicitly he would wrong someone else and bring down the stain of sin on himself, he said, *Take heed, perhaps it has been stolen.*[145]

These things, then, may be said about the natural order. Although we have not noted down in our remarks all the things people may licitly use, from those we have mentioned,

---

141 1 Co 11:20–21
142 1 Co 11:21
143 1 Co 11:22
144 1 Co 10:28
145 Tb 2:13

anyone who investigates carefully will discover the moderation that should be kept in other areas. Now let us glance at other matters in the necessary order.

Chapter 33. The measure of satisfaction and amendment in the necessary order is described.

79. Necessary order means that someone who has committed illicit acts should restrict himself in the use of things licit. In this restriction, two things should be considered: the measure of satisfaction, and the need for amendment. The measure of satisfaction, so that the severity of the mortification may be proportionate to the measure of the fault and that, attentive to the voice of the Baptist, *we may bear fruit befitting repentance.*[146] I will refrain from saying anything more about the kind of satisfaction, since it pertains to pastoral care. Books have been written on the subject by our holy Fathers and obligations prescribed.

Not only must a moderation of satisfaction be maintained, but the need for amendment should also be analyzed. Not only must we show restraint in things licit solely for satisfaction's sake, but we must also pursue laborious efforts to get rid of, or to diminish, any passions which have taken root in us because of bad habits. The disciplines of the outward person are tools for the inward person. By them the vice-ridden passions that infect the very soul itself are more easily cut way, and the smudges on our inward countenance are more completely cleansed away, as if by some rather harsh detergent.

The first thing necessary for a person concerned about his amendment is to turn his attention to those passions by which he is attacked, then to look at those which weary him most, and finally, with sagacious vigilance, to analyze the tools by which to counteract these passions more effectively. After

---

146 Mt 3:8

examining these things, to each passion he should oppose an appropriate tool. To whatever attacks him most he should apply himself with unremitting persistence that he may overcome it.

Restricting the stomach easily subdues the passion of sensual desire. The fatigue of vigils strengthens the wandering and unstable heart. Silence tempers anger, and application to work holds tedium of mind at bay. All one's energy should not be bent on extinguishing one single passion to the point that our tool, the body, is not up to subduing the others. Nor should one work so stubbornly that no passion at all is felt, but so that when passion does raise its head it may be curbed in keeping with the judgement of reason.

We need touch on the measure of amendment only briefly. Over and beyond this, anyone who wants to know more about how to combat vices and remedy them should read the book of John Cassian entitled *Instructions for renunciants.*[147] There, with his brilliant pen, he has described their origin, the means of combatting them, and the remedy for getting rid of them.

Chapter 34. What the voluntary order is, and the measure to be observed in it.[17*]

80. It follows that we should next examine the voluntary order, about which the psalmist said: *How willingly shall I offer sacrifice to you.*[148] There is an unforced holocaust,[18*] an acceptable offering, a voluntary sacrifice,[19*] when someone makes his way with liberty of spirit upward from the things that are conceded through those which are prescribed, to those which are proposed to all who long for the rewards of greater glory. To this pinnacle of perfection the Saviour

---

147 *De institutis coenobiorum,* Books V–XII.
148 Ps 53:8 (54:6)

invited the more fervent when he said, *If you want to be perfect, go, sell what you own, and give the money to the poor, and come, follow me.*[149] And elsewhere, *There are eunuchs who have made themselves that way for the sake of the kingdom of heaven, Let anyone who can accept this, accept it.*[150] Renunciation of the world, a resolution to observe chastity, and profession of a stricter life are therefore reckoned among voluntary sacrifices. Although entrance into the kingdom of heaven is not open to someone who looks back after renouncing the world, although no defilement of the flesh is licit after a promise of chastity, although it would be ruinous to slide back into more lax habits after resolving to lead a stricter life, still, be careful to reckon this perfection of life—[a life] which one undertakes not under compulsion but willingly— not to be among things necessary and obligatory, but rather among the voluntary. This necessity, which no one has imposed on him against his will, but to which he has spontaneously submitted himself in his desire for perfection, should be called voluntary and not compulsory.

81. Let someone who applies himself to these lofty and sublime pursuits first look carefully into the norm of his promise or resolution, that is, into what it consists of and what it demands. Then let him weigh it in the scales of his experience and discern the strength of both the outward and inward person. I call inward strength that by which he may combat the onslaughts of temptations by daily practice, and outward strength that by which he may endure the burdens of physical toil with an indefatigably even temper. Granted that in any state of life toil of both the inward and outward person is necessary for anyone making progress, still physical discipline (*corporalia*) cleanses the soul of the stains of the passions in a special way, while spiritual discipline (*spiritualia*), like some

---

149 Mt 19:21
150 Mt 19:12

heavenly aromatic spices, steep it in the pleasantness of spiritual fragrance.

Since the sweetness of that ointment is not fitting for someone soiled by the squalor of vice, it is certain, then, that affliction of the outward man is more necessary for a person still under attack from the passions of the flesh. Once these passions have been lulled or quenched, one may temper one's outward discipline a bit and practise spiritual exercises more persistently and fervently. Yet not in such a way that he presumptuously exceeds the norm of his profession or abolishes or changes around the distinctions of fixed times prescribed by the Rule to which he has submitted himself. Rather, observing the times designated for each discipline, he is to practise them either more quietly or more fervently, as he knows them to be useful to himself.

Chapter 35. Refutation of a letter of a certain person about the rule and profession of monks.

82. Although it may not seem completely pertinent to our subject, I think it advisable for us who are called monks to take into account and examine more closely the force of our rule. Since many things are said there about things spiritual and physical, let us investigate by careful questioning which of these the force of the rule and the norm of our profession consist of most particularly.

I read a letter on this subject by a certain person who replied as follows to someone who had questioned him on this:

I do not hesitate to say that the rule of the monastic state, yes the virtue of the monastic order, indeed, the essential character of monastic profession itself, consists in those practices which make the monk when all others cease to exist, and without which the others, I will not say do not *make* a monk, but do not even give an idea of what a monk is.

83. But what are these? The things we have solemnly promised and whose stability and observance we have sworn to God and his saints [to keep]. And what are they?

Stability in the monastery, he says, conversion of our life, and obedience according to the Rule of Saint Benedict. And further on, [he adds]: I want to go back to Saint Benedict's book for monks and I will point out in it how the things which we have already stated constitute the essential character of our rule and, even more, of our monastic profession, so my mind may comprehend them as necessary; I will strive with complete devotion to fulfill my promises and those things which I have vowed—to the extent that the Lord will grant this to me. But as for the other things, I will try to accomplish them, not as part of the body of our rule, but as practices which support and sustain it.

84. We would perhaps be in doubt as to what those other things are, had he not himself introduced them afterwards: not to go out of the cloister, to practise manual work, the quantity of food and drink, the number of dishes and their variety. the bedding, the use of trousers[20]* only by those sent on a journey.

What then, he says? If these are of the essential character of monastic profession, dispensing someone from them or changing any of them on occasion would not be allowed, would it? Otherwise, no essential character exists, and I am discovered not to be a monk once I have destroyed in myself what is essential to being a monk.

At the end of his tractate, he says:

So then, beloved brother, so then, since it is permitted to give dispensation in these matters, just as blessed Benedict himself also dispensed monks of delicate health to eat meat, and those sent on a journey, at least, to wear trousers, so also, I say, that because these matters admit of dispensation and change, they are not part of the essential character of profession.

That is what he said.

85. Whether what he has said about the use of trousers and the use of meat ought to be called dispensations or institutions of blessed Benedict, he really should see for himself. Certainly he taught compassion for the aged and children, not as a dispensation but by the authority of the Rule.[151] The authority of the Rule, he says, makes provision for them. But let us return to what we were previously discussing.

What he has called the body of the Rule and the essential character of monastic profession is clear: stability, conversion of life, and obedience according to the Rule of Saint Benedict. But I wonder why he said nothing about *lectio*, when he talked about the things that he called not the Rule itself but support for it. Since *lectio* can be dispensed, it is clear that, according to him, it does not pertain to the body of the Rule.

Since therefore manual labor, the quantity of bread and beverage, the number of portions, the way of dressing, the length of vigils, the quality of the bedclothes, the heaviness of the silence, the length of reading, the inflection of psalms, the prolonged fasts, and reception of guests, and anything else of this type should not be considered either the body of the Rule or essential to monastic profession; and since in these matters many dispensations and changes can be discovered—to the point that most monasteries practise none of them in a way that is in every detail prescribed by the Rule—where, I ask you, where in the Rule am I to find the body of the Rule and the essential character of monastic profession? Is the Rule as a whole not composed of all these together and indeed almost of these alone?

86. You will say, only those things we profess do I call the body of the Rule or the essential character of monastic profession; that is, the three things we mentioned above.

Can no dispensation be given for a change of place? Why is it then that, after the Rule had already been written and imposed, Father Benedict himself sent Maur into Gaul? If I had read a reference to a change like this in the Rule, I would think

---

151 RB 37

it should be called not a dispensation from, but rather an institution of, the Rule. But now that I find this was not prescribed by the Rule, but done after the Rule had been instituted, why should I not freely call it a dispensation, since he classifies eating meat, which the authority of the Rule grants in a general way to the sickly, as a dispensation? Do we not hear about dispensations like this being granted by our abbots every day? How often monks are transferred by a dispensation from their abbots, I do not say from monastery to monastery, but even from region to region.How then can stability of place susceptible to such frequent dispensations pertain to the body of our Rule and the essential character of monastic profession?

Why is it that those raised to the clerical state are ordinarily freed by ecclesiastical authority, I will not say from stability as concerns place, but from obedience to their own abbot? Doesn't so great a change destroy the essential character of the monk? What is the dispensation connected with stability that will, if granted, destroy the essential character of the monk?

He will perhaps answer: if a monk moves around from one monastery to another without his abbot's consent, when no danger to his salvation compels him to do so. Is this really a dispensation, and not more a prevarication? If it is not prevarication, I continue to insist that such a change does not destroy 'the monk'.

87. Perhaps he will think better of his argument then, and affirm that these three elements constitute the essential character of monastic profession not because they do not admit of dispensation, but because the monk professes these alone.

For the time being let us concede this. Let us say that the body of the Rule and the essential character of a monk consist of stability, conversion of life, and obedience according to the Rule of Saint Benedict. I ask that we shake hands for now and look more closely into what this stability, conversion of life, and obedience are.

88. I would still like to know whether he thinks that the monk professes the first two according to the Rule in the same

way as he does obedience, or whether these are professed simply in an indeterminate way. I would not think the question worthy of inquiry at all, had I not come across some monks who claim they have made profession in such a way—that is, that they have promised only obedience according to the Rule and the other two not according to the Rule but in some indeterminate way.

Since the Rule of Saint Augustine, to which the canons [regular] submit when making profession, is one thing, and the Rule of Saint Benedict, to which monks submit, is another, I ask what difference there is between profession of each? Both [canons and monks] profess stability, conversion of life, and obedience. If the first two are made in an indeterminate way, the Rule of Saint Benedict would seem to differ from other rules only as regards the profession of obedience.

Then is obedience one thing according to the Rule of Saint Benedict, and another according to the Rule of Saint Augustine? Blessed Benedict recommends obedience, which he wants to be neither tardy nor tepid, neither morose nor grumbling, unwavering in the face of injuries and adversities, and unflagging even in the face of death. Is it something different according to the Rule of Saint Augustine? Is what a priest owes a bishop, a bishop an archbishop, an archbishop the bishop of bishops any different? May that be either tardy or tepid, morose or grumbling? May it waver in the face of injuries or adversities? May it flag in the face of death?

What constitutes the difference between these professions, therefore? Or does obedience according to the Rule perhaps mean being subject to this Rule's precepts, for which those professing other rules are not accountable? In that case, what are these precepts?

89. If he is speaking about things having to do with charity, humility, patience, and other virtues, who—I do not say what canon, but even what Christian—is not obligated to these precepts? Does Benedict recommend one kind of charity in his Rule and Augustine another in his? Does not each recommend that charity which Christ recommends in the law and

the Gospel? We can ask the same thing about the other virtues. Who in his right mind, in exhorting others to virtue, will say that these precepts are his and not rather those of Christ? What difference will there be then among the precepts of the different Rules? Surely, how to eat, dress, work, read, keep vigil, sing psalms, correct and be corrected, and other things like this, because they are found to be different in the different rules. Consequently, things said to be especially characteristic of Basil or Augustine or Benedict are not imposed on all Christians by gospel authority, but are simply proposed to them. To those who profess these rules, however, they are no longer simply proposed, but they are also imposed on them.

90. If these are not the things, what are? Obviously, everything they put into their rules about charity, humility, and the other virtues, they recommend not as their own precepts, but as the Lord's. They invite not only monks but all Christians to follow them, not as being their own (for who would believe them?), but as being Christ's. If obedience according to the Rule of Saint Benedict means obeying the precepts of his Rule, and if the precepts of his Rule consist of the things we have enumerated above, how can anyone who does not keep them keep the essential character of the monastic profession, since that obedience we profess is the essential character of monastic profession?

91. He will perhaps say what certainly ought to be said: that we also profess the first two according to the Rule, and he will affirm that it is not in stability of place or obedience that diversity among the rules lies—since these same things are binding on monks, clerics, canons, and bishops—but solely in conversion of life. Is not one and the same obligation to stability incumbent upon all? Would anyone be so presumptuous as to transfer from one place to another without the consent of his superior? Furthermore, if we do profess conversion of life, not according to the Rule but simply in an indeterminate way, those who are called penitents in the Church do the same, as do those who flee the shipwreck of fornication

for the port of marriage. Who among them does not promise
conversion of life?

92. It remains for us to inquire what conversion of life
according to the Rule of Saint Benedict is. If we resort to
virtues here, so that, for example, a once proud person is
hereafter humble and a once hot-tempered person meek,
surely we can say that this conversion of life is enjoined not so
much on monks by the Rule of Saint Benedict as on all
Christians by the Gospel. Hence for some diversity to be
found among the diverse types of conversion of life which are
professed according to the diverse rules, there is nothing to
which we may have recourse except those traits which constitute the diversity among the diverse rules. On that we have
already said enough.

How then can anyone who does not keep these things keep
to his profession? Someone will say: if someone is proud,
stubborn, impatient, and yet observes all the things mentioned
above, must we say that he keeps the Rule of Saint Benedict? I
maintain that if a monk has committed any of these faults
against God's law, he will not be guilty of transgressing his
profession if he makes amends for them according to the
means prescribed by the Rule.

93. But what if someone looks at the Rule of Saint Benedict
as a tool for pruning away vices more easily and fulfilling the
gospel precepts more carefully, and yet, as could happen,
abusing this excellent tool, he neither prunes away his vices
nor acquires virtues by it. Does he not keep the Rule to his
peril then, and still not fulfill Christ's precepts? Does blessed
Benedict not allude to this? *We are going to establish*, he says,
*a school of the Lord's service, in which we hope not to institute
anything harsh or burdensome. If, however, some things are
rather strict...etc.*[152]

94. Now, first I ask: what is this strictness which he encourages beginners not to fear? He certainly confirms that what
he has established is situated in this strictness. If patience,

---

152 RB, Prologue

humility, and the other virtues were meant, would he say he was going to establish them, as though they were something new? Assuredly, there is nothing to which we have recourse except to the new practices he institutes. Neither the law nor the prophets nor Christ himself gave these precepts.

To beginners, of course, this strictness seems not inconsiderable when they think about the meager, paltry quantity of food and drink, the roughness of the clothing, the discomforts of fasts and vigils, the wearing grind of daily work, and all the other things we find he instituted in the Rule. If anyone does not agree that the Rule consists of these alone, at least let him admit what cannot be denied except by stubborn obstinacy: that our profession and Rule consist of both, that is, of virtues and observances, and let him therefore not refuse to admit that we necessarily practise both. However, the author of the Rule himself, in the words we have begun to consider, may seem to declare otherwise: *If following the dictates of sound reasoning,* he says, *for the correction of vices and the preservation of charity, something should turn out to be rather strict...*[153] I ask you, why are we seeking darkness in light? Why are we hunting for a knot in a bulrush?[154] Why are we groping along at noon as if it were night?

Is it not true in every institution that the institution itself is one thing and the reason for the institution another? Did he not make a very clear distinction between the institution and the reason for the institution? Does he not declare that the reason for his institution is the preservation of charity and the correction of vices?

95. Look now, another fellow at his side is speaking up.

Why do you throw the Rule up to me, he says. Have charity and do what you want.[21*]

Let us eat and drink, then, not because tomorrow we die, but because we are full of charity. Of charity, I ask, or vanity?

153 RB, Prologue
154 Cf. Terence, *Andria* 5.4.38

Well, you reply, if someone has charity, is he not fulfilling the Rule?

How many holy canons, holy priests, holy bishops, and also holy couples sense that they possess charity, but are very aware that they have not promised profession and do not keep the rule for monks? If, however, we are speaking about those who have made profession of the Rule itself, what is being said is true—if, that is, he understands what he is talking about.

Why then, you say, do you obligate me by the authority of the Rule to these harsh practices?

If you have charity it is not necessary for you to be forced to fulfill the promises which your lips have uttered.[155] If you scorn fulfilling the things you promised by putting your signature to them and calling on God and his saints as your witnesses, you can be very sure you do not have charity. For do you love someone you mock? If anyone does other than he has promised, he said, let him know that he will be condemned by the God whom he mocks.[156] What then? Do we condemn the dispensations granted in the Rule by our fathers, or those granted today? On the contrary, we allege that they can reasonably be granted because they arise from the precepts of a man, but not of God. But it is not within the prerogative of any man that he change or diminish any of the divine precepts.

We must carefully ward against letting a dispensation—a modification or variation—become in any way destruction. Since the reason for the institution itself is the safeguard of charity and the correction of vices, the dispensation will obviously be reasonable if it furthers this purpose. If, on the other hand, vices are fostered by the dispensation more than by the institution, charity is violated. Even if it may do no harm in itself, the dispensation is surely not without danger.

---

155 Cf. Ps 65(66):13
156 RB 58:18

Chapter 36. The measure to be kept in the voluntary order is likewise described.

96. Anyone who aspires to the summit of perfection in the voluntary order should first of all, and unceasingly, have in view that charity by which especially we approach God, indeed, by which we cleave to God and are conformed to him. In it the fullness of all perfection resides.[157] It is, as it were, the goal toward which he should direct his whole course. Next, he should strive with tireless alacrity of spirit toward its fullness by the way which the norm of his promise and profession prescribes for him. Let abstinence fight for this end, vigils serve it, *lectio* be alert for it, and daily toil sweat for it. If we realize that any one of them violates the charity for which they all have been established, then necessity obliges the one to whom granting dispensations has been entrusted so to adapt and arrange everything that this charity—the reason for them all—be not forsaken, but that its fruits be sought in all things. But unless some extreme necessity obliges him to do so, he should not so arrange things that any established practices are omitted, or that the fixed times assigned for certain disciplines are shifted around. Otherwise, it will be not dispensation, but disintegration. Yet he may modify certain exercises at certain times to the aptitudes and mental states of each person.[22*]

97. This is what the saint himself meant when he set out the rule about manual labor: *Let him so adapt and arrange everything that souls may be saved and that the brothers may do what they do without grumbling.*[158] And elsewhere: *Let all things be done with moderation because of the faint-hearted.*[159] Did he say that this or that should be omitted because of the faint-hearted? *Rather,* he said, *even to those who are sickly or delicate let some craft be assigned, so they will not be idle or discouraged by the hardness of the*

---

157 Rm 13:10
158 RB 41:5
159 RB 48:9

work.[160] Therefore, let those who are sickly and delicate do work, but let their work be tempered so they do not become discouraged. Whom, I ask you, has he completely freed from the work to which he obligated even the sickly or delicate?

It is obviously useful for everyone to observe moderation in these exercises, to do each so that he is not found wanting in others. Still, a person should practise with greater fervor the one that he feels is more profitable to him.

With regard to this, I have at hand the words of a certain sage, and I think it more suitable to insert here what I have before me than to compose some new declarations on the same subject.

Reflection on habits, he says, *considers first of all what is obligatory, whether they arise from a commandment or a vow. It decrees that we should first accomplish the things which are meritorious if we do them, and make us blameworthy if we do not do them. Things which cannot be set aside without fault should be done first. After these, if anything is added as voluntary practices, it should be done in such a way as not to hinder what is obligatory. Some people who cannot manage to do what they are obliged to do, want to do what they are not obliged to do. Others, although they manage to do what they ought to do, create willful impediments by wanting to do what is not obligatory. Likewise, in good actions one should especially be wary of two evils: anxiety and preoccupation. By anxiety, evenness of mind is embittered; by preoccupation, tranquillity is shattered. Anxiety occurs when, by impatience, a person frets about things he cannot manage to do. Preoccupation when, by intemperance, he is agitated when doing the things he can do. So that the spirit may not be detrimentally embittered, let it patiently endure its incapacity. So that it may not be detrimentally preoccupied, let it not push its capacities beyond their limits.*[161]

---

160 RB 48:24
161 Hugh of St Victor. *De meditatione* III,7; ed. R. Baron, SCh 155:57–59.

Chapter 37. What a person owes to himself, and what to his neighbor; an explanation of whether one should prefer himself to his neighbor or his neighbor to himself.

98. These things may be said about the measure to be observed in each degree, by which we strive toward the One who we realize should be loved above all else. We are concerned about the salvation of our soul and we allow the body what is owed it by nature. Moreover, since divine authority teaches us to love our neighbor as ourselves, it is first necessary for us not to fail to understand which order is appropriate for each [person]. Next, great care must be expended not to exceed the prescribed way of living in any given order. Still, because it is evident that some persons are superiors, others are subject to them, and others are peers,[23*] when any of these oversteps the legitimate measure, one who is subject should mention it to [his] superior, one peer should correct another, and a superior should even, if necessary, constrain a subject. The suggestion, or correction, or constraint, should itself be adapted to the nature of each person so that submission may be experienced in the suggestion, love in the correction, and compassion in the constraint.

Anyone who lives legitimately in a lower order may be advised to accede to a higher one, but he may not be forced [to do so]. Anyone who has freely submitted himself to a superior ought to be treated according to the measure of his profession, but he should not be compelled to [go on to] stricter measures without having his wishes taken into account. So also, in loving his neighbor, whom one ought to love as oneself, let him be careful not to exceed the measure of the love he ought to have for himself. This he does when he neglects the One whom he ought to love more than himself.

99. Nor should he listen to those who think that the words *you should love your neighbor as yourself*,[162] should be taken

---

162 Mk 12:31

[to mean] that a man should love each person as himself, and two or more persons more than himself, and consequently that he ought to will his own damnation, in preference to that of others. *What will a man give in exchange for his soul? For what will he gain if he wins the whole world*—even for salvation—*and suffers the loss of his own soul?*[163] We should also notice that according to the foregoing reasoning everything added to brotherly love would surely be subtracted from divine love. When love of self is weighed according to the measure by which a person loves God, he loves himself less only when he loves God less. Besides, someone who loves himself, whose damnation will he not prevent? How can someone who does not love himself love another as himself? When the Apostle said: *I would willingly be separated from Christ for the sake of my brothers in the flesh,*[164] he was revealing his attachment so he could draw them to salvation by manifesting his admirable charity; he was not expressing a well-considered decision.[165]

But we have adequately shown above how reason and attachment suggest different things to the same mind.

100. Hence, when the apostle said: *I would willingly be separated from Christ for the sake of my brothers,* he did speak the truth, because he was expressing the attachment he felt. If he had afterwards said, 'I would prefer that the whole world perish rather than that I alone be separated from Christ,' he would have spoken the truth no less, because he would have been revealing a well-considered decision of reason. Our Saviour himself, because of that attachment by which nobody has ever hated his own flesh[166]—that flesh which he voluntarily assumed from us and for us—also hoped that the hour of his passion would pass. By a well-considered decision of reason, however, he caused it not to pass.[167]

---

163 Mt 16:26
164 Rm 9:3
165 *consilium*
166 Eph 5:29
167 Cf. Mt 26:39

Scripture purposely does not say: '*You shall love your
neighbor as much as* yourself, but *as yourself*.[168] It prescribed the measure of love; it did not indicate how much
love. Yet let someone's love for himself be shown in such a
way that he has concern first of all for the salvation of his soul,
which is the principal part of himself, and then for what is
necessary for the body. If necessity occasionally obliges him
to disdain one of the two, let him suffer even destruction of
the body as long as he does not suffer loss of his soul. This is
not hating the body but, in love, preferring the soul to the
body. So let a man never draw back from love of himself, but
rather, holding on to it steadfastly and perseveringly, let him
arrive with sureness at concern[169] for his neighbor.

101. Let him adopt a measure for this concern by the rule by
which he concerns himself with himself. As much as possible,
let him deal with his neighbor, therefore, that he may be
sound in body and healthy in mind. If he neglects either of
these, he certainly does not love his neighbor who is composed of both.[24*] But if his neighbor is such a person who
cannot attain salvation of soul without some detriment to the
body, let him endure with compassion and heartbreak the
destruction of his [neighbor's] flesh that his spirit[170] may be
saved on the day of the Lord. Certainly, by no reason
or precept is he obligated to procure the salvation of his
brother's soul at the expense of his own soul, or to avert the
destruction of his brother's body by the destruction of his
own. That we are commanded *to lay down our souls for our
brothers*[171] refers to scorn for life, not loss of soul. It is laid
down not for perdition, but for salvation. Hence, laying down
one's soul this way is the same as having concern for one's
soul. Those who ward off the temporal death of their temporal
masters by their own temporal death do this rightly when they
do it not so much for the safety of the other person's body as

---

168 Mk 12:31
169 *consulendum*
170 *spiritus*
171 1 Jn 3:16

for the salvation of his soul. Their conscience is so convinced that they should keep faith with their masters that in such danger they think their lives are to be preferred to their own. Those, however, who do this not to keep faith, but to grasp glory or avoid dishonor, do it foolishly. They do it not to save the other person's body but to gain the reward of a reputation for themselves. It can happen, perhaps praiseworthily, that for love[172] alone a person may sacrifice his own body for the body of another. Yet for him to suffer the loss of his own soul—not, I say, for the salvation of one soul, but even for the salvation of the whole world—cannot happen as long as the order of true love is kept intact. Loss of the soul means withdrawing from the love of him who should be loved above all else.

102. Who will say that this can sometimes be done commendably or, at least, irreprehensibly? Someone surely withdraws from God's love when he either does something deserving damnation or omits doing something without which he cannot be saved.

There are, moreover, certain means such as *lectio,* meditation, manual work, fasting, the pleasantness of prayer, and other things of this type, all of which should be arranged, varied, changed, and sometimes even omitted for the sake of a brother's salvation. About these the apostle said: *No one seeks his own interests, but those of others.*[173] And in like way: *Just as I try to please everyone in everything I do, seeking not what is useful to me but useful to many others, that they may be saved.*[174] Lastly, that he said, *I would willingly be separated from Christ for the sake of my brothers*[175] can also be interpreted not inappropriately to mean that from the secrecy of his prayer, at which he reposed pleasantly in Jesus' embraces, from that ineffable height of contemplation where, with utterly pure eyes, he gazed upon the secrets of heavenly

---

172 *dilectio*
173 Ph 2:4
174 1 Co 10:33
175 Rm 9:3

mysteries, from the sweetness of the utterly grace-filled compunction which bathed with the soothing dew of spiritual attachment his soul thirsting for things of heaven, he would have chosen to be drawn away to the din of the world for his brothers' salvation. No-one who, according to his own measure, remains at leisure and tastes how sweet the Lord is,[176] and how blessed is everyone who hopes in him,[177] doubts that being called away this way must be termed separation from Christ. Anyone who chooses to be separated from Christ, either because he is urged on by brotherly love or because he consents to it when obliged by the authority of his superiors, must watch out for himself, so that this necessity not overwhelm him and sweetness not be lost.

What we have said about *lectio* and prayer should also be understood about bodily comfort, even about the body itself, so that one may realize that everything to be spurned or employed or changed for the sake of one's own salvation should also be done for the salvation of one's neighbor.

Chapter 38. Among neighbors, who should be given precedence is distinguished.

103. In reflecting on charity we have shown, according to its law, what a person owes himself and what he owes his neighbor. Although the great multitude does not permit us to provide for everyone's temporal needs, it still remains for deliberative reason to discern who should be given precedence over whom. So let us consider the breadth of our heart as though it were a spiritual ark,[25*] tightly built of undecayable timbers, that is to say, of good habits and virtues. Let us put compartments in it and three decks, that is, three spiritual holds. In these different holds, let us place each person by worth and order.

---

176 Ps 33:9(34:8)
177 Cf. Ps 39:5(40:4)

In the lowest hold let us enclose the beasts, that is, those who by bestial habits unleash their fury and thirst with fierce rage for our blood: obviously I mean our enemies. To them let us offer the solace of our prayers and to them, after others, the aid commonly needed in life.

104. Because there are both inside and outside compartments, let those on the outside suffice for that kind of people who remain outside, and let access to the inner compartments not be refused those who share—even if only in appearance—our common faith.

The place above these is accorded to reptiles and beasts of burden: those who defiling themselves with greed of the belly and the filthiness of sensual desire, savor things of the earth and debase themselves to a sub-human level, yet do nothing inhuman, nothing cruel to us, and nothing against us. To these let us offer the remedy of our prayer, the aid of our encouragement, the cautery of our correction, and, more than to those below but less than to those above, something additional to what they need. Among these latter, let those closer to us by kinship or human relationships be allotted the compartments closer to us on that deck. Let the others, however, not be excluded from the outside compartments.

105. Now on the top deck let us place human beings, especially those who, even if not raised above human level by a desire for perfection, do not fall headlong among the wild beasts by their ferocity nor among the brute beasts by their sensual desires, nor among the reptiles by their vileness. On this deck, too, to the degree someone is closer to us by blood, or dearer by friendship, or better disposed by the generosity of kind deeds, let him be closer to the center in the abode of our heart.

106. Then let a place still higher be granted to birds, who are borne aloft above man on the spiritual wings of virtues. To the degree that they are closer to God they ought to be higher in this spiritual ark. Let those among them who are joined to us by the sweetest bond of spiritual friendship be more pleasantly hidden in the innermost and secret recesses of our

breast. Let them be more closely bound to us and more fondly cherished.

There remains yet one place higher than all the others. Jesus, who has both built and restored this spiritual ark, sits there alone in his beauty, without peer. By his gentleness he keeps all lower creatures in order. May he give savor to all of them, fill all with his fragrance, enlighten all, shed upon all his splendor, and bring the whole lower span in a straight line to that single cubit of his love.[178] 26*

He alone in all, he alone above all, both captures our attachment and demands our love.[179] He claims for himself a place in the abode of our heart; not only the most important place but the highest; not only the highest but also the innermost.

Let this rationale be kept in these distinctions, that maintaining our will to have concern for all persons, even though our present indigence does not let us do enough for all people, let the higher level may be given precedence over the lower, and at each level let those closer to us be shown more concern.

Chapter 39. Those whom we can enjoy in this life.

107. One thing still remains that the rationale of these divisions compels us to discuss. We have said that charity consists in this: that the mind chooses what it ought for its enjoyment, is moved as it should be, and uses [what it has chosen] appropriately. As far as this present work is concerned, we have done enough about the choice and the motion. But if the choice is healthy and the motion sound, will the use be bad? In tending toward the person loved, intention can be altered and judgement can be deceived. Then, too, with a righteous intention and an appropriate motion, someone may procure the presence of the one whom he has

---

178 *dilectio*
179 *amor*

chosen for his enjoyment. Yet in the enjoyment[180] itself he can change his intention, alter the motion, and exceed measure. Since we have already given rank to our neighbors on different levels and by diverse merits, we must surely state whether we ought, or whether we can manage, to enjoy all of them or only some of them.

108. There is a temporal enjoyment by which we can enjoy one another in this life, as Paul enjoyed Philemon;[181] and there is an eternal enjoyment by which we shall enjoy one another in heaven, as the angels enjoy one another, in pure unity of mind. Moreover, since to enjoy means to use something with gladness and delight, I think it evident that at present we by no means can enjoy everyone, but only a few persons.[27*] It seems to me that we can use some people for testing, some for instruction, some for consolation, and some for sustenance. We use our enemies for testing, our teachers for instruction, our elders for consolation, and those supplying our needs for our sustenance. Only those whom we cherish with fond attachment, no matter which of these categories they may be in, do we use for sweetness of life and delight of spirit. These [persons] we can enjoy even at present, that is, we can use them with joy and delight. Wherefore, charity can be shown to everyone by everyone in this life, as far as the choice and development in the action are concerned, but as far as enjoyment is concerned, it can be shown to everyone only by a few, or even by no one at all. There are few people, if there are any at all, who cherish every sort of human being not only with a rational but even with an attached love.

Finally, charity in both choice and development is shown toward God himself by many persons to whom the enjoyment of love is not granted in this life, but is reserved for the ever-blessed vision of him after this life. There are some, too, who in the light of contemplation and the sweetness of compunction experience a beginning of this sweet enjoyment. If you

---

180 *fructus*
181 Phm 20

are looking toward future joys, these persons should not be said to enjoy God himself, but rather to use him. We have shown well enough above how he grants the ever pleasant taste of his sweetness to a good number of people more as a support for their weakness than as a fruit of their love.

109. Moreover, it is no mean consolation in this life to have someone with whom you can be united by an intimate attachment and the embrace of very holy love, to have someone in whom your spirit may rest, to whom you can pour out your soul;[182] to whose gracious conversation you may flee for refuge amid sadness, as to consoling songs; or to the most generous bosom of whose friendship you may approach in safety amid the many troubles of this world; to whose most loving breast you may without hesitation confide all your inmost thoughts, as to yourself; by whose spiritual kisses as by medicinal ointments you may sweat out of yourself the weariness of agitating cares. Someone who will weep with you in anxiety, rejoice with you in prosperity; seek with you in doubts; someone you can let into the secret chamber of your mind by the bonds of love, so that even when absent in body he is present in spirit. There, you alone may converse with him alone, all the more sweetly because more secretly. Alone, you may speak with him alone, and once the noise of the world is hushed, in the sleep of peace, you alone may repose with him alone in the embrace of charity, the kiss of unity, with the sweetness of the Holy Spirit flowing between you. Still more, you may be so united to him and approach him so closely and so mingle your spirit[183] with his, that the two become one.

110. In this present life we are able to enjoy those whom we love[184] not only by reason but also by attachment. Among them, we especially take enjoyment in those who are linked to us more intimately and more closely by the pleasant bond of

---

182 *animus*, spirit is *spiritus*
183 *animus*
184 *diligo*

spiritual friendship. Lest someone think that this very holy sort of charity should seem reproachable, our Jesus himself, lowering (Himself) to our condition in every way, suffering all things for us and being compassionate towards us, transformed it by manifesting his love. To one person, not to all, did he grant a resting-place on his most sacred breast[185] in token of his special love, so that the virginal head might be supported by the flowers[186] of his virginal breast, and the fragrant secrets of the heavenly bridal-chamber might instill the sweet scents of spiritual perfumes on his virginal attachments more abundantly because more closely. So it is that even though all the disciples were cherished by the sweetness of supreme charity by the most blessed Master, still it was to this one that he accorded this name as a prerogative of yet more intimate attachment: that he would be called that *disciple whom Jesus loved.*[187]

Chapter 40. How we should enjoy one another.

111. Let anyone who finds it pleasant to enjoy his friend see to it that he enjoy him in the Lord, not in the world or in pleasure of the flesh, but in joyfulness of spirit. But, you ask, what does it mean to enjoy 'in the Lord'? About the Lord, the apostle Paul said: *By God he has been made for us wisdom, sanctification, and justice.*[188] Since the Lord is wisdom, sanctification, and justice, to find enjoyment in the Lord is to find enjoyment in wisdom, sanctification, and justice. By wisdom worldly vanity is banished, by sanctification the vileness of the flesh is foresworn, and by justice all flattery and fawning are checked. Then it is charity, if it comes, as the apostle says, *from a pure heart, a clear conscience, and unfeigned faith.*[189]

---

185 Cf. Jn 13:25
186 Cf. Sg 2:5
187 Jn 13:23
188 1 Co 1:30
189 1 Tm 1:5

A pure heart accepts wisdom, modesty calms the conscience, and unfeigned faith adorns justice. There are those who take enjoyment in vain and ludicrous things, in worldly pomp and mundane spectacles, in the pursuit of vanity, and in revelling in falsehood. They do not enjoy themselves in wisdom, nor in him who is the strength of God and the wisdom of God. Others, although not worse, are certainly more vile. In them there is almost nothing human. Obscene depravity has transformed them into beasts who find enjoyment in self-indulgent banqueting and impure desires. Since they do not enjoy themselves in the sanctification which consists of the gentleness of charity, they do not, of course, enjoy the Lord who was made our sanctification by God.[190]

There are others who take enjoyment in flattery, patting each other on the back and conniving with each other. While taking care not to offend one another, they incur each other's ruin because they do not enjoy themselves in the liberty of justice or in the Lord.

112. If our mutual exchange of words is delightful, let our talk therefore be about our habits and about Scripture.[28*] Let us now grieve together over the miseries of the world, now rejoice together in the hope of future happiness. Let us now refresh one another by confiding our mutual secrets, now long together for the blessed vision of Jesus, and for heavenly well-being.

If we relax our tense spirits[191] with some pleasant and less lofty subjects, as is sometimes useful, let these moments of relaxation be filled with rectitude and free of frivolity. Although these subjects may not be weighty, let them never lack constructiveness. Let us enjoy one another in sanctification, so that each may know how to possess his vessel—that is to say, his own body—in sanctification and honor, and not in the passion of desire. Let us take enjoyment in justice, so we may mutually encourage one another in the spirit of freedom.

---

190 Cf. 1 Co 1:30
191 *animus*

Let us correct one another, knowing that wounds from a friend are better than an enemy's deceitful kisses.[192]

113. Most beloved Father, these are my meditations on charity. If its excellence, its fruits, and the appropriate way of showing it are by them made—like an image of it—to appear, this book may be called a *Mirror of Charity,* as you have directed. Yet I beg you not to display this mirror in public, for fear that instead of charity gleaming from it, the likeness of its author may make it dingy.

If, to my great embarrassment, as I fear, you do publish it, by that sweet name of Jesus I entreat the reader not to think that I undertook this work out of presumption. A father's authority, love for my brothers, and my own need drove me to it. Not to obey one's superior is a dangerous thing, but it is sweet and pleasant to converse in spirit on this sort of thing with someone very dear who is absent. I thought it necessary for me to bind together the wanderings and useless digressions of my spirit[193]—frolicking hither and yon—by the links of these meditations.[29*]

If by reading these pages anyone draws profit for either his attachments or his thoughts, may he repay me for my efforts by interceding with the just and merciful judge for my numberless sins.

HERE ENDS BOOK THREE

---

192 Pr 27:6
193 *animus*

NOTES

1 Aelred built his doctrine of the degrees of charity on the three sabbaths prescribed in the book of Leviticus: the seventh day (Lv 23:3), the seventh year (Lv 25:4), and the fiftieth, jubilee, year (Lv 25:10). He follows as well the account of the six days of creation given in Augustine's treatise *De Genesi ad litteram*, where no less then fourteen chapters of Book Four are devoted to God's rest. Aelred quotes this treatise (XI.24.31) explicitly in his sixteenth sermon *De oneribus*. PL 195:427C. Aelred grasped that in these chapters Augustine was expressing his theology on the human person's end and final rest in the peace of divine love.

2 See Abraham Joshua Heschel, *The Sabbath: Its Meaning for Modern Man* (New York, 1951).

3 Sg 1:3. Cf. Bernard *SC* 23 (CF 7:25f).

4 Cf. Aelred, *Annun*, ed. C.H. Talbot, *Sermones inediti*, p.88.

5 Cf. Augustine, *Enarr. in Ps.* 132.1. Cf Luke M.J. Verheijen, 'L'Enarratio in Ps. 132 de St Augustin et sa conception du monachisme', in *Forma Futuri*, Studi in honore Michele Pellegrino (Turin, 1975) 810–811. See also, Augustine, *In Ioh. tract.* 7.13.

6 Cf. Bernard, *SC* 14.2 (CF 4:99): *Oleum effusum nomen tuum*.

7 Cf. Aelred, *In pentecosten*, ed. Talbot, *Sermones inediti*, p. 110.

8 Cf. *Spir amic* III.2.17–18: *Amor sine amicitia esse potest, amicitia sine amore numquam*. CCCM I:317.

9 *Usus-fructus*, Cf. Augustine, *De doctrina christiana* 1.3.3–1,4,4, and Bibliothèque Augustinienne, *Oeuvres de Saint Augustin*, (Paris) vol. 11, note 18,pp.558–561.

10 *Circuitus impiorum*. Cf. Bernard, *Dil* 7.19–20 (CF 13:112–113); Aelred, *Spec car* I.**15**.47; I.**16**.48.

11 *affectuosus, discretus, fortis*. Cf. Bernard, *SC* 20.4 (CF 4:149)

12 Cf. Bernard, *Csi* 4.6.21 (CF 37:135) and *Conv* 20.34–35 (CF 25:72–74).

13 Cf. *Inst incl* 17.193–210. CCCM 1:642–43 (CF 2:52).

14 Cf. *Inst incl* 17,550–560. CCCM 1:653 (CF 2:66).

15 Cicero, *Pro rege dejotaro*, 26, cited by Augustine, *De beata vita*, 31.

16 *Tres ordines*. This is augustinian vocabulary, found in Augustine's treatises against the Manichaeans, notably in *De libero arbitrio*, Book Three, where the natural and voluntary orders are distinguished. See Bibliothèque Augustinienne, *Oeuvres de Saint Augustin*, vol. 6, note 25 on *liberté, volonté, libre arbitre* (p.510–511), and note 27, 'L'optimisme augustinien' (p.514–515). The order of nature is created by God. Aelred says that grace is due to nature. The necessary order is applied here to penance, with an allusion to the Penitentials circulating at Aelred's time, and in another sense as well: once penance has been performed, one must correct his faults and here, the monastic vocabulary of *exercitia necessaria* (cf. *Oner* 25; PL 195:463) as well as the reference to Cassian gives meaning to the 'necessary order'. The voluntary order is the order of love which brings the human person back to God. See Bernard, *Dil* 12.34 (CF 13:125–126): *Caritas vero convertit animas quas et facit voluntarias*; and *Div* 3.9; Cassian, *Conference* 11; and Aelred, *Spir am* III.101.790. CCCM 1:340.

17 *Ordo voluntarius*: Bernard, *QH* 9.1 (CF 25:182–183).

18 Cf. Aelred, *In adventu Domini*, PL 195:216AB.

19 Cf. Bernard, *OS* 1.8 and *SC* 42.7–8 (CF 7:215–216). See also *Pre* 1.2 (PL 182:862): *vovere voluntatis, reddere necessitatis* (CF1:106).

20 *Feminalium usus*. Cf. RB 55:13: *Femoralia hi qui diriguntur de vestiario accipiant.* Although one wants spontaneously to correct Aelred's *feminalia* to the more correct *femoralia*, all the manuscripts agree in using the latter word. Biblical language in this case may have been given preference to that of Saint Benedict. In numerous Old Testament passages we find directions for the High Priest's trousers (Ex 28:42, Lv 16:4, Ezk 44:18). See Jerome's detailed commentary to Fabiola (Ep 64.10,20,22; PL 22:613).

21 *Habe caritatem, et fac quidquid vis* harkens back to Augustine, *Commentary on the First Epistle of Saint John, Tract.* 7.8 (PL 35:2033). This phrase is also found in Peter the Venerable's letter to Saint Bernard (Ep 28; PL 189:118D–119A, repeated in 156A; Giles Constable, *The Letters of Peter the Venerable*, I (Cambridge, Massachusetts: Harvard, 1967) 98). The text of Augustine, on the contrary (*Ep. Ioh.* 7.8) is: *Dilige, et quod vis fac.* Aelred's passage may refer, directly or indirectly, to Peter the Venerable rather than to Augustine.

22 Cf. Aelred's *Orat past* 7; CCCM 1:761 (CF 2:113–115).

23 Cf. Bernard, *SC* 23.6 (CF 7:30). See above, the end of the Introduction, part one, where this passage on the novice master or abbot is quoted.

24 Cf. Aelred, *Nat Dom*, PL 195:226.

25 *quasi arcam*. Noah's ark was considered a foretype of the Church. See Augustine, *Enarr. in Ps.* 103, 3.2; *De doctrina christiana* I.37.28–29.

26 *cubitum illum unum*. See above, I.33.93, final lines. On the dimensions of the Ark, see Origen, *Homily XXI on the Book of Numbers* (Sch 29:418): 'In the construction of Noah's ark, the dimensions of which are given by revelation from above, the lowest hold should measure three hundred cubits in length and thirty cubits in width. But as the construction rises higher, it is made compact and is reduced to a small number of cubits, right up to the summit which is brought to completion in the space of one cubit. The reason for this is that the lower parts, where large and vast spaces have been arranged, received the beasts and the flocks, and the higher ones, birds. As for the summit, narrow and compact, it is joined in one sole measure because everything converges in Unity. But Unity itself signifies the mystery of the Trinity by the number three hundred, and the human being is placed very close to this symbol. as [being] rational and capable of receiving God.' See also a parallel passage in Origen's *Homily II.1* (SCh 7).

27 Cf. III.**7.**10, and *Spir amic* I.19.113–115. CCCM 1:292.

28 Cf. Walter Daniel, *Vita Ailredi*, XXXI; Powicke, p. 40.

29 See John Cassian, *De Institutis* 5.10.

TABLE OF SCRIPTURAL REFERENCES

Aelred: Mirror of Charity

Column one indicates Scriptural passage. Column two indicates the Book, **Chapter**, and paragraph of *The Mirror of Charity*. For the convenience of readers wishing to consult the Latin critical edition, column three identifies the passages in the *Corpus Christianorum Continuatio Mediaevalis*, volume 1.

Genesis

1:5	I.**19**.54	825–826
1:8	I.**19**.54	826
1:22	I.**32**.91	1544–1545
1:31	I.**2**.5	65
1:31	III.**7**.20	384
2:1 cf	I.**19**.56	855
2:2	I.**18**.52	782
2:2	I.**19**.53	813–815
2:2	I.**19**.56	856
3:19	I.**34**.108	1837–1838
9:25 cf	I.**26**.73	1163–1165
9:26 cf	I.**26**.73	1165–1166
12:1	I.**34**.100	1711–1713
22	III.**29**.69	1268–1272
37:28	III.**29**.70	1302
39:12	I.**34**.101	1737–1739
42:24	III.**14**.37	667–668
42:24	III.**26**.63	1173
47:29	III.**14**.36	652–653
47:30	III.**14**.36	652–653

Exodus

2:2	III.**15**.38	691
2:16ff	III.**13**.35	632ff
3:22	I.**29**.84	1372–1373
5:7 cf	I.**1**.1	14
15:23 cf	II.**15**.37	705
15:27 cf	II.**15**.37	706
16 cf	II.**15**.37	706–707
16:18	II.**15**.38	725
17:7	II.**15**.36	680
17:8–16	II.**15**.39	729–731
20:12	III.**4**.9	188
20:13	I.**29**.84	1369
20:14 cf	I.**29**.84	1375

Leviticus

23:3	III.**1**.1	7
23:8	I.**26**.77	1236–1237
25:3	III.**1**.1	7
25:4	III.**1**.1	7
25:8ff	III.**1**.1	8
25:10	III.**6**.18	329
26:6	I.**33**.95	1616–1617

Numbers

12:1–13	III.**29**.70	1303–1305
16:32 cf	II.**14**.34	635–636
22:23 cf	II.**14**.34	634–635
23:10	II.**9**.22	387–388
24:4	II.**9**.22	389–390

Deuteronomy

6:5	III.**9**.27	502–503
6:13	III.**9**.26	492–493
6:16	II.**24**.73	1357
32:10	I.**5**.15	211
32:13	Bernard, Ep.¶4	44–45

Judges

2:4	II.**9**.22	397
16:21	I.**15**.47	701

1 Samuel

15:23	Bernard, Ep.¶1	14–15
17:50 cf	III.**12**.33	610
18:1	III.**12**.33	613–614
20	III.**29**.69	1272
20:41	III.**29**,70	1310–1311
23:17	III.**29**.69	1283–1284
23:17	III.**29**.69	1287
23:17	III.**29**.69	1297
23:17	III.**29**.69	1308

2 Samuel

1:22	III.**29**.70	1295–1296
11:2	III.**15**.38	697–699
11:17	III.**15**.38	700–701
13	III.**11**.32	581
15	III.**11**.32	583
18:5	III.**14**.37	672
18:33	I.**34**.104	1782–1783
19:1	III.**29**.71	1333–1335
19:6–9	III.**29**.71	1335–1337

1 Kings

2:7 ff.	III.**13**.35	636ff
2:25	III.**29**.70	1305–1307
3:16ff	III.**14**.36	653 ff
3:26	III.**14**.36	660–661
3:26	III.**14**.36	663
11	III.**15**.38	701–704

Tobias

2:13	III.**32**.78	1475

33:9 (34:8)	III.**37**.102	1988
33:22 (34:21)	I.**34**.104	1786
35:9 (36:8)	I.**1**.2	26
37(38):13 cf	I.**34**.108	1847
37(38):14 (cf)	I.**34**.108	1848–1849
38:7 (39:6)	I.**4**.13	176–177
39:3 (40:2)	I.**5**.15	209
39:3 (40:2)	I.**18**.51	774
39:3 (40:2)	Bernard, Ep ¶5	52
39:5 (40:4)	III.**37**.102	1989
41:3 (42:2)	I.**5**.15	222–223
41:5 (42:4)	II.**11**.28	485–486
41:5 (42:4)	I.**34**.114	1988
42(43):1	I.**15**.47	695–696
43(44):22	II.**15**.36	692–693
44:3 (45:2)	II.**12**.30	520
44:3 (45:2)	III.**5**.14	279–280
44:3 (45:2)	I.**34**.100	1716
44:8 (45:7)	I.**34**.100	1717
44(45):11	I.**34**.100	1732
44(45):14	II.**24**.71	1317
45:11 (46:10)	I.**18**.52	784
48:18 (49:17)	I.**5**.15	217
48:21 (49:20)	I.**2**.6	90
48:21 (49:20)	I.**4**.11	151+157
50:6 (51:4)	I.**29**.84	1363
50(51):5	I.**26**.77	1242
50:19 (51:17)	II.**20**.63	1147–1148
53:8 (54:6)	III.**34**.80	1523
54:7 (55:6)	I.**5**.15	223–224
64:14 (65:13)	Bernard Ep ¶4	43
65(66):13	III.**35**.95	1802
65(66):14	II.**15**.36	675
67:10 (68:9)	I.**15**.44	655
67:14 (68:13)	I.**8**.25	362
67:14 (68:13)	II.**15**.38	719
67(68):16	II.**12**.29	510

139(140):9	I.**16**.48	707–708
140(141):4	II.**17**.52	966
140(141):5	II.**17**.46	868
143(144):7	II.**11**.27	460
145(146):8	Bernard, Ep.¶5	55–56

Proverbs

14:33 cf	Bernard,Ep ¶20	56
26:11	I.**30**.86	1424–1425
27:6	III.**40**.112	2175
31:6	II.**6**.16	303
31:7	II.**6**.16	304–305
31:7	II.**6**.16	312

Qoholeth

1:14	I.**26**.77	1231–1232
2:1	I.**26**.77	1217–1218
2:4	I.**26**.77	1218
2:5	I.**26**.77	1219
2:7	I.**26**.77	1220–1221
2:8	I.**26**.77	1221–1222
2:8	I.**26**.77	1223
2:10	I.**26**.77	1224–1226
2:11	I.**26**.77	1228–1230
5:9	I.**24**.68	1074
5:9	I.**23**.67	1065–1067
5:11	I.**23**.66	1051–1052
5:12	I.**23**.66	1043–1044
7:17	III.**24**.56	1043

Song of Songs

1:3	I.**18**.52	790–791
1:3	I.**7**.22	317–318
1:3	I.**34**.100	1715

11:36	I.**34**.112	1935–1936
12:15	I.**7**.22	313–314
12:25	III.**26**.61	1139–1141
13:23 cf	II.**17**.49	914–915
13:23	III.**39**.110	2133–2134
13:25 cf	III.**39**.110	2126
13:34	I.**8**.24	351
14:21	II.**17**.49	911
14:21	II.**18**.54	1001
14:23	II.**15**.36	682–684
14:23	II.**17**.49	910
14:23 cf	II.**18**.56	1036–1037
14:24	II.**17**.49	912
15:5	I.**13**.39	583
15:9–10	Aelred Ep ¶3	117
15:10	I.**20**.57	886
15:20	I.**20**.57	884
21:7 cf	II.**14**.34	630

Acts

5:41	II.**2**.4	65–66
11:26 cf	III.**4**.9	208–209
13:2	III.**24**.56	1050–1051
14:22	II.**15**.37	697–698
14:22	II.**17**.42	772
17:28	I.**8**.26	367–368
17:29	I.**8**.26	367–368

Romans

1:24	I.**26**.75	1197–1199
2:6	I.**11**.34	502–503
5:5	I.**9**.27	393
5:5	I.**10**.28	409
5:5	I.**27**.78	1266
5:5	III.**6**.19	346
5:5 cf	II.**18**.53	985
6:12	I.**7**.22	328–329

2:9 cf	III.**32**.77	1436
4:3	III.**32**.77	1427–1428
4:4	III.**32**.77	1425
5:8	III.**4**.9	177–178
5:8	III.**14**.36	647–649
5:8	III.**26**.60	1108–1109
5:8	III.**26**.61	1122–1124
6:9	I.**24**.69	1083–1084
6:10	II.**1**.3	31
6:10	III.8.**24**	451
6:17	I.**24**.68	1077–1078

2 Timothy

1:3	III.**24**.56	1055
1:4	III.**24**.56	1056
2:4	II.**14**.33	604–605
3:1–2	III.**26**.61	1125–1126
3:2	III.**26**.61	1127–1128
3:4	III.**26**.61	1128–1129
4:7	I.**11**.33	488–489
4:8	I.**11**.33	495–497

Titus

1:15	III.**32**.77	1424
2:12	III.**31**.74	1375–1376
2:12	II.**18**.56	1034
2:12 cf	III.**24**.56	1038

Philemon

20	III.**9**.28	524
20	III.**39**.108	2072

Hebrews

4:12	I.**34**.113	1947–1948
4:12	II.**1**.3	47–49
5:12	Aelred, Ep ¶2	96
10:34	I.**24**.69	1092

11:23	III.**15**.38	691
James		
2:1	II.**14**.33	612–613
3:14	II.**14**.33	613–615
3:15	II.**5**.9	172
3:16	II.**14**.33	615–616
4:1	II.**4**.7	148–149
4:4	II.**14**.33	616–617
4:11	II.**14**.33	618
1 Peter		
1:4	I.**31**.87	1446
1:24	I.**31**.87	1450–1451
1:25	I.**31**.87	1451–1453
2:1	II.**14**.33	621–622
2:11	II.**14**.33	619–620
3:3	III.**32**.77	1436
4:8	I.**27**.78	1264
4:11	II.**14**.33	622–623
4:13 cf	II.**6**.15	285
5:2	II.**14**.33	624
5:3	II.**14**.33	625
5:5	II.**14**.33	626–627
5:8	I.**1**.1	3
5:8	II.**14**.33	629
2 Peter		
1:4	II.**14**.33	628
1:17	I.**20**.57	887–888
1 John		
2:4	II.**14**.34	631–632
2:15	II.**14**.34	632–633
2:16	I.**28**.79	1174
2:16	II.**1**.2	25–26
2:16	II.**4**.7	129–130

2:16 cf.	II.**25**.74	1365–1366
2:16	III.**26**.61	1146–1147
2:16	I.**28**.79	1273–1274
2:16	I.**34**.98	1667–1668
3:15	II.**14**.34	633–634
3:16	III.**37**.101	1948–1949
4:1	II.**17**.47	899
4:18	II.**12**.29	502–503
4:20	III.**2**.3	74–76
5:3	II.**17**.49	914–915
5:3	I.**30**.86	1424

Jude

1:11	II.**14**.34	634–636
1:12	II.**14**.34	636–637
1:16	II.**14**.34	637–638
1:23	II.**14**.34	638–639

Revelation

1:4	I.**20**.58	903–904
3:17	II.**17**.52	968–970

Errata

Page 308, column 1
    Psalm 4:8 (7) *should read* 4:9(8)
             22(23)4 22(23):4

Page 308, column 2
    1.6 & III.**22**.52 III.**22**.52

Page 309, column 1
    65(66):13 65(66):13-14
    65(66):14 65(66):13-14

Page 309, column 3
    1363 (ref. Ps 50:6) 1364
    1242 (ref. Ps 50:5) 1241

Page 310, column 1
    72(73):22 72:23 (73:22)
    83:13 80:13

CISTERCIAN PUBLICATIONS INC.

Kalamazoo, Michigan

TITLES LISTING

THE CISTERCIAN FATHERS SERIES

Texts and Studies in the Monastic Tradition

THE CISTERCIAN STUDIES SERIES

MONASTIC TEXTS

CHRISTIAN SPIRITUALITY

MONASTIC STUDIES

CISTERCIAN STUDIES

* *Temporarily out of print*   † *Forthcoming*

---

* Temporarily out of print   † *Forthcoming*

Saint Gregory Nazianzen: Selected Poems

Eight Chapters on Perfection and Angel's Song
(Walter Hilton)

Creative Suffering (Iulia de Beausobre)

Bringing Forth Christ. Five Feasts of the Child
Jesus (St Bonaventure)

Gentleness in St John of the Cross

Distributed in North America only for Fairacres Press.

DISTRIBUTED BOOKS

St Benedict: Man with An Idea (Melbourne Studies)

The Spirit of Simplicity

Benedict's Disciples (David Hugh Farmer)

The Emperor's Monk: A Contemporary Life of
Benedict of Aniane

A Guide to Cistercian Scholarship (2nd ed.)

*North American customers may order
through booksellers or directly from
the publisher:*

    Cistercian Publications
    St Joseph's Abbey
    Spencer, Massachusetts 01562
    (508) 885–7011

    Cistercian Publications
    Editorial Offices
    WMU Station
    Kalamazoo, Michigan 49008
    (616) 387–5090

*Cistercian monks and nuns have been
living lives of prayer & praise, meditation
& manual labor since the twelfth century.
They are part of an unbroken tradition
which extends back to the fourth century
and which continues today in the Catholic
church, the Orthodox churches, the
Anglican communion, and most recently,
in the Protestant churches.*

*Share their way of life and their search for
God by reading Cistercian Publications.*

*A complete catalogue of texts-in-
translation and studies on early,
medieval, and modern Christian
monasticism is available at no
cost from Cistercian Publications.*